Scott Tinley's
Winning Guide to
Sports Endurance

Scott Tinley's Winning Guide to Sports Endurance

How to Maximize Speed, Strength & Stamina

By Scott Tinley
Three-Time Ironman World Series Champion
and Ken McAlpine

Rodale Press, Emmaus, Pennsylvania

Notice

This book is intended as a reference volume only. The information given here is designed to help you make informed decisions about your exercise and fitness program. It is not intended as a substitute for professional medical or fitness advice. As with all exercise programs, you should seek your doctor's approval before you begin.

Cover Designer: Charles Beasley
Book Design: Ayers/Johanek Publication Design
Cover Photographers: Peter Read Miller (top), Gary Randall (lower left),
  David Madison (lower right)

Library of Congress Cataloging-in-Publication Data

Tinley, Scott.
(Winning guide to sports endurance)
   Scott Tinley's winning guide to sports endurance: how to maximize speed, strength & stamina / by Scott Tinley and Ken McAlpine.
   p. cm—
   Includes index.
   ISBN 0–87596–106–1 paperback
   1. Physical fitness. 2. Physical education and training–Physiological aspects. I. McAlpine, Ken. II. Title. III. Title: Winning guide to sports endurance.
GV481.T56   1994   93–28410
613.7—dc20   CIP

Distributed in the book trade by St. Martin's Press

        8   10   9   7   paperback

———— OUR MISSION ————

We publish books that empower people's lives.

———— RODALE 🌱 BOOKS ————

To my children,
Torrie and Dane. Long may you run.
S. T.

To my wife, Kathy.
Her unwavering support has given me the
rare opportunity to do what I love.
K. M.

Contents

Acknowledgments

A book of this scope couldn't have been written without the contributions of dozens of experts. Unfortunately, acknowledging them all would be a book in itself. Instead, we can only extend our heartfelt thanks to everyone who gave their time so generously. Without their efforts, this book wouldn't have been possible.

However, special thanks are due on several fronts. First, we would like to thank Mike Plant, whose expertise and writing helped complete portions of this book. We would also like to thank experts Ken Sparks, Ph.D., exercise physiology, Susan Kleiner, Ph.D., nutrition, and Joe Ellis, D.P.M., podiatry, for reviewing the book to help ensure that the information we give you is up-to-date and accurate. We would also like to extend a very special thank-you to Rodale editor Claire Gerus. Claire's energy, efficiency and unflappably pleasant manner made the editing process a smooth one.

Last but not least, we would like to thank our wives, Virginia Tinley and Kathy McAlpine. Writing a book isn't an easy job. They provided the understanding, support and encouragement we needed to, well, endure.

Introduction

As a boy, I loved books about adventure. It didn't matter in what activity or what context—it didn't even matter if the story had a happy ending—so long as it brought images of adventure. It didn't matter if the hero found the treasure or rescued the girl, just so long as the wind was in his face during the thrill of the hunt.

Thirty years later, I haven't really changed that much. As a grown man with children of my own, I've chosen a career that's rooted in adventure and challenge. In some ways my life's calling as a professional endurance athlete is an oxymoron. Overcoming a challenge was always thought of as a deeply personal thing and was as far from the crass image of professionalism as it could be. Yet somehow the two became intertwined, and I became one of the lucky few who can claim their passion as their payday.

Along the way, I've had to explain my situation to countless people in countless ways. I now fully understand why, when Sir Edmund Hillary was asked why he chose to climb Mount Everest, he answered, "Because it's there." I don't feel compelled to explain how I can support a family by swimming, cycling and running. But I do feel a small sense of responsibility to offer something back, not only to a profession that has done me well but also to all those individuals who seek some type of fulfillment in the challenge of endurance activities. Each person makes the decision to experience uncomfortable situations while in search of whatever it is that they're looking for. I offer no commentary in that regard. What I do offer in this book is some advice, some knowledge gathered in research and a bit of insight gained from 20-plus years of just going out and doing it.

As an endurance physiologist once said, the best scientists in the world are the athletes themselves, who, through long years of trial and error, have arrived at the most important conclusion of all: What works and what doesn't. Explaining myself has become easier over the years. It may be because I've learned to say just enough about endurance without sounding gushy. But I think it's probably because more and more people have jumped on the bandwagon. If you think about it, there are few human activities as likely to draw attention to themselves as an act of physical endurance. Promise to go faster, longer, higher, farther than anyone has gone before, and you're likely to draw not only a crowd but a reporter or two as well.

Man has been fascinated by feats of long-suffering courage for at least as long as he's been able to put pen to paper—or charcoal to cave wall, for that matter. Our prehistoric ancestors very likely sat around the fire and swapped stories of life on the trail. Of angry storms and fierce beasts with huge teeth and bigger appetites, and of course, great heroes—some returned and some not.

In recent times, though, life for many of us has become rather easy, at least from a physical standpoint. We lack the opportunity (though at the time they might not have called it that) that early Americans had to explore new lands, deal with the unexpected and face challenges head-on. I honestly believe that a good percentage of men and women have an innate desire to test their limits of physical endurance, of courage, of sacrifice in order to gain the benefits that come with successfully meeting a personal challenge. Yet those opportunities don't exist on a daily basis. Truth is, most of us have to go out and create them. Thus the surge in the popularity of marathons, triathlons, ultra this and ultra that.

There's a bit of the would-be stoic in us all. We all seem to attach nobility to a person's willingness to endure pain and fatigue; this transcends even the concept of victory, rising above even our natural tendency to cheer the winner and ignore the also-rans.

It's a fascination that is unlikely to disappear as long as there are men and women around to tell the tales and do the deeds—and in this last decade of the twentieth century, there are more people than ever who are willing, and able, to do the deeds. Besides marathons and triathlons and duathlons, there is mountain biking, rock climbing, mountain climbing, stair climbing, wilderness vacations and on and on and on . . . .The allure of heroism, even private heroism, is difficult to resist, and the opportunities are endless. If you want to dress up like Greg LeMond and ride 100 miles on Sunday, you can do it—and you can probably find a buddy to do it with you.

In any case, we have this experience called endurance. And we have millions of people who see great benefit in pushing themselves beyond normal limits. But what we don't have is a tool to help us draw the line between courage and stupidity.

I've seen dozens of cases of athletes who have replaced preparation with perseverance. But unless your goal is to be a posthumous hero, knowledge, not courage, is the key to endurance.

Endurance is as much a thing of the mind as of the body. We can easily see greater wisdom in a well-planned and rehearsed assault on our endurance goals than in a seat-of-our-pants, till-the-bitter-end approach.

Still, where would our sentiments and gut feelings lie as would-be heroes (in our own minds) in this day and age? Are we more intrigued by the sight of the smiling winner crossing the finish line at the Ironman Triathlon in Hawaii or by lens-to-the-nose footage of the guy in 500th place, on his hands and knees, crawling desperately toward the end, a victim of his own ignorance or lack of preparation? Before you answer, think back to the media coverage of the women's marathon in the 1984 Olympic Games in Los Angeles. Which woman did you see more of, winner Joan Benoit Samuelson or Gabriele Andersen-Scheiss, stumbling around the L.A. Coliseum track in an exhausted stupor?

Errors such as this have great dramatic impact if you're sitting in front of a TV with a cold beer in your hand. It's not so exciting if you're the one halfway up the side of the mountain in a T-shirt, with night falling and freezing temperatures on the way. Any endurance activity can become an act of supreme will. The trick—if you're the one enduring—is not to let it get to that point.

How far can we go? What are the boundaries of human endurance? Hell, I don't know. There was a time early in my career when I thought that going under nine hours for an Ironman distance race (2.4-mile swim, 112-mile bike ride, 26.2-mile run) was the ultimate. Now I'm hoping to go under eight hours before I'm put out to pasture. People who put limits on their performance are destined to stay within those limits.

Nor do the boundaries lie just in the mind. No amount of guts or grit is going to make up for good, solid preparation—work, plain and simple. Oh, you can squeak out a few minutes or a few inches here or there, but in the end, luck is where preparation and opportunity meet.

The link that binds the two is knowledge. The best examples of this are the world's top athletes. There are lots of talented people who don't train hard or don't train right. And there are lots of folks without any talent who train hard and right but lack the basic skills to make it to the top. The few who combine skills with knowledge and work make it to the big time.

Getting to the big leagues isn't every weekend warrior's dream, but I doubt any of us would put time and effort into an activity knowing that much of it will be wasted by spinning our wheels in the wrong direction.

In fact, the greatest limiting factor is knowledge, pure and simple. What you don't know in the endurance business can hurt you; what you take the time to understand may even keep you alive. You won't make the papers or the six o'clock news, but you'll have a heck of a lot more fun and you'll be back to try next time, and that's what really counts.

With that in mind, I embarked on this book project. It's no secret that a lot of folks are taking their fitness very seriously, often in the form of endurance sports. But finding good word-of-mouth advice along the way is not enough. Where do you go for good information? When I look back on some of my training programs of the late 1970s and early 1980s, I can't help but shake my head in disbelief. Did I really ride my bike a whopping 500 miles a week at times? Did I really think that a paltry 2,000-yard workout in the hotel's kidney-shaped pool would be enough to make me a top swimmer?

There was simply no easy way for a semi-serious weekend endurance junkie to find out what was right and what was a waste of time. But it really didn't matter, because we were pioneers, and it was the adventure that counted. Things change, though, and steady improvement is a big part of the constant reinforcement necessary to avoid mental burnout.

Sure, you could go to the library and check out 12 books on 12 different sports. Or you could subscribe to (and even read) seven different magazines. You could even watch any number of training videos. Like most busy folks, though, you probably wouldn't go to all that trouble.

Oh, but to have a sourcebook of clear, concise information on various aspects of endurance sport—all in one place. What I wouldn't have given for that! And here it is—everything I've ever wanted to know about endurance and have been asking for years, but didn't quite get to in my early days.

Open *Scott Tinley's Winning Guide to Sports Endurance*, and look up the information you're seeking. What's a bonk? Can dehydration really kill you? What are the early warning signs of heat injury? What's the real lowdown on lactic acid? What do female athletes really need to know about iron? Why would you want to do an Ironman? And what might you learn from those who have? How can you go as long, as hard and as fast as you possibly can?

So here it is, but with some words of advice before you jump in. As with any encyclopedic book, this one cannot offer the definitive text on any one topic, but each entry will give you a dependable and authoritative starting point. Frankly, the science and psychology of endurance are vast, largely unexplored territories—you won't get much more than a head start no matter where you look. The real knowledge comes in the doing, the practical application of the basic concepts you'll learn in this book. You'll be the one to mold each one to fit your lifestyle, your temperament and, most of all, that marvelous piece of equipment that defies all catch-all solutions to even the most simple problems: your unique body.

If this kind of book had been around when I did my first triathlon in 1976, I probably wouldn't have read it. But two years later, when I had become thoroughly smitten with all aspects of endurance sports, logging a handful of marathons, open-water swims and off-road bike races in the process, I would have kept it in my pocket. I would have written in the margins, dog-eared the thing to death and made sure all my training buddies read it as well. I hope you do the same.

Scott Tinley

Part 1

The Biology of Endurance

Your body is a complex marvel. This incredible machine will power your every activity, and as an endurance athlete, you'll want to know how it works. How else can you make your body function at its optimum ability? Unfortunately, terms like adenosine triphosphate and capillarity will turn most athletes off faster than last month's meat loaf.

You wouldn't choose a mate, buy a home or take a job without some practical information. After all, charging blindly into any endeavor can have unpleasant consequences. Becoming an endurance athlete is no exception. Understanding the basics of glycogen metabolism can mean the difference between finishing strong and falling flat on your face.

In this section, we've presented the rudiments of how your body produces physical effort and meets endurance demands. We've also included working tips. So an entry on maximum heart rate will tell you not only what it is and why it's important. It'll also explain how to calculate it and use it to gauge fitness and performance.

Whenever possible, we've aimed at giving you the information you'll need in clear, practical terms. The sooner you can apply it, the closer you'll be to maximizing your potential as an endurance athlete.

Adrenaline
The fuel boost for endurance athletes

W hen you hear the word *adrenaline*, you summon up the image of the jolt you get when you have a near-collision with a careless driver. But adrenaline has a positive effect on those who exercise—including enhanced mental alertness and improved contraction in the heart and skeletal muscles.

Unfortunately, adrenaline, also known as epinephrine, can't be produced at will. It's only secreted by the adrenals after signals are sent from the sympathetic nervous system—the body's "fight or flight" response. The sympathetic nervous system is part of the autonomic (automatic) nervous system. As is often the case, the best things in life are outside our control. Apparently, however, through training, we can increase our adrenaline output when our nervous system calls for it.

Adrenaline's most important function during exercise is to impede the secretion of insulin. Why is this important? Insulin slows the breakdown of your body's two most important energy sources—carbohydrates and fats. The faster fat and carbohydrate are turned into fuel for your muscles, the better off you are. You might view adrenaline as a sort of "energy decongestant," freeing up your energy pathways so they can operate more efficiently.

Your capacity to secrete adrenaline diminishes with age. But there is a silver lining. The more endurance exercise you do, the more adrenaline you'll produce. And researchers have observed an exaggerated adrenal response during actual endurance activity.

Could it be the thrill of the chase?

ATP
Without this, you're going nowhere

Y ou might never have heard of it, but ATP affects everything you do, from giving you the energy to read this entry to enabling you to sprint across the finish line.

ATP (adenosine triphosphate) is our primary energy currency, fueling most of the cellular activity in every living thing. Every time you blink, breathe or blow bubbles, molecules of ATP within the involved muscles break down into their two basic components—ADP (adenosine diphosphate) and phosphate ions. Released in this breakdown is the energy that powers the contraction of your muscle fibers.

Remember that old physics dictum—energy can be neither created nor destroyed? In truth, energy is passed along, and we receive it wrapped in the foods we eat, encased in carbohydrate, fat and protein molecules. ATP is produced when these three energy sources are metabolized by the body.

You already have a limited supply of ATP in your muscles—energy you can tap into without relying on the breakdown of foods. The problem is, this supply is extremely limited—it's exhausted in just a few seconds of running up the stairs. Once that's gone, one of two things can happen. You'll stop, or you'll tap into the carbohydrate, fat and protein supplies in your body, which will give your muscles the energy to push on.

You've probably heard that your body "burns" carbohydrate, fat and protein to provide energy for your muscles. Not exactly. What your body really does is break these down—step by step—to create energy.

Carbohydrate, for example, is broken down into components you may be familiar with—glucose and glycogen. These are further broken down to produce ATP, which breaks down into ADP, phosphate ions and energy.

Fats, meanwhile, are broken down into free fatty acids and then into ATP and, finally, energy. Protein's amino acid building blocks can also be broken down and used for energy. However, protein's role as an energy source during exercise is usually minimal.

Another plus for aerobics

There are two ways your body can break its ATP down into energy: aerobically (with oxygen) or anaerobically (without oxygen). Aerobic metabolism wins hands down for efficiency.

Take the breakdown of carbohydrate. Anaerobic metabolism produces only 2 molecules of ATP from each glucose molecule. Aerobic metabolism creates 38 molecules of ATP—far more energy. This explains, in part, why you can run a long time at a comfortable pace, sucking down a bountiful supply of oxygen, yet you'll come to a halt after a short, oxygenless sprint up the stairs.

Sprinting up stairs also illustrates another clever adaptation our bodies have made. A cell completely out of ATP will die. Fatigue will then force you to stop your activity, preventing you from exhausting your muscles' stores of ATP. When the muscle stops contracting, critical ATP stores are preserved. You survive to run up the stairs another day.

Although this remarkable process is quite technical, we've tried to give you a simple explanation that will help you put the pieces together as you learn about other facets of the endurance equation—nutrition, training and pacing. They all tie in to ATP and the athlete's most crucial ally—energy.

See Also: *Aerobic Exercise, Anaerobic Exercise, Carbohydrate, Fat, Glucose and Glycogen, Protein*

Capillaries
More are better

E ndurance training will not only build your body, it will also build up your supply of capillaries. And that's all to the good.

Your hard-working muscles need as many of these mini-vessels as they can get to supply them with the oxygen they need. Growing muscles need to be fed, and the larger the muscle, the more oxygen it requires. Enter the capillary delivery service, assuring your needy tissues of an adequate supply of the vital substance.

Capillaries are minute blood vessels, tiny "twigs" at the end of your circulatory system's branching network. These vessels serve two important purposes: They deliver oxygen and other nutrients, and they remove waste from the body.

Because they're incredibly narrow—imagine a pinhead a hundred times smaller than normal—only a single drop of blood can pass through at a time. In the process, molecules of oxygen, carbon dioxide, nutrients and other gases and fluids diffuse back and forth through the walls of the capillaries and in and out of the tissues.

Now imagine yourself during a workout. Thanks to your increased capillarity, your muscles can produce the energy you'll need to pedal that bike or swim those lengths. You'll also produce less lactic acid.

More capillaries also mean that your muscles can remove heat and waste by-products more quickly. In short, bless those little caps—they'll result in more efficient energy production.

The great capillary controversy

There's no doubt among physiologists that exercise increases the number of capillaries, but controversy arises when it comes to the amount of increase. Research has shown that endurance athletes have an average of 40 percent more capillaries than sedentary folks. Because these vessels are so small, it's difficult to measure the increase in precise terms.

The implications for athletes are still not clear. Yes, endurance training will doubtless increase your capillary count. But sportsmedicine experts are still not sure how this translates for the individual athlete.

John Duncan, Ph.D., associate director of the Exercise Physiology Department at the Cooper Institute for Aerobics Research in Dallas, offers a not-so-final word on exercise and its effect on the capillaries.

"It does seem that moderate to vigorous activity is associated with increased capillarization," says Dr. Duncan. "But does it occur in everyone? Is it select to certain sports? Is there some kind of threshold you have to exercise at to experience the increase? We don't know."

Endorphins
Painkillers or mood-alterers?

*I*f you've had the misfortune of being cornered by a fitness zealot, you've likely been introduced to endorphins. Athletes prattle on about these wondrous peptides as if they could raise the dead, or at least have you joyously high-stepping your way to the horizon.

Endorphins are actually painkillers that are released by our bodies to combat physical and mental stress. Numerous studies have shown increased levels of endorphins in the blood during strenuous exercise, but the scientific community has yet to agree on their precise function in battling stress.

To wax scientific for a moment, endorphins are actually part of a group of naturally produced opiates known as "endogenous opioid peptides," or EOPs. They're endogenous because they're produced within the body; opioid because, like any opiate, they bind to painkilling receptors in the brain, dulling the body's perception of pain; and peptides because they're formed of strings of amino acids.

There are many EOPs with many different functions, but those most familiar to the layman are endorphins. Secreted by the pituitary gland, these act like morphine to dull your central nervous system's response to pain. For primitive man, a painful event might have been getting squashed by a mastodon. For athletes, there may be a point during endurance exercise when endorphins are produced to dull the pain of physical trauma.

"May"? Does the body produce opiates that dull the pain of exercise, or doesn't it?

Good question, says Peter A. Farrell, Ph.D., associate professor of applied physiology at Pennsylvania State University's Human Performance Laboratory in University Park. There's no doubt that endorphin levels in the blood rise during exercise, but whether those endorphins act to lessen the awareness of pain is still unknown.

"Some studies clearly show that endorphins are involved in modulating pain during and after exercise, and other studies indicate they have no effect," says Dr. Farrell.

What about "runner's high"? A runner himself for almost 20 years, Dr. Farrell allows that on rare occasions while running, he has felt as if he were on "cloud nine." Were endorphins responsible? Again, no one knows. Plenty of studies have shown that exercise reduces anxiety. Whether endorphins play a role in that reduction, science can't say. Some studies say yes, but even more studies indicate that increases in endorphins during exercise play no role whatsoever in anxiety reduction and positive mood changes.

Dr. Farrell brings up a final interesting point. His studies, and the studies of others, show that endorphins may act to dampen the reaction of the sympathetic nervous system, the "fight or flight" response that "excites" the body during exercise.

However, at this point, the final word on endorphins is anything but. Concludes Dr. Farrell: "The jury is still out."

Glucose and Glycogen
The sugars that matter

*I*t's an ugly sight and one long remembered. A wobbly, weak-kneed, glassy-eyed cyclist staggers toward the convenience store counter, grabs an armload of sugary treats, then promptly shovels the entire lot down with the etiquette of a Troglodyte.

These folks can be forgiven their excesses; they're simply trying to replace what their body craves, namely sugar. For the endurance athlete, sugar means energy, and energy, of course, means everything.

Two kinds of sugar provide the fuel your body needs: glucose and glycogen. Glucose, a simple sugar, or monosaccharide, is the end product of carbohydrate digestion. When you're exercising, it's the primary fuel for your muscles because it's readily available. When your body needs fuel, glucose is the source it first calls on, siphoning it from the bloodstream and shuttling it to the working muscles.

Glycogen can be viewed as a secondary fuel source. It's made up of chains of glucose molecules, or polysaccharides, which are stored in the liver and muscle cells. When you eat carbohydrates, the glucose molecules that don't go directly to the cells after digestion are carried off to the liver. Here they're combined and stored as glycogen.

When your liver and muscles are filled to the brim with glycogen, the liver converts excess supplies to fat and stores it in fatty (adipose) tissue. These "fatty" reserves can be an invaluable ally to the endurance athlete.

Tapping into your sugar supply

You've wolfed down your carbohydrates, and now you've got glucose in your bloodstream and muscles and glycogen in your liver, muscles and fatty tissues. As your exercising muscles demand more fuel, the stored glycogen is broken down into individual molecules of glucose, jettisoned into the bloodstream and whisked off to the demanding muscles.

Your body first uses the glucose available in your muscles and bloodstream. When those supplies are exhausted, it turns to stored glucose tucked away in the liver and the muscle cells. After depleting those sources, your body frees up the glucose stores in fat, as well as some glucose from protein.

Though protein supplies a small amount of glucose compared to carbohydrate and stored fat, it's not inconsequential. Researchers believe the glucose removed from protein-building amino acids in the blood contributes up to 5 percent of the total energy used during vigorous exercise.

This wealth of storage compartments might make it seem as if there's a boundless glucose supply just waiting to be tapped. In fact, there's just enough glycogen stored in the liver and muscles to fuel between 90 and 120 minutes of hard, aerobic exercise.

Thus, you'll have to be careful to replenish these supplies with carbohydrate-rich food or drink. Otherwise, this void becomes brutally apparent. Most endurance athletes have experienced this "bonk"—drained, they totter along as if auditioning for *Night of the Living Dead*. It's an unpleasant image, but one that's easily avoided by wise use of your energy reserves.

See Also: ***Bonking, Carbohydrate, Fat, Pacing, The Wall***

Lactic Acid
Befriending the fire

F ew things are more misunderstood than lactic acid, probably because it tends to play a Jekyll and Hyde role in exercise. Most athletes are familiar with lactic acid's Dr. Jekyll role—the pooling of lactic acid that makes muscles burn and the mind scream, "Quit!" But less well known is lactic acid's benevolent Dr. Hyde role.

First, a quick review of the Jekyll side. Lactic acid is a by-product of anaerobic metabolism—it accumulates when there's not enough oxygen to break down carbohydrates to create energy.

And yes, once the levels of lactic acid rise in your muscles, you'll find your energy peters out and your fatigue snowballs. That's because lactic acid in big doses prevents your muscles from contracting and blocks important enzymes in the muscles.

But there's more to the lactic acid story, and the latest installment is cause for grins instead of grimaces. Sums up George Brooks, Ph.D.: "A lot of what we thought about lactic acid and metabolism was wrong."

Acid in, acid out

As director of the Exercise Physiology Laboratory at the University of California at Berkeley, Dr. Brooks has done much to set the lactic acid story straight. For one thing, he says, lactic acid isn't produced only when you exercise anaerobically. Your body actually produces lactic acid while resting. Even as you read this, lactic acid is being formed in your intestines, skeletal muscles, red blood cells and parts of your liver.

Why, then, aren't we pickled in the stuff? Responds Dr. Brooks, "We now know that lactic acid is formed and removed continuously and frequently at rapid rates, even at rest."

But the level is low at rest because it's constantly being removed. You can compare it to a flush toilet—the level is always the same, but the water is being fully exchanged.

The muscles rid themselves of lactic acid in two ways. First, it's broken down by the muscles to produce energy. Second, it's removed through the liver and kidneys.

Polishing a tarnished image

Most of the lactic acid you produce turns into much-needed energy. In fact, during steady exercise at a comfortable aerobic pace, it's Dr. Brooks's estimate that about 75 percent of the lactic acid you produce is quickly turned into energy. When lactic acid is removed through the liver, it becomes glycogen and is stored for later use as energy.

But it's lactic acid's boost for the heart that really spruces up its image. According to Dr. Brooks, lactic acid is the heart's main source of energy. And during endurance exercise, it bolsters your body's most critical variable—cardiac output.

If lactic acid is so wonderful, why does it make our muscles burn as if they're being worked on by an army of mini-welders? It falls under the heading "having too much of a good thing." The point at which you feel pain when you push hard isn't the actual point where you begin to produce lactic acid—it marks the point where you can no longer get rid of it fast enough.

Staving off lactic acid buildup

As athletes, we don't need to be overly concerned with the complex biochemistry of lactic acid. Our concern is simple—how can we manage our lactic acid pool so it doesn't overflow and drown us?

Your body uses a two-pronged approach to keep lactic acid levels low—it tries to minimize its production, and it clears out what is produced as efficiently as possible. With proper training, you can improve your body's ability to do both.

Your best approach to improving the clearing mechanism is simple—train in hard intervals. When you begin increasing your load of lactic acid, your body will be forced to find better pathways to get rid of the stuff.

High-intensity training such as intervals also improves your ability to take in oxygen, and with more oxygen present, you won't be forced to produce as much energy anaerobically. Presto, you'll create less lactic acid.

As an added benefit, hard efforts improve your circulatory capacity, allowing lactic acid to be whisked away more quickly.

Bouts of long, slow distance training will also help prevent lactic acid buildup. Long runs and rides at moderate effort teach your body to burn fat instead of carbohydrate. This works to your advantage because the less carbohydrate you burn, the less lactic acid you'll get as a by-product.

Conditioning—your best buffer

Studies have shown that the better conditioning you receive, the better chance you have of preventing excessive lactic acid buildup. While experimenting with rats, Dr. Brooks found that untrained and trained rats produced the same amounts of lactic acid. However, the trained rats were more than 100 percent better at clearing it from their bloodstreams.

It's much the same with people. Your overweight neighbor will produce lactic acid while huffing up the stairs. (Lactic acid begins to accumulate beyond the 65 percent effort level.) In contrast, an elite runner like Olympic gold medalist Frank Shorter can push at 80 to 90 percent effort without creating lactic acid levels that will affect performance. Thanks to supreme fitness and proper training, lactic acid removal has been honed to a highly efficient process.

"You may produce more lactic acid at high power, but proper training allows you to get rid of it," explains Dr. Brooks. "You develop a mechanism for lactate clearance."

Common sense will also help you regulate your lactic acid levels. Athlete John Howard has made three Olympic cycling teams and won eight national road championships and the 1981 Hawaii Ironman Triathlon. He has done so, in part, by carefully marshaling his resources. When Howard competes, he often eases into the race, then picks up his pace as the event unfolds. If he feels lactic acid building up early in a race, he'll turn down his pace a notch until the burning goes away.

Walking the tightrope

Successfully competing in endurance events, says Howard, often boils down to a tightrope walk between aerobic and anaerobic effort.

"Treading that fine line between anaerobic and aerobic is the way you go fast," says Howard. "If you push too hard too early, lactic acid buildup will shut you down."

Yes, lactic acid can contribute to muscular fatigue. But athletes would do well to consider its positive contribution to performance.

"Everyone used to think of it as a poison to be avoided, but lactic acid is now recognized for its important metabolic functions," says Dr. Brooks. "The current concept is that it's like fire. You can't have civilization or progress without fire."

See Also: *Aerobic Exercise; Anaerobic Exercise; Anaerobic Threshold; Fat; Long, Slow Distance Training*

Maximum Heart Rate
An honest measure of honest effort

*T*wo runners, both doing intervals on a track, are equally convinced that they're laboring mightily. One runner carefully monitors her heart rate; the other bases her assessment on a heart that feels as if it's about to leap from her chest. Are both expending the same effort? Probably not.

Subjectively measuring your own physical effort is a bit like rating your own job performance. Odds are, you're not working as hard as you think.

But your heart rate never lies. Your mind may be dizzy with effort, your muscles buzzing with strain, but your heart thumps along implacably. It's the seat of objectivity and your most accurate measure of effort. This is precisely why a sound understanding of maximum heart rate (MHR) is an invaluable tool for the training athlete.

Two things make your MHR the best yardstick for measuring the intensity of your effort. First, unlike other measures of aerobic fitness, which change quickly as you get fitter, your MHR won't change much over the short term. Second, it's easy to measure.

And it's well worth the effort. Knowing your heart rate is the best way to ensure that you're getting the workout you want.

Measuring your "horsepower"

The most common way of measuring your maximum heart rate is simple—subtract your age from 220. Are you 40 years old? Your MHR is about 180 beats a minute.

But exercise physiologist Mary O'Toole, Ph.D., director of the University of Tennessee's Human Performance Laboratory in Memphis, warns that this simple measure of MHR can be off by as many as ten beats a minute. This is a substantial difference that can skew your measure of your effort.

What to do? You can sidestep this variation, says Dr. O'Toole, by borrowing or buying a heart rate monitor. Then go to the track. Take an easy two-mile warm-up. Begin to run a progressively faster quarter-mile, picking up the pace as you go until you're sprinting all-out for the final 100 yards. Check your heart rate immediately after you finish. This should be a reasonably accurate measure of your MHR.

Peg your effort to your heart rate

Once you've calculated your MHR, you can use it to specifically measure your level of effort.

As a general rule of thumb, you'll have to exercise at at least 60 percent of your maximum heart rate to achieve effective aerobic conditioning. Let's say your MHR is 180 beats a minute. Sixty percent of 180 is 108 beats a minute. If your heart rate drops any lower, you won't be getting much aerobic benefit at all.

To be honest, however, this 60 percent figure isn't a hard-and-fast one. In the case of a slightly fit person, a decent aerobic training effect can be achieved with a sustained heart rate as low as 40 percent of maximum. The more fit you become, the higher training stimulus you'll need to get results.

Many serious endurance athletes train at 80 to 90 percent of their MHR. Obviously, this is a highly individual decision, taking into account your degree of fitness, the sport involved and your inherent ability to sustain these training levels.

You'll know when you've crossed from aerobic to anaerobic territory; a queasy feeling will overtake you, your body won't be able to replenish oxygen fast enough and you'll lose your ability to keep up the pace.

Though anaerobic exercise has its place, it's sustained aerobic exercise that offers the benefits most exercisers want. It burns lots of calories, helps control cholesterol levels and reduces the risk of heart disease.

Calculate your heart rate reserve

If you want an even more accurate method than calculating your percentage of effort, consider the "heart rate reserve" method. First calculate your resting heart rate. Simply take your pulse for 60 seconds before arising in the morning. Next, apply the heart rate reserve formula:

220 – age – resting heart rate × percent effort + resting heart rate = target heart rate

In fact, assuming that every 30-year-old has the same maximum heart rate is about as logical as assuming that every 30-year-old has the same shoe size. Because it incorporates your own resting heart rate, the heart rate reserve method is a more accurate way to gauge your efforts.

It's also important to remember that your MHR is *not* a measure of your fitness—for the most part it's the product of your age. An elite 30-year-old marathoner has approximately the same MHR as a 30-year-old couch potato. What separates the two is the ability of the conditioned marathoner to run much faster at the same effort.

When the couch potato begins to engage in a regular running program, his level of fitness will improve. His maximum heart rate won't change, but he'll be able to run farther and faster with less effort.

The myth of the declining heart rate

For years, sports physiologists and other fitness professionals assumed that a person's MHR declined after age 25. This inevitable decrease in aerobic potential, decreed the experts, was partly due to the aging heart's less elastic muscle fibers. More recent studies suggest that this is not entirely the case. In fact, lifelong high-level fitness may minimize, or even stall, the drop in MHR seen in sedentary folks.

Many current theories about aging are being reexamined. These most recent findings cast even more doubt on the MHR formula of 220 minus age. For now, however, its simplicity makes it the best formula we have to work with.

See Also: *Aerobic Exercise; Anaerobic Exercise; Long, Slow Distance Training; Perceived Exertion*

Maximum Oxygen Uptake (VO$_2$ Max)
The gold standard of aerobic fitness

Maximum oxygen uptake (VO$_2$ max), also known as maximum aerobic capacity, is the buzzword of aerobic sport. The only problem is, most athletes can't tell you precisely what it is.

VO$_2$ max is actually the amount of oxygen you're putting to use. It's a measure of your body's ability to take in oxygen, move it through the bloodstream and make it available for the breakdown of carbohydrates, fats and proteins. These provide the energy that keeps you going. After all, if you can't deliver oxygen to your muscles and put it to good use, you can't perform.

In large part, your body's ability to use oxygen is genetic—some people are born with more aerobic ability than others. Age is also a factor. Your VO$_2$ max begins to decline after age 25—from 5 to 10 percent with each decade. The rate of decline can, however, be eased somewhat through training.

Your VO$_2$ max is also affected by your muscle mass. If you're male, your muscle mass will be greater than your female counterpart's, and you'll need more oxygen to fuel muscular activity. Thus, men have higher VO$_2$ max measurements than women.

Even the efficiency of your working muscles' metabolic enzymes helps determine your VO$_2$ max.

The good news is that not all is left to fate. Hard endurance training can increase your VO$_2$ max dramatically—up to 30 percent—especially if you're new to exercise. And that's good news for older people, who are just as capable of raising their VO$_2$ max. In fact, studies indicate it may take them even less effort to do so.

Measuring your max

How is VO$_2$ max measured? Sorry, no one's yet invented a simple do-it-yourself formula, so you'll have to visit a local lab to get your results. VO$_2$ max can only be measured with proper monitoring equipment. Fortunately, the procedure is quite simple—you run on a treadmill or pedal an exercise bike while your heart rate and breathing are measured on a machine.

VO_2 max is expressed in milliliters of oxygen per kilogram of body weight per minute (ml/kg/min). The average VO_2 max for a 25-year-old man is 45 ml/kg/min; for a 25-year-old woman, it's 39 ml/kg/min. At the far end of the scale, top male endurance athletes score in the 80s and top women in the 70s.

There's really no compelling need to be tested. If you're not obsessed with this sort of thing, just keep training and forget the test. You might, however, want to measure your max as a benchmark of your progress. If, after six months, your aerobic capacity hasn't improved, take a second look at your training routine.

Maximizing your max

If you weren't genetically gifted with the VO_2 max of an industrial-strength vacuum, don't despair. It's what you do with your aerobic capacity that counts. The trick to successfully competing is being able to perform as close as possible to your VO_2 max without collapsing. Sure, it takes a good set of genes to win the Boston Marathon. But it also takes long years of training to prepare yourself to run 26 miles at 90 percent of your aerobic capacity.

"Performance is not just a function of VO_2 max," says Jim Rippe, M.D., a cardiologist at the University of Massachusetts Medical School in Worcester. "When we studied competitive cyclists in the lab, VO_2 max was one of the poorest correlators with performance. What correlated best were years of experience in riding."

Another expert adds: "A cyclist who's able to ride for two hours at 75 to 80 percent of a relatively modest VO_2 max is going to blow the doors off a more gifted rider working at 50 percent of VO_2 max."

See Also: *Aerobic Exercise, Muscles and Muscular Endurance, Staying in the Game*

Muscle Fiber Ratio
Your personal endurance factor

T wo athletes stand side by side, both well muscled, both in excellent condition. What's the factor that will determine which athlete will be a sprinter and which will be a marathon swimmer?

Believe it or not, the deciding factor could be the predominance of fast-twitch or slow-twitch muscle fibers. Slow-twitch fibers, which contract more slowly, contain an active capillary network that delivers lots of oxygen to the muscle. Slow-twitchers are your *aerobic* muscle fibers, which need oxygen to burn fuel in order for the muscle to contract. When these fibers get enough oxygen and energy, these muscles can work steadily for a long time.

Fast-twitch fibers move two to three times faster than their slower counterparts. They're larger and stronger, but with far fewer capillaries delivering blood.

These are your *anaerobic* muscle fibers—they don't need oxygen in order to work. But because they function anaerobically, their rapid contractions also produce lactic acid, causing them to fatigue more rapidly. Hence runners like Olympic gold medalist Carl Lewis can proceed at warp speed for only so long.

We all have both types, but to better understand how they work, let's assign them personalities.

Carl Lewis exploding from the blocks, accelerating down the track like a gust of wind, then quickly tapering off, represents the fast-twitch muscle—it gives a short, sweet burst of raw power. Four-time Ironman winner Mark Allen, flowing through the miles at a smooth, steady clip, personifies the slow-twitch muscle fiber—dogged, resolute and enduring.

An athlete with a predominance of fast-twitch fibers will feel right at home in events requiring raw speed and power but will be short on the staying power needed for events that require stamina and endurance.

On the flip side, an athlete who's heavy on the slow-twitch fibers might lumber out of the starting blocks but will get to that finish line come hell or high water.

It's all in the genes

Every muscle contains elements of both Lewis and Allen, with fast-twitch and slow-twitch fibers lying next to each other. Fiber ratio is solely a matter of genetics—you're born with a specific number of each, and the ratio doesn't change, regardless of athletic prowess.

Most people have equal amounts of each type of fiber, but the exceptions can vary widely. It's not unusual to find an elite marathoner with 80 percent slow-twitch fibers in the muscles. A track sprinter, on the other hand, will probably possess 80 percent fast-twitch fibers.

Amazingly, muscles in various areas of the body can have different fiber ratios. If you're endowed with a nice supply of slow-twitch fibers in your legs, you could be a natural for long-distance running. On the other hand, if your arms contain lots of fast-twitch fibers, they could be well suited for pulling you through water.

A biopsy is the only way to determine each muscle's fiber ratio. This lab test involves injecting a needle into the muscle and removing a small sample to examine under a microscope. This is somewhat painful and is usually done only for scientific study.

One such study involved top runners at Ball State University's Human

Performance Laboratory in Muncie, Indiana. Lab director David Costill, Ph.D., noted that many top long-distance runners, such as Frank Shorter and Steve Prefontaine, had muscles made up of 79 percent slow-twitch fibers. Elite middle-distance runners—half-milers to two-milers—averaged only 62 percent slow-twitch fibers. This made perfect sense, since these runners would need more fast-twitch muscles, and speed, to succeed in their events.

Dr. Costill concluded that our muscle fiber ratio genetically predisposes us to excel in certain events. "We've shown that you're never going to be a long-distance champion unless you've got a lot of slow-twitch muscle fibers."

Boosting fiber fitness

As you get older, your "twitch quotient" begins to change. Explains Christopher Scott, research associate at the Cooper Institute for Aerobics Research in Dallas, "This probably occurs due to both the aging process and the inactivity that accompanies it. Total muscle mass can decrease as much as 40 percent as we age. Most of this occurs in the fast-twitch muscle fibers, but slow-twitch muscle fibers are lost, too."

Though you can't change or restore your fiber ratio, you can improve the capabilities of the fibers you have. Long, steady efforts will strengthen your slow-twitch fibers. Hard, fast efforts—such as interval work on the track or hill climbs on a bike—can greatly improve the ability of your fast-twitch fibers to use oxygen. Your muscles will also be able to work longer before grinding to a halt.

There's more good news. Studies have shown that athletes who indulge in consistent endurance cycling have fast-twitch fibers that can handle almost as much oxygen as the slow-twitch fibers of the untrained. Apparently, steady endurance training increases the number of capillaries in the fast-twitch muscles so they can transport more oxygen.

Every athlete performs within limits, and muscle fiber ratio is one contributing factor. But you can maximize your abilities by putting both speed and endurance work into your program. In this way, you'll be confident that your muscle fibers are working to the best of their ability.

See Also: *Aerobic Exercise, Anaerobic Exercise, Capillaries, Maximum Oxygen Uptake, Muscles and Muscular Endurance*

Muscles and Muscular Endurance
Making the most of what you've got

*I*t's Hawaii, 1982. We're at the 140-mile Ironman Triathlon. Julie Moss of Carlsbad, California, leads the women's race. Yards from the finish, Moss wilts to the ground. Over the next several minutes she struggles back to her feet several times, only to fall again. A huge crowd of spectators cheers and pleads, hoping to will her across the finish line. Moss finally opts to crawl to the finish. As she bumps along on elbows and knees, fellow Californian Kathleen McCartney sprints past her.

As moving as that scene was, replayed again and again on "ABC's Wide World of Sports," it is also fascinating from a physiological point of view. Most people assumed Moss was suffering from heat injury and had lost touch with reality. Quite the contrary. Moss was tired, yes, but otherwise she felt fine. She was lucid, her brain was working and her arms were working. Only the muscles in her legs wouldn't respond.

"The real panic came the first time I fell and I tried to get back up," recalls Moss. "That was frustrating. I was giving it everything I had from the waist up, but my legs weren't working. They felt like wet spaghetti.

"The last time I fell, I just crawled. It was surprising, because crawling wasn't bothering my legs at all. It was just the effort of getting up."

Moss recovered quickly after the race, looking amazingly fresh at a television interview within the hour. Ironman medical director Robert Laird, M.D., believes Moss wasn't suffering from heat injury or severe electrolyte imbalance but rather from simple muscular exhaustion. Moss had pushed herself to the limit.

A close look at the muscles of endurance

To understand how you can get the most from your muscles, let's take a brief look at how they work.

Muscles are organs that allow the various parts of your body to move. There are three kinds of muscles:

1. Smooth or involuntary muscles, which are found, for instance, in the walls of the digestive tract.
2. Striated or skeletal muscles, which are attached by tendons to the bones and are under voluntary control.
3. Cardiac muscles, which are similar to skeletal muscles but are not under voluntary control and are found only in the heart.

As endurance athletes, we need to concern ourselves primarily with the muscles we can control—the skeletal muscles. Cut through a section of TV cable and you'll get a good idea of what skeletal muscle looks like—many thousands of intertwined strands, ranging from 1 to 45 millimeters long.

Like a TV cable, the muscles are composed of smaller and smaller "wires." Progressing from large to small, you have the muscle, composed of intertwined strands of muscle fiber; the muscle fiber, composed of strands of myofibril; and the myofibril, composed of strands of myofilaments.

When these myofilaments contract, fueled by the body's energy currency, ATP (adenosine triphosphate), your muscles move. Bereft of ATP and unable to contract, Julie Moss's leg muscles might as well have been made of rubber.

A quick skeletal survey

Skeletal muscles come in three fiber types, each with a different ability to contract. You've probably heard of the sprinter's fast-twitch muscles and the marathoner's slow-twitch muscles. Actually, science divides skeletal muscles into the following three categories.

Type I, or high-oxidative, slow-twitch red fibers. These fibers react slowly to nerve impulses, but they can produce great quantities of ATP (energy) over long periods of time. Type I fibers fatigue slowly and are ideally suited to endurance activity. These are the fibers you would call on during a slow jog.

Type IIA, or high-oxidative, fast-twitch red fibers. These fibers react quickly to nerve impulses. They can produce a lot of ATP quickly, but they fatigue far more rapidly. These are the fibers you would call on when you up the pace from a jog to a run.

Type IIB, or low-oxidative, fast-twitch white fibers. These fibers also react very quickly to nerve impulses, but they fatigue far more rapidly than the other two types. Unlike the other two fibers, which require oxygen to produce energy, these fibers produce ATP almost solely in the absence of oxygen. These are the muscle fibers you'd call on during a sprint.

What do all these fiber types mean to the endurance athlete? Each type comes into play during different types of activity. On a casual bike ride or a long, slow run, your legs rely mostly on slow-twitch fibers. During a fast, racing-pace marathon that calls for speed and stamina, you'll use both slow-twitch and fast-twitch muscles.

An argument for cross-training

First a word about what training doesn't do. Training does not increase your original number of muscle fibers. Thanks to genetics, you're endowed with a certain number and distribution of slow-twitch and fast-twitch muscles that are yours for life. Carl Lewis is Carl Lewis and you are you. No amount of training will change that.

What you *can* do is strengthen the fibers you have and, most important from an endurance perspective, make those fibers much better at producing energy. If you continue to stress certain muscle fibers, they'll eventually become far more efficient at burning fat and carbohydrate for fuel. This, of course, allows you to push harder and faster without falling on your face.

It's also important to realize that any type of training is highly specific. To be successful in your chosen sport, you need to stress the muscles and fibers unique to that sport. How specific are training's effects? Tell the world's best marathoner to dash about on a racquetball court for an hour or so. Guaranteed, you'll hear about a case of sore legs when the game is over.

Once you understand the slow-twitch/fast-twitch distinction, it's easy to understand why you need to vary your training. Long, slow endurance training promotes precisely that, stressing the slow-twitch muscle fibers and improving their ability to produce energy. Fast-paced, interval-type effort conditions your muscles' fast-twitch component, refining their ability to produce energy quickly. If you train properly and condition your muscles to quickly produce whopping amounts of energy, there's little else you need—except an agent to represent you on the professional circuit.

Rest—overlooked and underrated

Stress strengthens, but too much stress can bring even the fittest athlete to collapse. Your muscles need rest.

Unfortunately, rest is one of the most neglected components of an endurance training program. In the minds of many endurance athletes, more is better, and even more is better still.

Wrong, for two compelling reasons.

First, it takes about 24 hours to replenish your stores of muscle glycogen after sustained periods of intense exercise. Continuous hard training, especially if you're doing more than one workout a day, will inevitably send you on a downward energy spiral. Eventually, you'll be plodding through your workouts with the verve of someone slogging through a bog.

Second, and more important, intense exercise causes real physical damage to muscle fibers. The fibers strain and tear, capillaries break and cell membranes rupture. If you don't give your body time to mend, the risk of more serious damage—connective tissue injuries, nasty muscle tears and strains—increases astronomically.

World-class athletes, who have decidedly more reason to be compulsive about training, understand the need for rest.

"The most important thing about training is the work-to-rest ratio," says mountain bike star Ned Overend. "A lot of people heap on the miles, and they'll work at, say, 75 percent of their maximum all of the time. They should be working at 85 percent on the hard days and then at 40 to 50 percent on the easy days."

To allow for recovery, many athletes choose a hard/easy training program, following a day of intense training with one that's more recreational than purposeful. You can also alternate sports. If you're a runner and opt to do a hard interval workout on Tuesday, give your legs a break on Wednesday and spin easy on the bike.

For the same reason, serious weight trainers who work out six to seven days a week try to alleviate the strain. They'll work specific muscle groups on specific days—a chest and back day, for example, gives the legs a day of rest.

If you're training in more than one sport, you can still use the hard/easy concept, although you'll have to be a bit more creative. If the morning calls for a hard run, make the most of it. Then swim in the afternoon (great for loosening up) and use the following morning for a long, easy bike ride.

Whatever the pattern, the idea is the same. You don't ever want to stress the same muscle groups twice in a row.

Muscular fatigue: avoiding meltdown

No matter how well conditioned your muscles are, eventually you'll experience muscular fatigue. After all, it comes with the territory when you're building endurance.

The primary cause of muscular fatigue in endurance athletes is glycogen depletion. Runners "hit the Wall." Cyclists "bonk." Suddenly the only fuel available to the muscles is fat. Though abundant in supply, it can't be broken down quickly enough to supply energy for high levels of aerobic performance. Once fatigue sets in, your pace will fall to a fraction of what it was earlier in the race.

Other factors can bring on muscular fatigue and collapse. Dehydration, for example, may lead to electrolyte imbalances, producing severe cramps. Dehydration can also reduce blood plasma levels and impede circulation to the point where lactic acid can't be flushed from the muscles. At this point, the muscles will simply refuse to contract.

The truth is, muscular fatigue can be a good thing. It's another mechanism that stymies our best efforts to destroy ourselves. Fatigue prevents us from doing irreversible damage to our muscles and other organs—including the brain, which hopefully will know better next time.

See Also: *Bonking; Cross-Training; Glucose and Glycogen; Interval Training; Lactic Acid; Long, Slow Distance Training; The Wall*

Perceived Exertion
Your guess is better than you think

*P*erceived exertion is hardly a new concept; you've been using it ever since you first hauled a big load of grocery bags from the car into the house, dropped them on the kitchen counter and proclaimed, to no one in particular, "Whew! Those were heavy!"

Well, back in 1982, a Swedish psychologist named Gunnar Borg developed something called the Borg or RPE (rate of perceived exertion) scale. This scale assigned numerical values from 6 to 20 to exercise intensities ranging from "very, very light" to "very, very hard." The ratings were then correlated to percentage of maximum heart rate (MHR).

A "moderate" workout, for instance, would merit an RPE rating of 12, which corresponds roughly to 70 percent of MHR. A very heavy level of exercise—16 and above on the RPE scale or 90 percent or more of MHR—would be speed training or racing.

Estimating your exertion

If you don't have access to a lab and you're not ready to plunk down money for a heart rate monitor, don't despair. Controlled studies have found that many experienced endurance athletes can accurately assess the intensity of their workouts through perceived exertion.

The key word here is *experienced*. If you've just started training, everything will feel hard. But if you're a regular exerciser, familiar with effort and honest with yourself, your perception of your effort is apt to be close to the mark. No less august an authority than the American College of Sports Medicine calls the RPE scale "a valid tool in the monitoring of intensity of exercise training programs."

Using your perceived rate of exertion, you can estimate your heart rate fairly closely. Simply multiply your rate of perceived exertion by ten.

Let's say you're pushing just a bit hard—an effort of about 14 on the RPE scale. Your heart rate is probably hovering around 140 beats a minute. If you want to test the accuracy of this measure and don't mind interrupting your workout, stop, count your pulse rate for ten seconds and multiply by six.

When it comes to assessing an endurance training program, most of your exercise will usually fall within the moderate to heavy range, with an RPE of 14 to 16, or 80 to 89 percent of your maximum heart rate. This is the level that builds your all-important aerobic base. Unfortunately, many recreational athletes feel compelled to push themselves to the limit every day, a misguided inclination smart athletes avoid.

"You don't need any more than three hard workouts a week to achieve top condition," attests Olympic gold medalist Frank Shorter.

See Also: ***Heart Rate Monitors, Maximum Heart Rate***

Second Wind
A breath of fresh air

The scientific community can't quite put its finger on second wind, but there's no doubt it exists. It's that sudden shift, early in exercise, from the agonies of the Inquisition to a feeling of breezy bliss.

"The problem isn't that people don't believe in second wind," says Richard Coast, Ph.D., an exercise physiologist at Texas A&M University in College Station. "I think even the most dyed-in-the-wool, prove-it-to-me scientist who has ever exercised believes in second wind. It's just that it doesn't come about predictably enough to study it."

You can't call it up at will, but the scenario is still a familiar one to many athletes. You start a run. You feel good. Then you feel bad. Your legs ache, your breath comes in gasps and your heart pounds out the rumba. Suddenly, presto, your body seems to make an adjustment, and you're on cruise control.

Glenn Town, Ph.D., offers the most agreed-upon assessment of what's happening here. An exercise physiologist and athlete (he once placed 24th at the Hawaii Ironman Triathlon), Dr. Town believes the second wind phenomenon is a simple matter of paid-off debt.

A debt repaid—and a bonus

Here's how it works. When you begin at a pace too fast for your body to adjust to, your body needs more oxygen than it's getting. Your heart's forced to beat faster to circulate the limited oxygen available as fast as possible. Meanwhile, your lungs strain to bring in more air. Since there isn't enough oxygen available to burn carbohydrate and fat aerobically, your body has to work anaerobically to produce energy and its lactic acid by-product. Now your muscles are starting to burn.

Eventually, you'll reach a point where your body starts to take in enough oxygen to replace what it lost. Suddenly, you feel good again. That's second wind.

Well-conditioned athletes, says Dr. Town, rarely experience second wind because they don't go into oxygen debt in the first place. Their fit systems provide more than enough oxygen from the get-go.

The best advice for less fit folks, says Dr. Town, is to start slowly. If you plan to run, begin with a brisk walk, move to a light jog and then up the pace gradually to your running speed.

"You need to move into aerobic work at a slow pace so you don't develop this huge indebtedness," says Dr. Town.

Fit athletes, too, can benefit from a slightly juiced-up version of this walk/jog/run premise. Even when Bill Rodgers was winning the Boston

Marathon on a regular basis, he'd start his training runs at little more than a matronly shuffle. Dr. Town agrees that this snowball strategy is a good one.

"There's strong evidence that you need to go through a slow progression to get to your optimal heart rate," says Dr. Town. "Everyone can benefit from this."

See Also: *Aerobic Exercise, Anaerobic Exercise, Pacing*

Staying in the Game
It's not over 'til it's over

alt Stack arrived at the 1981 Hawaii Ironman Triathlon full of piss and vinegar. This did little to differentiate Stack from his fellow Ironmen, except that Stack, then 73, had marinated longer in the stuff. The irascible San Franciscan hitched up his britches and steadfastly plowed through the 2.4-mile swim, 112-mile bike ride and 26.2-mile run. He finished 15 hours behind winner John Howard—at 26 hours, 20 minutes.

Stack's was the slowest time in the Ironman's history. It didn't bother him, however. He even stopped for a few roadside beers, not to mention breakfast and dinner.

Completing an event of the Ironman's scope at half Stack's age is a remarkable accomplishment. Stack and others like him force us all to reconsider the limits of age. So what's new? These days stories about 70-, 80- and even 90-year-old athletes litter the sporting world.

At 92, Dr. Paul Spangler finished the Boston Marathon. His time, almost nine hours, led him to huff, "I'm too damned old. And I went out too fast." Spangler was 67 when he took up running.

Perhaps closer to home, members of the 40-something crowd are turning—nay, snapping—heads, pummeling athletes half their age. At age 39, Jimmy Connors made the semifinal of the U.S. Open, producing a series of come-from-behind five-set victories. Running against the best women in the country, 39-year-old Francie Larrieu-Smith made the 1992 U.S. Olympic marathon team—which was not particularly surprising since one year earlier she had set the American record for 10,000 meters.

Good news for older athletes

When it comes to aging and endurance, the news is good. There are certain declines you can't escape. You can, however, through regular training, slow these spirals considerably.

One long-held standard is that your maximum oxygen uptake (VO_2 max) declines at a rate of 10 percent per decade after age 25. However, researchers have found that fit men and women over 50 lose their aerobic capacity only half as quickly—at a rate of 5 percent per decade.

There's more encouraging news. Yes, your maximum heart rate (MHR) declines with age. But research suggests that athletes over 50 can exercise at

Training Keeps You Young

Despite age-related declines in aerobic ability and muscle mass and strength, research has shown that even sedentary women and men in their sixties plus can benefit from endurance training programs. In fact, they may improve to as great an extent as athletes 40 years their junior.

One research study showed a 16 percent increase in VO_2 max among a group of 70- to 79-year-olds after only a 13-week training program. Another study, conducted at the Human Nutrition Research Center at Tufts University in Boston, had a group of volunteers, average age 90, improve their leg strength 174 percent after eight weeks of training.

Take Greek runner Christos Vartzakis, now pushing 80, who's been competing since 1927. His VO_2 max resembles that of a 40-year-old nonathlete, his cardiovascular fitness level is equivalent to that of a 20-year-old youth, and his blood lipids place him at minimal risk of atherosclerosis. Awed researchers who studied Vartzakis attribute his superb condition to a lifetime of competitive athletic activity.

Perhaps the best evidence, and certainly the most interesting, is anecdotal. Take Norton Davey of Oceanside, California. Davey was a 55-year-old financial officer for Continental Airlines when a company physician recommended he start running. Davey's reaction was typical.

"I thought he was crazy," he recalls, "but I gave it a try and it worked. I felt better, took off some weight and dropped my blood pressure. Then the worst thing of all happened: I got competitive."

Eighteen years later, at 73, Davey was a seven-time finisher in the Hawaii Ironman Triathlon, with an off-season "maintenance" program that would reduce most youngsters to rubble: 40 miles of running per week, 150 miles on the bike and 15,000 yards of swimming.

Davey's advice to the over-60 beginner?

"First, get yourself checked by a physician. Then start slowly. Buy a good pair of running shoes and walk 20 to 30 minutes two to three times a week and see how you feel. Then gradually increase your time and distance until you're walking and jogging for about half an hour, three or four times a week. If running isn't your thing, buy a bicycle. You've got to enjoy what you're doing."

higher percentages of their MHR before lactic acid accumulates in the blood. We do slow with age. But we recoup some of that loss by being able to exercise at levels closer to our physical potential.

Age and endurance are by no means mutually exclusive. In fact, when it comes to operating at our high end, older people who exercise are better prepared than their younger counterparts.

"Older, sedentary people produce lactate at a higher percentage of their VO_2 max than do young, sedentary people," says James Hagberg, Ph.D., whose work at the University of Maryland Center on Aging in Baltimore has focused largely on athletes over 50. "We see it consistently. So there's at least one adaptation with aging that's beneficial."

The fact that aging declines can be minimized by regular endurance training is no surprise to folks like Larrieu-Smith, Spangler and Stack. Studies have shown that regular endurance training favorably affects all sorts of things, including blood pressure, glucose tolerance, HDL cholesterol, the strength of the heart muscle and bone density.

Your maximum endurance prescription

Training, like athletes, varies widely. A day of training with Larrieu-Smith would reduce most folks to Jell-O. However, there are some general exercise guidelines for developing and maintaining cardiorespiratory and muscular fitness. Developed by the American College of Sports Medicine (ACSM), these guidelines can be applied, with minor variations, to an exercise program whether you're 45 or 85.

The ACSM recommends training three to five days a week at 60 to 90 percent of your MHR. Continuous aerobic activity is the best conditioner; the ACSM recommends exercise sessions of 20 to 60 minutes. Any aerobic activity will do, but the best activities are the ones that involve large muscle groups—hiking, running, cycling, cross-country skiing, dancing, jumping rope, rowing, skating, climbing and swimming, to name a few.

Because muscular strength and fat-free mass decrease with age—a look at your waistline may convince you of that—the ACSM also stresses the need for moderate-intensity strength training. The ACSM minimum is one set of 8 to 12 repetitions of eight to ten exercises that condition the major muscle groups. Do these two days a week. Strength training can also strengthen bones, which is especially important for women, who tend to lose bone strength rapidly.

The ACSM also issues a familiar caution. Before you start a fitness program, get a physical checkup and a medical okay from a physician.

See Also: *Aerobic Exercise, Lactic Acid, Maximum Heart Rate, Maximum Oxygen Uptake, Weight Training*

Part

2

Training Tools and Techniques

*T*he endurance arena is still quite young. Yes, Pheidippides made the first, ill-fated marathon run over 2,000 years ago, but only within the past 20 years—as more and more athletes have taken up endurance sport—have we begun to learn what works in training and racing and what doesn't.

We offer here the nuts and bolts of successful endurance endeavor, information gathered in large part through the trials and errors of athletes who preceded you. Tapping into this experience, you'll be able to use the practices that work and, hopefully, avoid the mistakes.

Take heed before you begin this section. If there's one hard-and-fast rule when it comes to training and racing, it's that there *are* no hard-and-fast rules. No one method works for everyone. Experiment with the techniques we've offered. See how they work for you. Make adaptations.

None of this is etched in stone. One of the most exciting things about endurance sport is the newness of it all. The experiment continues, and you're a part of it.

Acclimatization
Working with the elements

T om Warren, winner of the 1979 Hawaii Ironman Triathlon, may be pegged by some as an "exercise eccentric." We prefer to offer him as an example of one who takes acclimatization seriously. To prepare for the sweltering weather that's synonymous with the Ironman, Warren rides his exercise bicycle. In his home sauna. Ask Warren about it and he won't cringe with embarrassment—he'll tell you precisely how far to place the bike from the rocks, the ideal temperature for training and how big the puddle of sweat under the bike should be before you get off.

Warren's premise is simple. It could never get as hot or as humid in Hawaii as it gets in his own sweat box. So, by the time he gets to Hawaii, Warren is ready for the worst. Quirky, yes, and we don't recommend Warren's regimen. Training in a sauna could cause extreme circulatory stress that could be fatal. But it's interesting to note that, with the exception of a mechanical problem one year, Warren has never failed to finish the Ironman.

Like it or not, many endurance events pit you not only against numbing mileage but also against extremes of hot and cold. The good news, as Warren so clearly illustrates, is that you can adapt your body to all of these through proper training. Granted, you'll run up against certain genetic limits. Men sweat more than women; larger people sweat more than smaller people with smaller sweat glands—but for the most part, your body is remarkably adaptable.

Our ability to acclimatize, or adjust to climate extremes, is evidenced by the wide range of our species. If not for our ability to genetically adapt, the French Riviera would be a crowded place. Eskimos, for example, react to falling temperatures with an almost instantaneous rise in metabolism that warms their skin and extremities and protects them from frostbite and hypothermia.

Of course, such genetic changes take place over thousands of years. We don't have that much time. For the athlete, acclimatizing is a matter of making the maximum adjustment in a minimum amount of time. Fortunately, the body adapts remarkably fast. For example, your body can better cope with heat after as little as seven to ten days of exposure to hot conditions.

Conquering the cold

Experienced cold-weather athletes believe acclimatizing to the cold is mostly a matter of mind over body.

"Just getting yourself used to the cold is the important thing," says mountaineer Gary Scott, world record holder for a solo climb of Alaska's Mount McKinley. "Get out there and run and hike in cold weather. I've trained on Pike's Peak every day, day in and day out, no matter what the conditions. Dealing with the cold is more psychological than anything."

Don Winant, Ph.D., an aerospace physiologist at Edwards Air Force Base in California, agrees that the physiological adaptations to cold are virtually nil.

"Other than the tendency some people have to put on adipose tissue (fat) during the winter months," sums up Dr. Winant, "there are no long-term adaptations."

Dr. Winant does not discount the need for cold-weather acclimatization, however. Experience in cold is crucial, he says. By being mentally prepared, knowing what to wear and knowing when and how much to drink, you can prevent yourself from falling prey to the cold.

Drinking properly during cold weather endurance events is especially important. Though you're not hot, the drier air common to cold temperatures can still absorb moisture quickly. This dehydration reduces both blood volume and cardiac output.

"Hydration is the big factor, because if you're dehydrated you can't transport heat to the extremities," says Dr. Winant.

Getting used to being in cold water also involves getting experience and developing a tough mental attitude.

If you've never been immersed in cold water, your baptism could be rough. Ask Tina Bischoff. In 1976, Bischoff set a men's and women's world record for swimming the notoriously numbing English Channel. However, on her first attempt she didn't finish, but passed out three miles off the coast of France.

Armed with that memory, Bischoff was a bit more meticulous in her preparation for her second, record-breaking attempt. First she added 15 to 20 pounds to her slender 115-pound frame. Then she made training runs through a snowy Cleveland, Ohio, winter in shorts, a couple of T-shirts and a hat.

"Most of the people I talked to who had done the Channel were big to start with—they had a lot of body fat," says Bischoff. "They didn't have a whole lot of trouble adjusting to the cold. Other than that, I think it's just mental."

Learn the art of heat management

It's 1981, the Hawaii Ironman competition. Scott Molina's riding the bike, wearing his father's T-shirt and black dress socks. A mobile solar panel, Molina self-destructs early in the run, passing out and executing a flawless asphalt face plant.

Seven years later, Molina returned to Hawaii, older, wiser and well-prepared. Part of that preparation was a two-week training stint in 108°

weather in Palm Springs, California. On the bike, Molina drank liberally. He skipped the black socks, opting instead for light-colored clothing that reflected the heat. On the run, Molina drank even more.

"I walked every aid station and drank three to four glasses of fluid at each one," recalls Molina. "Water, Coke, Exceed . . . everything they had. When I came through it was, 'Give me the works!' "

This time, Molina executed no face plants—and won the race.

Molina learned his lesson, and it's one all athletes can benefit from. Wherever there's heat, there's potential danger for the endurance athlete. Dehydration, heat exhaustion, heatstroke and severe electrolyte imbalances are a few of the serious—and potentially fatal—consequences of taking heat too lightly.

There's no getting around it—hot weather will always hurt your performance. Still, proper acclimatization can substantially reduce your risks and optimize your effectiveness.

For example, studies have shown that heat-trained ultra-endurance runners lose 90 percent less sodium in their perspiration than those who are not heat trained. Heat-acclimatized athletes also tend to start sweating sooner, and usually in greater amounts. This makes them less likely to suffer from most heat-related injuries, especially if they pay close attention to hot weather's golden rule.

"Drink, drink, drink," says Kathleen McCartney, who did exactly that on her way to her 1982 Hawaii Ironman win, sucking down half a water bottle every five miles and pouring the rest over her body. "If it's hot, it's just amazing how much you sweat. You've got to make sure you get enough fluids."

Take time to acclimatize

The general rule of thumb for endurance athletes off to a warm-weather race is to spend 10 to 14 days training in an equally sweltering climate. The greater the temperature difference between home and race site, the more important it is to acclimatize. If you're headed to Hawaii for the Ironman, and you live in Miami, there won't be as much need to adjust. If you're from Bismarck, North Dakota, give serious thought to arriving in Hawaii early.

Acclimatization is quite specific. If you train in 80° weather, you'll be prepared to race in 80° weather. And generally speaking, it's impossible to overacclimatize. The longer, hotter and more humid the event, the more time your body needs to adapt.

Robert Lind, M.D., medical director of the Western States 100 (as hellishly hot an event as you'll find), considers an ultra-endurance runner to be adequately heat trained after 10 to 14 days of 90-minute midday runs in 90° heat.

Vital to your training success is maintaining proper hydration and nutrition during your acclimatization period. You can't teach your body to deal with shortages of fluid and electrolytes through deprivation. All you'll develop is chronic dehydration and a much higher risk of serious heat injury while competing. When racing or training in heat, the same rules apply— drink plenty of fluids before, during and after.

In fact, fluid intake is a must regardless of weather conditions; you can also lose fluids quickly on a cool, overcast day simply through your exertions. It's therefore wise to go easy at first when acclimatizing—to either heat or cold. Don't make your first-day run in the heat a three-hour mid-day affair. Train easily those first few days.

And expect some dehydration, despite all your precautions, if the weather's hot. The body produces more sweat than can be replaced simply by taking in fluids.

Finally, keep in mind that, when it comes to temperature extremes, if the mind is willing, the body is remarkably adaptable. Dennis "The Coatman" Marsella, a quirky Floridian who likes to get attention, has run over 40 marathons and logged a marathon best of three hours, 26 minutes while running in a full-length, wool-lined winter coat. Certainly you'll think twice before following in "The Coatman's" footsteps. But Marsella, 41, sees no reason why heat should be an obstacle. He vows to continue running in his winter coat until he's 60. Then maybe he'll make a concession.

"After that," says Marsella, "I might cut out the lining."

See Also: *Altitude Training, Dehydration, Hyperthermia, Hypothermia*

Aerobic Exercise
The cornerstone of endurance

At Australia's 1990 1,010-kilometer Westfield Run from Sydney to Melbourne, Greek ultramarathoner Yiannis Kouros politely declined to start the race when the gun sounded. Kouros gave his 31 competitors an 8-hour head start, then promptly mowed them all down within 30 hours. For the first 24 hours, Kouros averaged a remarkable 6:40-mile pace.

Consummate sportsmanship, yes, but what Kouros really showcased was a mastery of aerobic effort second to none. Running at a pace that kept up his oxygen reserves, Kouros was a ruthlessly efficient aerobic machine, able to click along while his opponents collapsed and crumbled.

Simply put, aerobic exercise uses oxygen to help supply energy. But you'll need to understand why aerobic exercise is so efficient—how it allows a superbly conditioned athlete like Kouros to maintain a seemingly inhuman pace.

When you need energy, your body breaks down carbohydrate into glucose, a high-energy sugar. This is further reduced to ATP (adenosine triphosphate), your body's most important energy source. The aerobic process is far more efficient than the anaerobic version, producing 75 times more useful energy.

Anaerobic energy blazes brightly and fades quickly. It's invariably followed by fatigue. Activities such as power-lifting or short sprints are good examples of anaerobic exercise.

In contrast, aerobic energy provides fuel for long-term effort. It enables elite runners to run marathons in two hours and six minutes and lets triathletes persevere through eight hours and 140 miles of swimming, biking and running.

The benefits of aerobic exercise

The body is capable of remarkable adaptations; witness all the news stories about reformed chain smokers and plucky octogenarians who have run marathons.

And you can do it, too. Studies have long shown that regular aerobic exercise, as little as 20 minutes three times a week, can accomplish the following:

- Increase the total volume of your blood, making your circulatory system more efficient.
- Increase the number of your capillaries, the tiny blood vessels that carry oxygen and fuel to the muscles and cart waste products away.
- Enhance your ability to break down fat and carbohydrate and send them to the working muscles to supply energy.
- Strengthen your heart, thickening the walls and allowing it to pump more blood and oxygen to your system with each stroke.
- Increase the number of oxidative enzymes in your muscle fibers. More enzymes allow you to break down carbohydrate and fat faster, keeping you up and running longer.

On a more immediate front, sustained aerobic effort gives most exercisers what they want: It burns calories, raises HDL (good) cholesterol and reduces the risk of heart disease. John Duncan, Ph.D., associate director of the Exercise Physiology Department at the Cooper Institute for Aerobics Research in Dallas, sums up the benefits: "The heart can slow down because it's become a stronger pump. You'll have a higher energy level physiologically and psychologically, and you'll look better through reductions in body weight and changes in body composition."

All these, Dr. Duncan points out, "afford you the opportunity to turn back the hands of time."

Reaping the benefits

The best way to strengthen your aerobic system is through a regular program of sports such as swimming, running, cycling and cross-country skiing, which involve large, oxygen-hungry muscle groups.

You'll achieve the greatest aerobic benefits when you train at about three-quarters of your maximum effort for at least 20 minutes at a time.

Here's how to estimate that effort: Subtract your age from 220 to estimate your maximum heart rate. Then, while exercising, keep your heart rate at 60 to 80 percent of that maximum.

Want a simpler gauge? "If you can't carry on a conversation, you're going too hard," says Brian Sharkey, Ph.D., an exercise physiologist at the University of Montana in Missoula and a past president of the American College of Sports Medicine. "Exercise doesn't have to hurt to be good."

To be most effective, points out Dr. Duncan, aerobic exercise must be continuous. Basketball is great, except when you stop every 30 seconds to shoot a foul shot. Tennis, though a good conditioner, still has too many stops and starts. You can make up for this lack of continuity to some extent by exercising a bit longer, but in the long run nothing beats continuous exercise for aerobic benefit.

Aerobic exercise will help you, the endurance athlete, gain exactly what you're seeking—the ability to keep on going.

See Also: ***Anaerobic Threshold, Glucose and Glycogen, Maximum Heart Rate***

Altitude Training
From mountain high to valley low

*E*ndurance athletes have been singing the praises of altitude training for decades. The idea is, if you're scheduled to compete in the Olympics at, say, Mexico City, then training at a comparable altitude should give you an edge over others who haven't. At the very least, you'll be able to hold your own against competitors accustomed to training at similar altitudes.

In fact, the successes of distance runners from mountainous regions of Africa and Mexico have fueled strong interest in endurance training at 5,000 feet and higher. But does altitude training *really* make a difference? Can endurance athletes who train in the mountains of Colorado or Kenya become Amazons at sea level?

Despite vast amounts of anecdotal evidence that altitude training does work, data from the scientific community is mixed. For every researcher prepared to demonstrate its positive effects, there's another with figures showing just the opposite.

One thing's certain—the lower oxygen content of the air at altitude produces short-term physical changes that would *seem* to improve aerobic capacity. Within the first month of training at high elevation, the number of red blood cells increases and oxygen-carrying hemoglobin within them grows more dense. The network of tiny capillaries that delivers oxygen to the muscles and removes waste products becomes more branching and complex. There's also a greater concentration of enzymes that assist oxidation within the muscle fibers.

The challenge of alternate altitudes

On the other hand, it's harder to train at altitude, especially at first. The shortage of oxygen is impossible to ignore; at 5,000 feet you have to breathe 20 percent harder than at sea level to get the same amount of oxygen into your lungs. Aerobic capacity has been shown to drop roughly 3 percent for every 1,000 feet above 5,000 feet.

Thus, lowlanders moving up to the mountains to train are in for a shock if they try too soon to duplicate their best sea-level efforts. Instead of getting faster, they often drive themselves into chronic exhaustion, wiping out an entire season's worth of hard work.

Training at altitude also decreases the frequency of stride, as you have to train more slowly. This can impair performance by affecting the mechanics of your run.

The only logical solution is to train with less intensity than you would at sea level. Alas, therein lies the dilemma. Can the aerobic adjustments your body makes to altitude overcome your reduced capacity to train?

The answer is a qualified no. Most researchers have found sea-level performance to decrease, or stay the same, following training bouts of several weeks or more above 5,000 feet.

There are exceptions, however. In a study conducted in 1969 by exercise physiologist Jack Daniels, Ph.D., and Neil Oldridge at the University of Wisconsin, six world-class middle-distance runners recorded 14 personal best times at sea level after six weeks of alternate training between sea level and 7,600 feet.

Dr. Daniels, however, was not willing to go out on what he knew to be a long and shaky limb. "The 14 personal best times recorded by the six subjects during various sea-level trips clearly indicates that intermittent altitude training *does not hamper* sea-level performance," he wrote. (The italics are ours.)

It's worth noting that Dr. Daniels's subjects were working under very favorable conditions. They were highly motivated, well-coached individuals in a team environment and were under close medical supervision.

Furthermore, the personal best times in question were only fractional improvements over previous best times. Few of our readers would find such small increments to be worth the time and trouble.

Generally, training at altitude under any but the most rigidly controlled conditions will probably *not* improve your performance at sea level.

Still, if you're determined to try, remember that the optimum training elevation is 7,000 to 9,000 feet. The sharply reduced concentrations of oxygen at higher altitudes may cause oxygen deficiency (hypoxia). It will put so much stress on your body that you'll probably return to sea level in far worse shape than when you left. If you're above 10,000 feet, you may also experience reduced maximum oxygen uptake (VO_2 max), weight loss due to muscle atrophy, chronic dehydration and glycogen depletion.

Racing at altitude

While training in the Rockies isn't likely to help you run, ride or swim faster at the beach, it's a different story if you're going to race at altitude. Experts recommend a bare minimum of two to three solid weeks of acclimatization and training under conditions similar to what you'll see during the race. And the longer the event, the more important this extended training period becomes. A 200-meter sprinter can probably get away with flying in to Mexico City from San Diego the night before a race; a triathlete cannot.

What works even better, say the experts, is the Jack Daniels scenario—a six-month period during which you train five to six days per week at sea level and one to two days per week at altitude. Follow this with two to three solid weeks under race conditions at altitude and you're all set—assuming you can still pay for groceries after all the traveling and time off.

In any case, when racing or training at altitude, remember that additional stresses are being placed upon your body. Experts recommend extended warm-up and cool-down periods, careful attention to proper hydration and a conservative approach to pacing in the early stages of any competition.

The destressing factor

How can one explain the numerous athletes who swear by the effectiveness of altitude training? In the first place, for some people, altitude training simply *works*, period. For others, though, the impact may be more psychological than physical.

Many athletes who train at altitude move from a sea-level environment filled with urban distractions and stress to one in which the focus is on one thing: improvement. Clean air, scenic beauty and dedicated training partners may be as significant a factor in high-altitude improvement as tightly packed red blood cells.

"When I go to Boulder to train, there's not a lot going on. It's pretty low stress," says four-time Hawaii Ironman winner Mark Allen. "The phone doesn't ring as much as when I'm in San Diego and my mail doesn't get forwarded. There's also less environmental stress. If I take a three-hour bike ride in San Diego, I'm tense for two hours and 50 minutes—the time I spend in traffic."

For Allen, getting out of town helps him focus on his priorities. "I can spend time thinking about my legs, my muscles and the upcoming race."

Amphetamines
Speed at too high a price

A thletes have been looking for an edge on the competition since the first time a pair of Cro-Magnons raced each other back to the cave. And while tripping an opponent was probably the earliest example of un-ethical performance-enhancing conduct, it probably didn't take long for drugs to make their way onto the playing field. Stimulants of one kind or another—alcohol, coca leaves, caffeine and so forth—with their battle-proven ability to enhance courage and hostility and mask the pain of wounds, no doubt led the parade.

Today amphetamines, better known as "speed," are among the most com-monly abused stimulants in the endurance arena. It's easy to see why. Marathon runs, triathlons and ultradistance cycling are as much a matter of grit and mental toughness as of raw talent. Unfortunately, mental toughness is sometimes supplied via chemicals.

Scientists aren't sure exactly how amphetamines work, but the bottom line is that they stimulate the central nervous system. First used by doctors in the 1930s to treat obesity and narcolepsy (frequent, uncontrollable sleep), amphetamines increase your heart rate, make you more alert and aggressive and raise your body's metabolism. It's unclear whether or not they'll improve athletic performance, but they can improve the way an athlete *feels* about performing, which often amounts to the same thing.

Recognizing the risks

The risks posed by amphetamines far outweigh their benefits, however. Pain and fatigue are natural and important signals to your brain that something isn't right. To short-circuit that system is to invite serious injury—or worse.

Nor is the "feel-good" aspect of amphetamines the only concern. Imagine for a moment a fast marathon on a warm day in high humidity, then con-sider the following documented effects of amphetamines: increased blood pressure, increased oxygen consumption, cardiac arrhythmia (irregular heartbeat), thermo-regulatory failure and dehydration. That's a formula for disaster if ever there was one.

Amphetamine use by an endurance athlete is foolhardy, if not suicidal—and the longer and more rigorous an endurance event becomes, the greater the risk. Perhaps the best known example of the dangers of amphetamines occurred at the Tour de France bicycle race in 1966. Tom Simpson, Great Britain's first world champion, collapsed on a hot day during the 2,000-foot climb up Mount Ventoux. Simpson died on the way to the hospital of acute cardiac failure, caused by his use of benzedrine tablets during the competition.

For obvious reasons, amphetamines are banned by the International Olympic Committee (IOC) and most other national and international sports-governing bodies. Under IOC rules, an athlete who tests positive for amphetamines will be suspended from competition for two years; a second offense results in a lifetime suspension.

The bottom line: Don't even *think* about amphetamines as training aids.

Anabolic Steroids
Monsters in your medicine cabinet

*T*o most people, the word *steroid* conjures up images of bulging biceps, broad backs and the slick, suntanned washboard abdominals of world champion body builders.

But steroids are taken by athletes of all shapes, sizes and persuasions. In fact, a poll conducted by the World Health Organization showed that up to 20 percent of athletes in Western countries admitted using performance-enhancing drugs, including steroids. And while endurance athletes take steroids for different reasons than a four-time Mr. Stupendous might, they face the same risks to their long-term health.

Anabolic, or "tissue-building," steroids are synthetic versions of the male hormone testosterone. While they have legitimate medical uses, they're best known today for their appearance on the dark side of amateur and professional sport.

Taken regularly and combined with appropriate training methods, steroids help build lean muscle mass, increase strength and instill or enhance aggressive tendencies. These make an athlete more formidable in competition and more eager to train on a daily basis.

It's also widely believed that steroids allow an athlete to train harder and recover more quickly from strenuous workouts.

Not true, say the experts. In fact, the American College of Sports Medicine insists that "anabolic steroids do not increase aerobic power or capacity for muscular exercise."

Sex-change drugs you can do without

What's the flip side of steroids' allure? While they do build tissue, anabolic steroids are "androgenic"—they have a tendency to produce alternate sexual characteristics. Men's breasts can become enlarged, their testes may shrink and sperm counts can decrease, resulting in sterility. Women may develop facial hair and a deep voice. Baldness and acne have been noted in both sexes.

But these superficial changes are symptoms of more serious difficulties. Steroid use can lead to cardiovascular problems by raising blood pressure and serum triglyceride levels and encouraging cholesterol deposits on the walls of the arteries. Cancer of the liver, kidney, prostate gland and breast are also well-documented side effects.

"Steroid use is a very complicated attack on normal hormonal balance," says Robert Voy, M.D., former director of sportsmedicine and science for the U.S. Olympic Committee. "When we take a lot of hormone from an outside source, the body becomes confused. It turns off its own system and a lot of peculiar effects occur."

According to Bob Goldman, D.O., of the Chicago College of Osteopathic Medicine, "No safe dose of anabolic steroids for normal, healthy athletes exists. No test is available to determine which athletes have a genetic predisposition toward cardiovascular disease, liver cancer or kidney problems."

Anabolic steroids can be psychologically damaging as well. The same " 'roid-rage" that makes a 280-pound defensive tackle an unstoppable crowd-pleaser on game day can cause violence and full-blown psychosis off the field. And while anabolic steroids are not physically addictive like heroin or cocaine, they can become a powerful psychological crutch.

As warped as it may sound to the layperson, steroid users are typically unwilling to sacrifice their chemically enhanced physiques or lower their competitive expectations in the name of long-term health.

St. Louis orthopedic surgeon Herman A. Haupt, M.D., explains, "While taking steroids, athletes enjoy more intense training sessions, and they enjoy the euphoria well documented with any steroid use. . . . However, as the athletes discontinue the steroid . . . size and strength improvements quickly disappear, as does steroid euphoria. Most athletes cannot tolerate this withdrawal and quickly return to using steroids . . . they have become psychologically addicted to the steroid and its effects."

Fighting the steroid threat

The sale and use of steroids is strictly controlled in the United States and many other countries. In most states, it's a crime for a physician to prescribe steroids for nontherapeutic purposes. Steroids are also strictly forbidden under the rules of the U.S. Olympic Committee and most national and international sports-governing bodies.

Nevertheless, the drugs are still widely used and readily available from illicit domestic and foreign sources. A few years ago, one study found that 3 percent of male and female high school athletes interviewed used anabolic steroids and that more than 80 percent of the supply came from "black market" sources.

How can drugs so dangerous be so attractive? Look to the long-entrenched philosophy of high-level competitive sport for the answer. "Winning is all"—even more important than health and a sense of honor. Once we remove the concept of fairness from the competitive arena, the walls of good sense soon come crashing down.

Most competitive athletes (especially endurance athletes) see themselves as invulnerable to age, injury and defeat. They feel capable of rising above the crowd and succeeding where others have failed. To them, the long-term risks of anabolic steroids may seem small indeed compared with the rewards of an Olympic gold medal or a world championship. How do you tell a cyclist hurtling 60 miles an hour down a windswept, rain-soaked sliver of asphalt in the Swiss Alps that drugs are dangerous? For many, risk-taking is the very essence of sport; athletes who don't brave the odds don't win.

Facing the moral dilemma

Further complicating the issue is the perception—often accurate—that an athlete cannot compete at the highest levels without using drugs. "The pressure to take drugs is enormous," U.S. Olympic shot-putter Augie Wolf told *Time* magazine in 1988. "An athlete asks himself, 'Do I take drugs and win medals, or do I play fair and finish last?' "

Unfortunately, this pressure is intense at sports' upper levels. Drug accusations, veiled and overt, have become standard fare at the Olympics. At the 1992 Barcelona Games, several U.S. women swimmers questioned the sudden emergence of the Chinese in the sprint events.

Making things even more difficult is a win-at-all-costs environment in which coaches, doctors, teammates, friends and families ignore or even encourage the use of steroids and other performance-enhancing drugs. The athletes themselves are not the only ones who hunger for medals and world records.

Drug testing is clearly the only answer to the problem. In the 1980s, procedures for collecting samples and testing them in the lab were dramatically improved. In 1988, Canadian sprinter Ben Johnson was disqualified from the Olympic Games after his urine sample tested positive for the steroid stanozolol.

Following a public outcry for more vigilance, a period of strict enforcement followed as sports-governing bodies around the world attempted to prevent steroid use. Three years later, at the 1991 World Track and Field Championships, some analysts attributed the shortage of new world records at that meet to new, get-tough policies. "Times are up, bodies are thinner," said hurdling great Edwin Moses.

Resisting the lure of steroids

It doesn't help the workaday athlete to read news stories describing the latest scandal featuring steroid use. In fact, anabolic steroids are probably used today by numerous top distance runners, endurance cyclists, triathletes and other endurance athletes.

Spanish cycling star Pedro Delgado, on his way to victory in the 1988 Tour de France, tested positive for probenecid, an anti-inflammatory medicine used to treat gout. This drug is commonly used to mask the presence of anabolic steroids in urine.

Surprisingly, Delgado was not disqualified from the race. It seems that, although probenecid is banned by the International Olympic Committee, it wasn't on the banned list of the International Cycling Federation, under whose auspices the Tour de France was staged.

Apparently, the cycling community wasn't too concerned about Delgado's test results. Yet science continues to discount anabolic steroids as boosters of endurance or aerobic potential.

When the average recreational athlete considers the risks versus the benefits of using steroids, the answer is obvious. There's little but risk awaiting those who tinker with the notion of adding an artificial substance to their exercise kit bag. Though less exciting, a program of rigorous training and proper diet is a far stronger predictor of success.

See Also: *Cholesterol, Ergogenic Aids*

Anaerobic Exercise
An alternative energy system

M ost people associate anaerobic exercise with short, intense bursts of effort—a 100-meter dash, a dazzling kickoff return, a commuter chasing down a bus. It's impressive and functional, but hardly enduring stuff.

What does anaerobic ("without oxygen") activity have to do with endurance? Plenty. In some sports, such as tennis, it can play a big role. Tennis great Ivan Lendl plays center court under a hot sun, serving in a fourth-set tie-breaker of a five-hour U.S. Open final. Lendl is every bit an endurance athlete, yet his back-and-forth, side-to-side, serve-and-volley bursts use anaerobically derived energy almost exclusively.

Anaerobic effort is a part of any successful endurance attempt. Even within the longest events, you still need short bursts of speed. Often, races are won by the athlete who throws in an anaerobic surge no one can match.

Take the 1989 New York City Marathon. Thirteen miles into the race, Tanzania's Juma Ikangaa was running up front with a pack of nearly a dozen runners. Fed up with all this company, Ikangaa ran the 14th mile in four minutes, 34 seconds, leaving everyone else looking like a tour group that had suddenly wandered into a bog. No one ever bridged the gap, and Ikangaa won the race.

Of course, Ikangaa had cultivated these reserves with 200-mile training weeks. Should New York's average marathoners decide to storm from the start at such a pace, the event would collapse in a breathless, beet-faced, 17,000-person pileup. Even Ikangaa had to back off the pace.

Exercising without oxygen is inefficient—no one can operate anaerobically for long. But, like Ikangaa, you'll want to be able to call on this talent.

Creating energy without oxygen

Aerobic exercise delivers enough oxygen to the working muscles to generate a constant supply of the body's energy currency, ATP (adenosine triphosphate). But when oxygen can't be adequately supplied, ATP is produced through two chemical processes:

1. A reaction between ADP (adenosine diphosphate) and another substance in the muscle, creatine phosphate.
2. The breakdown of glycogen to lactic acid—known as anaerobic glycolysis.

Unfortunately, both are short-term solutions to the body's energy needs. Muscles store only enough creatine phosphate to fuel a few seconds of intense effort. Lendl's U.S. Open effort is a good example of this—most of the ATP used to power his bursts came from the ADP/creatine phosphate reaction. Dawdling about the baseline and glowering at the referees allowed Lendl time for recovery and resupply.

Glycolysis, which kicks in once creatine phosphate is exhausted, is a slightly more efficient means of providing energy, but not by much. Why? Glycolysis consumes huge amounts of your body's invaluable glycogen reserves and leads to a buildup of lactic acid. A 30-second burst can produce fatigue. It's a bit like flicking on a jet's afterburners—there's a burst of energy and a tremendous waste of fuel.

Avoiding flameout

Anaerobic energy production and its inherent waste can be avoided by combining smart aerobic and anaerobic training. Exercising at three-quarter speed can vastly improve your body's aerobic capabilities. Your muscles learn to produce energy more quickly. Your heart and lungs develop so they can supply more oxygen for that conversion. Your body becomes more efficient at removing lactic acid from the muscles and carting it off to the liver, where it's converted into a usable energy source.

Conditioned muscles can store more glycogen. And these muscles, just plain stronger, don't have to work as hard. That means you won't need to turn to anaerobic effort as soon.

Proper anaerobic training—intervals and fartlek, for example—schools your body in the same manner, teaching it to do more with less. Ikangaa's burst at the New York City Marathon is a good example. Hard anaerobic efforts in training not only raised Ikangaa's anaerobic threshold level to otherworldly heights, but when high levels of lactic acid did accumulate, his body was conditioned to flush them away quickly. This is precisely why he continued running away from the competition after his burst, rather than collapsing in a heap.

For most of us, a 4:34 mile is out of the question at any time, much less midway through a marathon. But Ikangaa's effort is a good example of how, through proper training, you can learn to maintain your own delicate balance between peak aerobic function and anaerobic disaster.

See Also: *Aerobic Exercise, Anaerobic Threshold, ATP, Glucose and Glycogen, Lactic Acid*

Anaerobic Threshold
Overcoming an internal obstacle

Y ou might think of your anaerobic threshold as the welcome mat to athletic excellence. Unfortunately, its telltale signs—the first sharp breaths, the first burn of discomfort, the initial chords of real effort—will make you feel anything but welcome. But unless you learn to step across this barrier, you'll never make the most of your athletic potential.

There are other yardsticks of fitness, but they have their limits. Maximum heart rate is mostly a function of age. Maximum oxygen uptake (VO_2 max) is influenced by genetics and training.

Anaerobic threshold, however, is the tool of the conditioned athlete. Many less gifted athletes have walloped more talented competitors simply by raising their anaerobic thresholds.

Before you set about doing this, you'll need a short course in what your anaerobic, or lactate, threshold is. Comfortable effort is aerobic effort. When you exercise aerobically, you're able to give your muscles enough oxygen to help break down carbohydrate, fat and protein into energy.

If you continue to push, however, you'll reach a point where your oxygen supplies are inadequate to produce the energy you need. This is your anaerobic threshold.

At this point, your muscles begin to produce energy without oxygen, or anaerobically. Lactic acid starts to accumulate in the blood. You begin to feel uncomfortable.

This is the point during energy production when your muscles begin to generate lactic acid faster than your capillaries can flush it away. As lactic acid accumulates, your muscle chemistry changes, triggering fatigue.

All this is designed to keep you out of trouble. If you weren't forced to ease up on your efforts, you could sustain muscle damage or even muscle cell death. The lactic acid effect ensures that you'll preserve those all-important muscle cells.

The good news is that you can raise your anaerobic threshold, improving your endurance as you begin to work longer and harder. In doing so, you can short-circuit the onset of fatigue that heralds the upper limits of your aerobic ability. You'll be able to exercise longer and faster at a comfortable pace. Improving your anaerobic threshold isn't easy, though, which is why many athletes don't make the most of this endurance ace-in-the-hole.

Keep tabs on your anaerobic threshold

Before you can improve your anaerobic threshold, you need to locate it. Elite athletes check their anaerobic thresholds by trotting off to a lab, where they offer blood samples to measure levels of lactic acid.

They also have their heart rates and respiration checked. The committed athlete will be heartened to learn that sports performance labs are sprouting up around the country, offering their services to anyone serious enough to pay for them.

Don't despair, though. If you want to do a self-check, you can get a fair idea of your anaerobic threshold by following the advice of exercise physiologist Mary O'Toole, Ph.D., director of the University of Tennessee's Human Performance Laboratory in Memphis.

"A good field test is to run a 10-K at just above your anaerobic threshold. An athlete can generally tell where that threshold is—your breathing increases a little more than is comfortable," she says.

Let's say you run the 10-K at that slightly uncomfortable speed. Your time is 36 minutes. You can safely assume that a 6-minute mile is somewhere around your anaerobic threshold pace.

Incidentally, 5- and 10-K races are usually run at the competitors' anaerobic thresholds, so try to train a bit faster than the race pace to be well prepared.

Push past your comfort zone

The best way to raise your anaerobic threshold is through high-intensity training. This will help you train your body to cope with less and less oxygen. For any serious athlete, breaking through the anaerobic ceiling is a painful but necessary time-honored tradition.

Before he broke the magical four-minute mile, Roger Bannister prepared by running 10 × 440 yards at 60 seconds. Later, miler and three-time

Olympian Steve Scott shattered Bannister's once-invincible four-minute barrier more than 130 times.

"Challenging yourself is what training is all about. If you're always training in your comfort zone, you can't expect to push through it when a race comes along," Scott counsels.

Once you identify your anaerobic threshold, you'll need to train at this pace. Hold your sustained efforts above the edge of aerobic effort. You can do this with long track intervals of two to five minutes. Or use fartlek efforts on the road, alternating hard pushes with slower bouts of recovery.

You can also do longer, consistent efforts, like Dr. O'Toole's 10-K run, holding your pace at the very beginning of discomfort.

Remember, you're not sprinting. You couldn't hold a sustained sprint over these distances. And all-out sprints would defeat your purpose: They hone speed, not anaerobic threshold. Rather than sprint, back off the throttle a bit, then maintain that pace over a sustained distance.

Obviously, there's a tremendous range of anaerobic thresholds, and endurance training is your key to reaching your optimum level. The delivery and use of your energy will become more efficient.

As always, it's your decision how far to go. The recreational athlete who never strays beyond the comfort zone might have an anaerobic threshold of 60 percent effort. A world-class marathoner might be able to operate aerobically, just below anaerobic threshold, at 90 percent effort.

Guess who's going to run faster.

See Also: *ATP, Interval Training, Lactic Acid*

Aspirin and Its Cousins
The pros and cons of pain relief

There's a story about a young female triathlete in San Diego who looked over at her boyfriend one morning a mile or so into a group fartlek workout. In midstride, she muttered, "You put aspirin in the coffee this morning, didn't you?"

"Yeah," the boyfriend replied. "How'd you know?"

"My stomach hurts," the woman answered.

Aspirin is known for its ability to relieve soreness and inflammation, and some consider it a blood-thinning agent that can reduce the risk of heart attack. It's also an extremely popular drug with competitive endurance athletes, who must train consistently, regardless of minor aches and pains, and recover quickly from hard workouts and harder competitions.

The catch is that aspirin is a potent medication with potentially serious side effects—especially under conditions common to endurance activities.

Athletes who rely on aspirin to ease pain should be aware of two of these side effects. First, aspirin can irritate the gastrointestinal tract, resulting in stomach pain, nausea and even ulceration and perforation of the intestine or stomach lining. The risks of taking aspirin rise when it's taken on an empty stomach. Second, high doses of aspirin can impair kidney function.

If you must take aspirin, do so only occasionally, and never actually *during* a hard workout or competition. Your best bet is to take aspirin with food, or at least with a full glass of water.

Alternatives pose similar risks

In 1989, the Food and Drug Administration (FDA) required that warning labels be placed on certain prescription and nonprescription painkillers. This decision highlights a much underpublicized risk to endurance athletes.

The medications in question are nonsteroidal anti-inflammatory drugs (NSAIDs), which include Motrin and Naprosyn, both popular among marathoners, triathletes, cyclists and other endurance athletes. They're used to ease the pain and inflammation of common wear-and-tear injuries like tendinitis and muscle strains. NSAIDs are listed as "allowed medications" by the U.S. Olympic Committee.

However, while these drugs don't enhance performance, the ruling says nothing about their across-the-board safety. Of particular concern is their potential for serious gastrointestinal difficulties. According to the FDA, up to 4 percent of those who use NSAIDs heavily over months or years may develop serious problems, including ulcers and intestinal perforation.

The question is, since endurance athletes use prescription-strength NSAIDs regularly, often train on empty stomachs and are almost always mildly dehydrated, are they at even greater risk than the general population?

Not necessarily, reassures Steven Brozinsky, M.D., a San Diego–based gastroenterologist. Short-term use of NSAIDs like ibuprofen, sold under the brand names Motrin, Advil and Nuprin, isn't likely to cause problems in a healthy person beyond the occasional upset stomach. He adds, however, that highly competitive athletes who take NSAIDs daily for weeks at a time are as much at risk as anyone from gastritis, ulcers or bleeding ulcers.

"One of the things that protects the stomach is the blood flow to the stomach, which tends to be superb in well-conditioned athletes," Dr. Brozinsky says. "It's probably even okay when the blood flow is being shunted away from the gastrointestinal tract during the height of competition."

But other physicians are concerned about that shunting away of blood from the stomach to the working muscles of the arms and legs during training and competition. "The tissue is far more likely to get injured under those circumstances," says Marvin Adner, M.D., medical director of the Boston Marathon.

Moderation is the key

It's an old story: Taken occasionally for minor injuries, NSAIDs can assist the athlete by reducing swelling and speeding healing. But use can become abuse when athletes take them far more often and in greater doses than recommended—including just before and even during long races in hot weather.

How much is too much? The answer varies with the medication. A good rule of thumb is, don't exceed the recommendations on the label. It's easy to end up taking more painkillers than you should. Just two acetaminophen tablets (sold under brand names such as Tylenol and Anacin-3) taken daily add up to a toxic dose in about three years.

In fact, a federal study concluded that the risk of serious kidney disease tripled in people who took two acetaminophen tablets daily for just one year. Check with your physician if you have questions about these drugs.

Downing NSAIDS before or during a race is an invitation to a number of problems. "I would think that popping nonsteroidals before a race would be hard on your G.I. tract," says Dotty Pease, a consumer safety officer with the FDA in Rockville, Maryland. "But upset stomachs are the least of the problem. Perforations, bleeding and ulcers are what we're usually talking about when we're talking gastrointestinal toxicity."

Complicating the situation is the fact that NSAIDs, like aspirin, tend to reduce blood flow to the kidneys. This can lead to kidney damage in endurance athletes who fail to drink enough liquids.

Pease points out the case of the NSAID suprofen (sold under the name Suprol), which came onto the market in December 1986. It was removed several months later following reports of flank pain, which was traced to kidney problems and seemed to be associated with dehydration. The pain, so severe that it sometimes required hospitalization, disappeared once the drug was discontinued. Subsequent studies indicated that the problem seemed to occur most often in men in their thirties and forties who exercised regularly immediately before or after taking the pills.

"I'd hate to see something like that happen with the drugs that are still out there," Pease says.

Keep in mind, however, that most people, including endurance athletes, use NSAIDs without incident. Nevertheless, before taking them, consider the following:

- Take medications like Motrin only when you need them to speed healing of minor injuries. Don't use them just for pain relief—you could be masking a serious injury.

- Drink plenty of fluids before, during and after racing or training.
- Never take NSAIDs just before or during long, hot races.
- If you start having chronic stomach pain or see blood in your urine or stool, haul yourself in to your doctor's office for a checkup.

"One of the reasons for our warning," Pease says, "was that if people realized how toxic this group of drugs is, they might consider not taking any of them, especially when they don't really need them."

See Also: *Anabolic Steroids, Dehydration*

Blood Doping
When recycling has its risks

lood doping (also referred to "blood loading" or "blood packing") has nothing at all to do with your circulatory system's I.Q. It may say something about your common sense, however, at a time when blood-borne diseases are making headlines almost daily.

The technique of blood doping involves drawing out a quantity of blood a month or so before a major competition, then reinfusing it just prior to race day. This can increase an athlete's aerobic capacity by up to 10 percent.

That's a huge amount by anyone's standards; blood doping would probably be universally practiced by world-class endurance athletes were it not banned as a performance aid by most sports-governing bodies, including the International Olympic Committee.

Unfortunately, no testing methods are available to detect blood doping in competitive athletes, so it's hard to tell how frequently it's attempted. Back in the late 1980s, Scandinavian distance runners were often charged with doping, but no concrete proof ever surfaced to support the charges.

The practice of blood doping is based on two physical phenomena. First, if you lose a less-than-fatal amount of blood through accident or some other means, your body quickly builds blood volume back up to its normal level—about 5½ quarts in an adult male. Second, red blood cells are the largest solid component of blood. The hemoglobin within them transports to the working muscles most of the oxygen they need and carries off waste products.

With those two facts side by side, it doesn't take a Madame Curie to see the possibilities.

What would happen if an athlete removed a "reasonable" amount of blood from the body (a quart is about right), waited until the lost blood was regenerated (two to four weeks), then reinfused the previously drawn blood? Wouldn't the increased density of red blood cells (and therefore greater concentration of hemoglobin) increase the blood's capacity to transport oxygen? And if that were true, couldn't the athlete run, bike or swim faster, longer and harder?

Indeed, that seems to be exactly the case. Studies have shown a significant increase in aerobic capacity after blood doping, although it's impossible to predict how long the effect will last. Reports range from a few days to two weeks and more, depending on the individual.

While there are no side effects from withdrawing and reinfusing blood, the technique is not without its risks. Specific medical procedures must be followed, and the blood must be properly stored in a licensed blood bank.

Even so, writes Bjorn Ekblom, M.D., of the Karolinska Institute in Stockholm, Sweden, "Medical complications including syncope (fainting), hematoma formation and infection can occur. . . . If the blood is donated by another individual, additional risks include transfusion reaction and disease transmission."

Dr. Ekblom was writing in the pre-AIDS years; today the risks of transfused blood are enormously higher. While it would seem absurd that an athlete would permit the infusion of another person's blood simply to enhance performance, this did occur as recently as 1984. Several members of that year's U.S. Olympic cycling team underwent illicit blood doping prior to the games in Los Angeles.

The bottom line is that blood doping, like illicit performance-enhancing drugs, gives one competitor an unfair advantage over another. The practice is unethical. Sadly, that fact alone isn't always the deterrent it should be at high levels of competition.

Cooling Down
Easing out of exercise

L ike the warm-up, the cool-down has an important function in the exercise equation. And, like the warm-up, it's usually neglected by endurance athletes.

That's too bad, because cooling down deserves more respect. It helps your body move smoothly and comfortably from hard effort to rest. During exercise, the blood vessels that sweep oxygen and nutrients to the working muscles are wide open. If you suddenly stop exercising, the blood begins to pool in these wide-open vessels and just sits there.

Remember the last time you hammered across the line and stopped like a deer blinded by a flashlight beam? Remember being dizzy and lightheaded? That was caused by the blood pooling in your extremities—especially the legs. It wasn't reaching your brain, possibly explaining why you didn't consider cooling down in the first place.

Light cooling-down exercise after hard effort also helps flush lactic acid from the muscles and the blood. As you cool down, your body gets busy restoring its supplies of ATP (adenosine triphosphate), refilling the muscles' oxygen stores and easing back on hormone and temperature levels. All this will eventually occur without a cool-down, but a proper one will make the process much quicker and easier.

The length and type of cool-down varies, often limited by practical realities. If you've just tottered across the finish at a marathon, the best you might be able to muster is a walk. If you've just finished an interval session on the track, you'll probably have enough energy for some light jogging.

Edmund R. Burke, Ph.D., associate professor at the University of Colorado, advises cooling down at 50 to 60 percent effort, wrapping up when your heart rate slows to just above resting rate. It's also a good idea, he adds, to toss in some light stretching to prevent muscle tightness, concentrating on the muscle groups you used during exercise.

Dr. Burke, who works extensively with swimmers and cyclists at the U.S. Olympic Training Center in Colorado Springs and was staff coach for the 1980 and 1984 Olympic cycling teams, explains that, in general, "the higher the intensity of the event, the longer the cool-down at a moderate pace." Therefore, he urges, "Use common sense. You're the best judge of when your body has recovered."

When athletes realize how important cool-down can be, many schedule it into their workouts. This may seem like a substantial chunk out of precious training time. But, as coauthor Scott Tinley points out, you'll probably make better use of the time left.

"A lot of people just ease into a workout and then keep on easing right through it," he says. "Even if you only have 90 minutes to train, it's better to include a warm-up and a cool-down with a hard effort in between than to expend a moderate effort through the whole workout."

See Also: *ATP, Hamstring Pulls, Muscles and Muscular Endurance, Stretching, Warming Up*

Cross-Training
Spicing up your program

J oy Hansen knows cross-training. In fact, there are few sports she's bypassed. Back in 1979 she ran for the University of Arizona, placing 15th at the NCAA Cross-Country Championships. Three years later she ran, rode, swam, fenced and shot her way to the U.S. Women's Modern Pentathlon Championship. In 1983 she took up triathlon training and immediately became a contender in that sport. Hansen's thoughts on the value of cross-training?

"People may balk at the idea of cross-training, but I know it works. It's given me variety and kept me challenged. I've found that by doing other sports I've gotten stronger and I'm injured less. And my running is still improving."

Hold that thought, because in sporting circles, fewer topics will create more of an uproar than cross-training. Exercise physiologists and athletes continue to harangue over the pros and cons of training in multiple sports.

Behind the debate are two constants. First, training is highly specific—to the point where you can actually train certain muscle fibers within a muscle. Logically, if you want to develop your running muscles, you'll run. If you want to develop your delts, you'll do weight training.

But, having said that, let's look at how training in other sports can provide substantial benefits and even improve your performance in your chosen sport, as triathlete Hansen has attested.

Reaping the benefits

If you're training for overall fitness, cross-training will benefit you most, conditioning you from head to toe. Let's face it—most of us train, in part, to improve our body image. Unless you relish the look of legs the size of Maine and an upper body as firm as saltwater taffy, your body sculpting will need more than a program of running or cycling. But toss in some swimming and some upper-body weight work and, presto, you're looking good!

Vanity aside, cross-training has numerous practical benefits. Runners can benefit from the upper-body work that sports like swimming, cross-country skiing and weight lifting provide. Top runners use their upper bodies when they run, driving with their arms. After doing some form of upper-body work, their arms tire far less quickly when they run.

Cycling and running can help improve the leg strength of swimmers, who spend most of their time dragging their legs along in the pool. Cycling can also help runners strengthen their legs by working those muscles neglected in running.

Running, of course, will improve cardiovascular strength, which will make for a stronger cyclist or swimmer.

Just as important, cross-training provides an invaluable break in the routine. No one can train hard all the time. If you do, you're sure to be injured or burned out. Top athletes alternate hard training days with easy ones; many do this by tossing in another sport.

"Cross-training makes avoiding injury easier," says Ray Browning, a top triathlete who specializes in the grueling Ironman triathlons. "If you're a runner, bike or swim on your easy day. Doing something else, whether it's riding a bike or cross-country skiing, is great for recovery during hard training. You'll come back to your hard training days recharged and ready to go."

Cross-training's role in preventing injury can't be overlooked, either. Endurance athletes have a tendency to overtrain in the first place. Cross-training gives the muscles that are usually pounded into oblivion a break.

How They Train: Three Approaches

Here are three distinct, and equally successful, case studies showing the variety and flexibility of endurance programs. You might find something here that can enhance your own. Remember, a successful endurance program fits the needs of the individual athlete.

From fitness dabbler to triathlete

Susan, a single, 26-year-old professional who enjoyed light swimming and jogging, decided to get into better shape. But how?

It was already June. Knowing she needed to commit to a training program, she set herself an impressive goal—an August sprint distance triathlon (880-yard swim, 13-mile bike ride, 3-mile run) ten weeks away. Actually, she had three goals: "To finish, to not finish last and to break one hour, 35 minutes."

Prior to her big decision, Susan had been swimming laps on her own at a nearby pool for about a year—two or three days a week, 30 minutes at a time. She was also jogging sporadically—30 minutes once or twice every two weeks. She wasn't cycling at all because she didn't own a bike.

"My first step was to join a Masters swim program on June 3," says Susan. "That was great. The structure and accountability kept me in the pool and focused for a full 60 minutes.

"My second step was to buy a bicycle on July 17—five weeks out! I rode on my own, usually for about an hour in the morning, but without ever really knowing how far or how fast I was going.

"My third step was committing to the running. I knew it would kill me, because I hate running. I started running to and from swim workouts—one mile each way—with long runs (45 minutes) on the weekends."

During her ten-week program, Susan averaged three hard, one-hour swim workouts per week and one to two moderately paced runs per week. Mixing her swimming and running was an endurance plus—the combination gave her a long, slow distance workout that encouraged her body to burn fat without the risk of injury.

And the stronger the athlete in general, the better the chance of avoiding injury.

Expanding your repertoire

Here's a word of cross-training advice. If you're doing two sports in one day, do your sport of choice first—you'll get more out of your first workout because you'll be fresh. Thus, if you're a runner, make your run the primary

---

As for cycling, she crammed that in at the end—three rides per week for the last five weeks. Since she went at an easy pace, content to simply develop her riding skills, there was little risk of injury or overtraining.

The end result? On race day Susan achieved all three of her goals. She finished 144th in a field of 292, in a time of one hour, 30 minutes—5 minutes faster than her target time.

"In hindsight, it wasn't really that hard, because once race day got closer and workouts became a priority, they were something I *wanted* to do, not that I had to do."

Ten months after the race, Susan maintained her aerobic base by continuing to swim with her Masters team and running and biking sporadically.

"For me, having the race as a goal was essential. Focus on a goal, and the momentum just takes over," she says.

From Colorado to the Himalayas

Gary is an accomplished mountaineer who lives and trains at altitude in Colorado. For him, maintaining an aerobic base means combining aerobic activities like running and cycling with a year-round program of vigorous weight training.

In early 1990, Gary decided to challenge the Himalayas. His goal was to reach the top of Mount Everest—altitude, 29,028 feet— without the use of supplemental oxygen. Only a handful of climbers had accomplished this feat.

During the year prior to his effort, Gary followed this routine.

Running: Three times a week, twice a week on trails with lots of hills (60 to 90 minutes each) and once on flat roads (60 minutes).

StairMaster: One to two times each week, 40 minutes each time. Gary's heart rate during both running and StairMaster sessions was consistently in the range of 80 to 85 percent of his maximum. He got variety by cross-country skiing or mountain biking, depending on the weather.

Weight training: Sixty to 90 minutes, three times a week with Nautilus equipment and free weights. He did about 35 different exercises, singly

(continued)

focus of the day. Then toss in an afternoon bike ride or swim, using it to help loosen you up from your hard run.

Remember to start out easy when you take up these new sports. If you're already fit, you may want to push too hard too soon. Many a runner has come to swimming with eager heart and lungs and promptly developed sore shoulders. Although cycling is traditionally a forgiving sport, you can damage your knees in a blink if you get on the bike the first time and hammer off in the highest gear. Take your time upping the volume or intensity of your workouts.

"It's hard enough to fit one sport into my schedule," you moan. "Now you're asking me to pick up more?" The truth is, in this hectic day and age, cross-training is the ideal fitness plan.

"The more congested your schedule, the more sense it makes to cross-

---

How They Train: Three Approaches — *Continued*

and in multiple sets, for 12 to 15 repetitions each. The last reps would bring the muscle group to exhaustion.

Short periods of rest between sets kept the aerobic quality of the workouts high—70 to 75 percent of Gary's maximum heart rate. "That kept me strong, helped me with my endurance and didn't build bulk," he explains.

Four months prior to his climb, with his endurance base firmly established and having achieved his maximum strength on this program, Gary cut his weight workouts from three times a week to two. He knew this was enough to maintain his level of fitness.

Gary continued his running and StairMaster routine but "with much greater intensity." He also introduced long, high-quality days, climbing 14,000-foot Pike's Peak as rapidly as possible once or twice a week with a 35-pound pack on his back. Gary used ski poles to keep his upper body involved and his heart rate up.

On those days, he was alone with the mountain for 11 hours at a time, adding a psychological factor to the intense aerobic workout.

How did Gary fare tackling Everest without supplemental oxygen? Unfortunately, he had more than his share of setbacks. Frigid weather, high winds and illness buffeted Gary and his expedition through most of their climb.

Still, he made one attempt at a rapid ascent. It was thwarted at 10:30 P.M. at 22,000 feet by the tiniest of incidentals—a headlamp problem.

The serious triathlete

Along with his wins through the years, coauthor Scott Tinley is also known for his heavy training schedule and his ability to avoid injury. He train," says six-time Hawaii Ironman Triathlon winner Dave Scott, who during his career as a professional triathlete juggled family, training and office hours. "Cross-training gives you more flexibility. You're not dependent on pool hours or weather conditions."

Cross-training also opens up whole new frontiers, making sport, well, fun again. If coauthor Scott Tinley doesn't feel like doing anything hard but still wants a workout, he'll hop on his bike and run errands around town. If he wants more of a workout, and the family is driving from San Diego to Palm Springs for the weekend, Tinley goes by bike. All 160 miles.

During his off-season months of November, December and January, Tinley takes spontaneity and play to greater lengths than most athletes. After tossing his running shoes and bike in the closet until next season, Tinley will

manages to pull these off by teaming common sense with a sound knowledge of injury's signs and symptoms.

Tinley strongly believes in year-round training. Base-building, as he sees it, is a career-long process. As a result, he rarely has to build up to speed after a long layoff.

"I've found it harder to come back after I stop than if I never stopped at all," he confirms.

Many recreational endurance athletes agree that a consistent fitness program will keep them in good shape all year long, rather than bouncing from one competitive season to the next. Tinley successfully applies this strategy to a high-intensity schedule without being constantly sidelined by injury and fatigue. It's an example other athletes will want to follow. By training year-round and applying a "building-block" approach to developing endurance, training athletes will make steady strides.

Tinley's maintenance sessions are almost always long—four to seven hours on the bike (twice a week) and 90 minutes or more on the run (at least three times weekly). He does these workouts over varying terrain that continuously shifts the training intensity from hard to easy. He often rides and runs with friends, both for the added challenge and for the diversion a group session invariably offers.

"It has to be enjoyable," says triathlete Tinley. "I tend to be of the school that says you have to put the time in," he says. "Sure, some days are worthless and you end up putting in junk miles, but the more time you spend on the road, the better chance there is of getting something done."

In the final analysis, Tinley believes in keeping the pressure on. "If you don't keep stressing your body," he says, "you can't get better. And if you're not getting better, then you're losing."

paddle, cross-country ski, skate and tackle anything else he fancies. As a result, he stays in better shape than most of us in peak condition, simply by playing hard.

For people who are determined to stay fit during the off-season, cross-training (sometimes called alternative training or supplemental training), is perfect. In effect, if you cross-train, you have no "off-season"! The in-between-seasons work keeps your cardiovascular system in good working order. So when it's time to resume your primary activity, you won't feel you have to make up for lost time, because so little was lost.

See Also: *Aerobic Exercise, Detraining, Duathlon, Triathlon*

Detraining
Bouncing back from a layoff

T ime off is a wonderful, and necessary, part of the endurance equation. Few people can train without a break, and those who can often suffer the consequences—a body and mind with all the pep of week-old soda.

Alas, time off means losing some of training's benefits. It's simple. Exercise regularly, and your body adapts to the increased demands on it. Quit, and your body quits too.

"An easy rule of thumb is that you get about a 1 percent decrease in physiological function for each day that you lay off exercise," says John Duncan, Ph.D., associate director of the Exercise Physiology Department at the Cooper Institute for Aerobics Research in Dallas. "You can lose most of your conditioning fairly quickly, in as little as six weeks."

These declines occur on all fronts—cardiovascular capacity, muscular strength and flexibility. After six weeks without training, you'll suffer an almost complete loss of any cardiovascular adaptations you gained.

Worse, your total blood volume starts to decline after just a few days of inactivity. The less blood circulating through your system, the less oxygen is available to produce energy. Muscle strength diminishes about 1.5 percent per day as unexercised muscle fibers lose stamina and size. And without consistent attention, your connective tissues—ligaments and tendons—quickly become less flexible.

Take the slow track back

The good news is that fitness seems to rebound almost as quickly as it disappears. A few weeks of training can markedly improve cardiovascular and muscular efficiency.

Coming back from time off, disgusted with the gelatinous goo that is you, it's crucial to remember three words: Rein yourself in.

"You'll get better results in the long term if you're patient and build slowly," says Mark Plaatjes, a physical therapist and runner from Boulder, Colorado.

Plaatjes practices what he preaches. A 2:08 marathoner, he resumes serious training each spring with the urgency of a repairman on an hourly wage. He does no hard work for at least two months, using this time to slowly build a base of strength and endurance. Plaatjes combines calisthenics with long, slow runs at no more than 70 percent effort and finds that building a strength and endurance reservoir gives him a solid training base and helps prevent injury.

But take it slow, Plaatjes cautions. Pushing too hard, too soon can produce a symphony of popping that will make Orville Redenbacher stand at attention.

"If you go straight into quality," says Plaatjes, "you're very prone to ligament or tendon injury."

Fools rush in

When you resume training, your muscles are your weakest links; therefore, your first sessions of running, swimming, cycling or any other aerobic sport should be half-speed affairs that simply reacquaint the muscles with physical effort. Plaatjes recommends keeping initial workouts to no more than 40 percent, in distance or duration, of your last peak accomplishments. Build slowly from there, increasing your distance or exercise time by up to 5 to 10 percent each week. Avoid all-out effort for at least six weeks.

Most experienced athletes also incorporate some form of whole-body strength training into their regimens. Muscle strength is crucial if you want to avoid injury.

If you're not much for weights, consider jumping rope—it works muscles in your chest, shoulders, arms, buttocks and calves, and it's a terrific cardiovascular workout. Other good conditioning calisthenics include sit-ups, chin-ups, push-ups, one-leg hops, leg lifts and squat jumps.

Remember, when lifting or hopping, don't strain! Stop as soon as you lose form. If that means three chin-ups in the beginning, fine.

Stretching, a good idea when you're fit, is downright crucial after a lay-off. Regular stretching produces minor lengthening of the ligaments and tendons that connect your joints. It also keeps the muscles supplied with needed blood and oxygen. Most important from a comeback standpoint, flexible muscles are less subject to pulls and tears.

Come back with cross-training

Even if it isn't part of your regular endurance training, returning from time off is a perfect time to do a little cross-training. When you aren't at peak condition, mixing sports is a terrific idea. Someone who runs one day and cycles the next is using different muscle groups—giving regularly used muscles a break while still getting an aerobic workout.

"Cross-training is a good idea for people who are coming back," says Brian Sharkey, Ph.D., an exercise physiologist at the University of Montana in Missoula and a past president of the American College of Sports Medicine, who is an avid cross-trainer. "Cross-country skiing won't make you a better runner, but it will keep your cardiovascular system working at a high level. You'll come back quicker, with less risk of injury."

In fact, the best way to move your cardiovascular system into high gear is through sports that involve large, oxygen-hungry muscle groups—swimming, running, cycling and cross-country skiing are good examples. And in keeping with the "start slowly" theme, the greatest aerobic benefits are gained when you work out at about three-quarters of your maximum effort—60 to 80 percent of your maximum heart rate.

A change can be as good as a rest

This probably isn't news to you, but endurance athletes can be neurotic about training. You may be afraid to take time off. If you're obsessed with doing something during the off-season, at least do something different.

During his annual vacation from triathlons, coauthor Scott Tinley drops running, biking and swimming for kayaking, surfing, mountain biking and just about any other activity that strikes his fancy. He stays fit. Far more important, when it's time to come back, he's ready to charge. Perhaps the best part of a comeback is the freshened enthusiasm that comes with it.

See Also: *Cross-Training, Stretching*

Drafting
Taking the path of least resistance

*T*he merits of drafting have never been so grandly displayed as when John Howard set the world land speed record on a bicycle. Howard, a member of three Olympic cycling teams and winner of the 1981 Hawaii Ironman Triathlon, has legs like ham hocks, but thunderous thighs alone can't account for the fact that he reached almost 130 miles an hour on a bicycle. How'd he do it? Easy. Howard set his record by drafting (i.e., trailing) behind a specially designed race car.

This isn't an experiment you should try, but it's an eye-popping example of the extremes to which you can take drafting. Even the most inexperienced athlete is well aware of the advantages of tucking in behind a moving object (usually another competitor), and enjoying the free ride. Out in front, you're forced to push through wind, or, in the case of swimming, water. Tucked just behind, you can breeze merrily along in the laborer's slipstream.

When it comes to endurance sports, cyclists receive the greatest benefits of drafting. Air can produce substantial drag. A cyclist riding at 20 miles an hour expends more than 50 percent of his or her energy just overcoming wind resistance. Studies have shown that cyclists can reduce drag by as much as 40 percent by tucking in behind another rider.

Watch a major cycling race like the Tour de France and this quickly becomes evident. See a lone rider break away from the pack. Watch him struggle valiantly on his own. See the pack mow him down with about the same effort they'd use to clear last night's dinner table.

To draft, or not to draft?

Swimming is another sport that lends itself to successful drafting. Although swimmers move much more slowly than cyclists, water is a denser medium; having someone in front of you creating a slipstream can make things appreciably easier.

In fact, drafting during a swim can reduce your efforts by 10 percent. Just tuck in behind a fast-moving pack of swimmers and the effect is magnified. Of course, most people don't appreciate doing all that work for your benefit. It's also a lot easier for a swimmer to slow down and kick the drafter in the teeth than for a cyclist to climb off a bike and punch someone in the nose.

There's a second danger to drafting during open-water swimming. Get behind someone whose navigation skills are lacking and you could quickly find yourself heading out to sea.

In the case of running, drafting serves as little more than a psychological ploy, unless you run into a strong headwind. Not that it isn't done. Watch any major road race and you'll see the lead pack maneuvering like Blue Angels. Tucking in behind a competitor allows you to eavesdrop on his or her condition, while your status is your own little secret.

Plus, for all but the most hardened athletes, the stress of having a potential threat lurking just over one's shoulder can affect equanimity—and performance.

Some sports have made drafting illegal. Triathlons, as a rule, don't allow drafting during the bike leg—which doesn't mean that triathletes still don't try to get away with it.

Drafting, however, isn't your only option when it comes to reducing resistance. Studies have shown that runners and cyclists can reduce drag by as much as 10 percent just by choosing the right clothing. This helps explain the popularity of skin suits and teardrop-shaped bike helmets that turn some races into Darth Vader look-alike contests.

Cyclists also shave their legs to reduce wind resistance (and make it easier to pluck gravel out of their skin after crashes), and serious competitive swimmers shave themselves from head to toe to reduce drag in the water.

The fact is, there's really no limit to what athletes will do to reduce drag. The former East German swim team occasionally trained in the nude and would likely have raced that way if competitors and television networks hadn't been so prudish.

Endurance Training
Going the distance

*T*om Warren is probably best known as the original Ironman, winner of the 1979 Hawaii Ironman Triathlon. A quirky soul who goes his own way, training is rarely separate from Warren's daily life. He'll drop his car off at the garage, reach into his trunk, pluck out his running shoes and run the ten miles home. He'll ride to a business appointment on his bike—from San Diego to Los Angeles.

Warren's been doing this sort of thing for years, which helps to explain how he returned to Hawaii ten years after his 1979 win and, at age 46, finished the Ironman in nine hours, 42 minutes. Even better, he did it 90 minutes faster than his first winning time.

When it comes to endurance training, Warren illustrates two important points: (1) there are a handful of hard-and-fast rules for successful endurance training, and (2) once you've followed them, the rest is up to you. This is precisely what makes endurance training such a challenge, and so much fun.

Get down with the ground rules

Endurance training is anything but scientific. Ask 100 endurance athletes—triathletes, ultramarathoners, century cyclists and so on—how they train, and you'll get 100 different answers. Everyone has his or her training secrets. Some, like Warren, even have the gall to share them.

Still, there are some basic ground rules and, yes, they're actually rooted in science. Consider these a foundation for your endurance program—then go off and tilt at your own windmills.

The official ground rules were laid down by the prestigious American College of Sports Medicine (ACSM). Its prescription is broad in scope, including those on both ends of the fitness scale. To develop and maintain aerobic fitness and build endurance, the ACSM suggests the following guidelines.

Frequency of exercise: Three to five days a week.

Intensity of training: 60 to 90 percent of maximum heart rate (MHR) or 50 to 85 percent of maximum oxygen uptake (VO_2 max).

Duration: 20 to 60 minutes of continuous aerobic activity (walking, hiking, running, bicycling, swimming, cross-country skiing, rowing, aerobics, etc.)

Type of training: Along with the regular program, at least two strength-training sessions of moderate intensity per week.

If you adopt these guidelines, a good, basic endurance training program might look something like this:

- Two weekly 30-minute runs at 70 percent of your maximum heart rate.
- Two 30-minute workouts of the same intensity in the pool or on the bike.
- Two weight-training sessions of 30 minutes each.

Look closely and you'll note several things about this program. For one, it doesn't demand the monastic devotion you thought was required of endurance training. It's only three hours of training a week.

Even the Pope could fit that into his schedule. In fact, Pope John Paul II does—at 74, he spends three hours a week walking in the Vatican's exercise yard.

There's more good news—the program doesn't require excessive suffering. Unless you're shooting for an Olympic marathon gold or planning an assault on Mount Everest, you can achieve a sound level of endurance through a gradual, enjoyable, relatively low-key effort over several months.

Motivation and goals come first

Before you charge out the door, it's important to decide just why you're getting involved in this scene.

"If you don't have a strong enough motivation to keep at it, you probably won't," cautions coauthor Scott Tinley, whose desire to extract the most from himself has brought him to his own limits of endurance.

Your reasons will be as unique as you are, driven by your priorities at the time you begin: shedding a few pounds, improving your quality of life or being able to run after your kids without risking a coronary.

It also helps to have some concrete goals. Concrete objectives make it a lot easier to stick with your program. The line between motivation and goals might seem thin, but there *is* a distinction. Motivation is what drives you. Goals are the direction in which you'll channel that drive. Your motivation could be a desire to lose weight or to trot upstairs without wheezing. Your goal might be a 10-K run by the end of six months.

Set up your endurance base

Time to get started. There are too many sport-specific programs to mention here, and thousands of training variations within each one. But whether your interest is marathon running or kayaking, consider the following to help you build and maintain an endurance base.

First, remember that the core of any endurance activity is, naturally, the ability to endure. So your main concern at first will be working up to the point where you can handle long distances and big chunks of training time.

Second, performance is *not* important in the beginning. The idea is to get from point A to point B with relative ease, and without injury.

Third, at the beginning, be open to more than one sport. Many world-class athletes spend their preseason indulging in all manner of sport. Mark Hodges, former United States Cycling Federation coaching director, used to have riders in his Olympic development program spend their first six weeks "just piddling around." Hodges's cyclists indulged in a plethora of play that would turn any summer camper green with envy—they'd hike, ride mountain bikes, swim, even play Frisbee football.

Your early season, or the first few months of your newly resolved fitness lifestyle, should be similar to theirs. If, like Hodges's cyclists, you're an experienced endurance athlete, you might want to dedicate six weeks to general play. If you're new to endurance training, you'll play longer. Because this all-around play taxes a wide range of muscles, you'll begin to feel the benefits of good aerobic conditioning.

You'll also have fun. By the time you've jettisoned ancillary sports and gotten around to the essence of your training program—the speedwork, the fartlek and the other hard efforts—you won't be bored with your chosen sport.

Tote that weight, lift that bale

Many endurance athletes are uninterested in weight training—reckoning, rightly enough, that it doesn't provide the aerobic benefits of a 25-mile bike ride. But experienced endurance athletes make sure they get some form of strength training early in the season—it's crucial to build up muscle for the hard efforts to come later.

If you're not one for hefting weights, Mark Plaatjes offers an innovative alternative. Early in the season, Plaatjes, a physical therapist and 2:08 marathoner from Boulder, Colorado, heads off to a field behind his home where he's set up a training circuit. He goes through 10 to 12 calisthenic stations and jogs easily from one to the other—doing sit-ups, push-ups, knee-bends, one-leg hops, squat jumps and the like. Although Plaatjes is out of the weight room, the premise behind his routine is the same.

"You've got to strengthen your muscles before you go into quality," he says. "If you don't, you'll be very prone to injury."

Here's an overview of what your base-building program should accomplish. It should:

1. Get you comfortable with your sport. Developing the neuromuscular coordination—or "getting the feel"—of your sport is an important first step toward higher levels of performance.
2. Allow your whole body to ease back into the specifics of your chosen sport. You may have spent the winter running up stairs and doing leg lifts, but if you're a cyclist tackling your first 100-mile training ride, your butt will feel as if someone cracked it with a hammer. On a more serious note, if you go too far or too fast on your first ride, the muscles specific to cycling will pay the price.
3. Establish a baseline of aerobic strength that will support you when it's time to push harder.

In the beginning, you'll be working at an easy pace. The fact is, this moderate-intensity training at 60 to 70 percent of your MHR will comprise the majority of your endurance program throughout the year. It's your daily bread-and-butter homework that helps you maintain a minimum long-distance capacity and strengthens your body for hard efforts like racing and speedwork.

In his book, *Galloway's Book on Running,* former U.S. Olympic marathoner Jeff Galloway proposes that a marathon runner's base training should equal at least half the permanent schedule. "If in doubt," says Galloway, "go slower."

This is good advice for all endurance athletes, whether your sport is swimming, cycling or cross-country skiing. Like enduring itself, building and maintaining an endurance base is largely a matter of just keeping going.

Stick with it

Staying with exercise is mostly a matter of personal discipline—if there were an easy formula for developing this ability, athletes everywhere would possess the drive of Japanese industrialists.

You can, however, use the following tips to stay on the training treadmill.

1. Plot out your program in black and white. It doesn't matter whether you're shooting to finish a marathon or a triathlon or just want to stay in shape. Get that weekly schedule down on paper—in advance. If you only do what turns you on at the moment, your program is doomed.

2. Find friends to train with. Some of the best endurance athletes would be lost if they had to train alone. The physical and emotional support of a group inspires you when times get tough. On the other hand, the endurance arena can offer welcome solitude.

3. Make your training program as logistically convenient as possible. Don't schedule track work at a location 40 miles away. The fewer difficulties you encounter, the less apt you are to throw in the towel.

4. Keep a record of your training—but don't let it take over your life. While some people will do anything to pencil in a few extra miles, the benefits of a training log far outweigh the risks, since your body is your best laboratory for testing what you can do. Notes about distances, diet, emotional ups and downs and performance quality are invaluable when you're tracking the overall success or failure of your program.

What did you do last week that made you feel so good? Why in the world do you feel so tired now? When did you begin doing speedwork for last year's half-marathon?

5. Add some zest to your plan. Lay out a training schedule and follow it, but allow some room for alternatives. When boredom gets to be a problem (because it will), be creative. Pull out the mountain bike, lace up the skates. Have some fun. Come back refreshed and ready to roll.

6. Start slow. We've said this before. We'll say it again. Give your body time to catch up with your ambitions. The endurance philosophy is one of patience and persistence. Results will come.

Cultivate consistency

In Pacific Beach, California, five miles from Tom Warren's home, there's a light pole at the end of the beach promenade. On the pole is a smudgy black ring, just about shoulder high. That smudge marks the spot where Warren has reached out, thousands of times, to swing around the pole and run back the way he came.

Triathlete Warren, of course, is a bit more zealous than most. Given the realities of life, most of us can't train day in and day out for years on end. But when it comes to exercise, some is always better than none. Missing a few days is no reason to chuck it all and head for the couch.

"Training, if only a day a week, will really help maintain what you've gained through regular exercise," says Edward F. Coyle, Ph.D., director of the Human Performance Laboratory at the University of Texas in Austin. "Get out there and do something, even if it's only for a short time, once a week."

See Also: *Cross-Training; Long, Slow Distance Training; Weight Training*

Scott Tinley's Training Table— Menu for a Week

Any athlete who wants maximum mileage from his or her reserves knows that optimum fuel for the body will enhance performance. The seven-day diet below reflects Scott Tinley's food choices. Check with your own doctor or nutritionist before starting any new diet program.

DAY ONE

7:00 A.M. Breakfast
Large bowl oatmeal w/brown sugar
2 oz. nonfat milk
2 pieces whole-wheat toast w/2 Tbsp.
  all-fruit jam
12 oz. orange juice
Large banana
Frozen waffle w/maple syrup

10:00 A.M. Snack
Medium apple
4 medium fig bars
12 oz. Endura

1:00 P.M. Lunch
Avocado and tomato sandwich
16 oz. fruit juice
Medium banana

5:00 P.M. Snack
6-oz. bag rice crackers

8:00 P.M. Dinner
Large plate whole-wheat pasta w/tomato sauce
2 pieces garlic bread, lightly buttered
Large lettuce and vegetable salad
  w/3 oz. fat-free dressing
2 12-oz. light beers

9:30 P.M. Dessert
Medium piece iced carrot cake

Calorie Count Breakdown
TOTAL CALORIES: 3,306

10% Protein
61% Carbohydrate
24% Fat
 5% Alcohol

DAY TWO

6:30 A.M. Breakfast
6-oz. bowl Grape-Nuts cereal
8 oz. nonfat milk
Medium banana
Cup coffee
Medium English muffin
w/2 Tbsp. all-fruit jam

10:30 A.M. Snack
Large bran muffin
2 whole-wheat bagels

2:30 P.M. Lunch
6 oz. nonfat yogurt

4:30 P.M. Snack
Power Bar
16 oz. Endura

8:00 P.M. Dinner
Medium mixed green salad
w/3 oz. fat-free dressing
5 oz. broiled boneless,
skinless chicken breast
2 cups brown rice
2 whole-wheat rolls
Large baked potato w/nonfat yogurt
and tomato sauce
12 oz. light beer

8:30 P.M. Dessert
2 small pieces bread pudding

Calorie Count Breakdown
TOTAL CALORIES: 3,141

19% Protein
63% Carbohydrate
15% Fat
 3% Alcohol

DAY THREE

7:15 A.M. Breakfast
2 6-oz. bowls rice cereal w/1 banana
4 oz. nonfat milk
Whole-wheat bagel
8 oz. nonfat yogurt w/fruit
2 cups coffee

1:00 P.M. Lunch
Medium enchilada w/low-fat cheese
12 corn chips
14 oz. apple juice

3:30 P.M. Snack   2 Power Bars

7:30 P.M. Dinner   6 oz. broiled boneless,
         skinless chicken breast
Large green salad w/4 oz. fat-free dressing
Whole-wheat roll
2 cups rice

9:00 P.M. Snack   6-oz. bowl cold cereal
4 oz. nonfat milk

Calorie Count Breakdown

TOTAL CALORIES: 1,989

21% Protein
52% Carbohydrate
27% Fat
 0% Alcohol

DAY FOUR

6:45 A.M. Breakfast   8-oz. bowl cold cereal
6 oz. nonfat milk
1 cup raisins
Cinnamon bagel

9:00 A.M. Snack   Box animal cookies
16 oz. Endura

1:00 P.M. Lunch   Large bowl mixed fruit
Medium green salad
     w/8 oz. nonfat yogurt

4:00 P.M. Snack   2 slices rye bread w/apple butter

8:00 P.M. Dinner   3 slices vegetarian pizza w/low-fat cheese
2 slices garlic bread
2 12-oz. light beers

Calorie Count Breakdown

TOTAL CALORIES: 3,583

13% Protein
72% Carbohydrate
11% Fat
 4% Alcohol

DAY FIVE

7:00 A.M. Breakfast	8-oz. bowl Grape-Nuts cereal 6 oz. low-fat milk Medium banana Medium whole-wheat cinnamon roll
12:00 P.M. Lunch	Medium piece lasagna w/low-fat cheese Whole-wheat roll 12 oz. apple juice
4:00 P.M. Snack	12 oz. low-fat fruit yogurt w/½ cup raisins Whole-wheat bagel 12 oz. orange juice
8:00 P.M. Dinner	6 oz. tabbouleh salad w/humus spread 2 pieces pita bread 8 oz. pasta salad 2 6-oz. glasses red wine

---

Calorie Count Breakdown

TOTAL CALORIES: 2,700

13% Protein
73% Carbohydrate
 9% Fat
 5% Alcohol

DAY SIX

6:00 A.M. Breakfast	3 medium pancakes w/maple syrup 12 oz. orange juice
9:30 A.M. Snack	3 oat bran cookies
1:00 P.M. Lunch	Medium plate beans w/2 whole-wheat tortillas

7:30 P.M. Dinner	Medium piece grilled fish
	  w/¾ cup rice
	Medium green salad w/3 oz.
	  fat-free dressing
	Medium baked potato w/nonfat yogurt
	  and chopped onions

9:30 P.M. Snack	Medium piece apple pie

> **Calorie Count Breakdown**
> TOTAL CALORIES: 2,595
> 18% Protein
> 55% Carbohydrate
> 27% Fat
> 0% Alcohol

DAY SEVEN

7:30 A.M. Breakfast

Large omelette w/3 eggs, cheese
   and vegetables
8 oz. nonfat milk
Piece whole-wheat toast w/2 tsp. all-fruit jam
Cup coffee

12:00 P.M. Lunch

2 medium apples
8 crackers

3:00 P.M. Snack

2 Power Bars
12 oz. cherry juice

6:30 P.M. Dinner

Large plate whole-wheat pasta w/tomato
   and meat sauce
Medium green salad w/4 oz.
   fat-free dressing
2 cups steamed broccoli
Whole-wheat roll

8:30 P.M. Snack

4 oz. low-fat frozen yogurt
   w/chocolate chips

> **Calorie Count Breakdown**
> TOTAL CALORIES: 2,167
> 19% Protein
> 43% Carbohydrate
> 38% Fat
> 0% Alcohol

Ergogenic Aids
A wary word on performance boosters

*H*ere's what you're offered: enhanced muscle growth, more endurance, improved energy production, faster recovery time, increased alertness and faster reaction time. Here's what you might get: faintness, gastrointestinal stress, diminished coordination, headaches, heart damage and reduced immunity. In extreme cases, even death can result.

One thing is certain, a discussion of ergogenic aids is anything but boring. There are literally hundreds of ergogenic aids—pills, potions, herbs and nutritional supplements purported to give you more of whatever you want in less time than it takes to read this entry—and their alleged benefits run the gamut from the fascinating to the fantastic.

Ergogenic means "tending to increase work." It's no coincidence that this all-purpose term has been applied to the purported athletic aids we're hearing so much about. No topic is more muddled. Therefore, caution is in order when considering using these substances, urges John Ivy, Ph.D., director of the Exercise Science Laboratory at the University of Texas in Austin.

"There are hundreds of ergogenic aids that haven't been shown to be effective via sound scientific research," says Dr. Ivy.

In 1989, the National Council against Health Fraud identified a wide range of deceptive methods that some suppliers of ergogenic aids use to dupe consumers. Among these are testimonials from athletes who were at worst bought off or at best duped by a placebo effect.

Another ploy is using outdated or poorly controlled research to substantiate claims. In some cases, the task force found suppliers who reported research that was never conducted.

At times, legitimate published research work may be taken out of context. As an example, Dr. Ivy points to a common claim that supplements of the amino acid arginine will raise insulin and growth hormone levels, boosting strength and performance.

Counters Dr. Ivy, "If you infuse (inject) arginine, that's true, but if you take it orally, it isn't." Suppliers, who sell arginine in pill form, neglect to mention this fact.

Cut through the confusion

There's no denying that some ergogenic aids are intriguing. Baking soda is supposed to help delay fatigue, while phosphate loading may help improve oxygen delivery to the muscles (scientists are still debating this).

Some aids, though effective, are illegal, such as the practice of blood doping—drawing off several pints of your own blood, letting your system replace it, then reinjecting the missing blood to boost your oxygen-carrying capabilities right before competition.

Other aids illustrate how easily confusion enters the picture. Quinine is sometimes used by doctors to treat cramps due to poor circulation. Some enterprising athletes have ingested quinine in hopes of preventing heat cramps, a misguided strategy (heat cramps are caused by dehydration and salt loss, and quinine has no effect on either). Instead, they end up with such symptoms as nausea, ringing in the ears and slowing of the heart.

And of course, there's no limit to the extreme measures some athletes will take. This gives rise to such ludicrous acts as shoveling down everything from beef testicles to blue-green algae.

Unfortunately, there are also deadly serious underpinnings to this improve-at-any-cost outlook. Purported aids like amphetamines, anabolic steroids and corticosteroids can cause permanent damage and, on occasion, death.

Faced with the heated claims of ergogenic aid suppliers, athletes may ignore substances that can genuinely help them. Do you know which performance booster is guaranteed to help regulate temperature, keep the body's chemical reactions working efficiently and stave off exhaustion? It's cheap, plentiful and guaranteed effective. Look no further than your tap—it's water.

Consumer, beware

How should you assess an intriguing ergogenic aid? Dr. Ivy offers a couple of tips. First, check to make sure the aid isn't banned—a substance is declared off-limits for good reason. Some may actually work, but at too high a cost. While injections of the hormone erythropoietin (better known as EPO) can boost the oxygen-carrying capacity of the blood, they're believed to have caused the deaths of more than a dozen professional cyclists.

Next, do some reading. Look for research that's been peer-reviewed, repeated and published in qualified professional journals.

Even proven ergogenic aids have varying effects. Carbohydrate drinks boost glycogen stores and help prolong endurance exercise. But if you drink a mix that disagrees with you, all that excess energy could be spent dashing for the bushes.

An aid's proven effectiveness is sometimes negated by a change in conditions. The caffeine in a few cups of coffee could help improve your performance at a 10-K on a cool autumn day, but its diuretic effect will be bad news on a hot, muggy summer day when fluid conservation is a must.

"Athletes need to test these aids beforehand, by simulating race conditions and seeing how they react," counsels Dr. Ivy.

Here's another caution. Even aids that are proven safe and effective hold an inherent danger. Once athletes find a product that offers a competitive edge, they tend to react like starving masses stumbling across an all-you-can-eat buffet.

"Often an athlete's mindset is 'more is better.' People can overdose on things that we know work and are generally safe," says Dr. Ivy. "With all these ergogenic aids, taking too much can be detrimental to your performance and possibly your health."

Resist the hype

It's often hard to resist the enthusiastic claims of other athletes, points out Dr. Ivy. "Someone will start doing something, and whether it works or not, people will start jumping on the bandwagon," he says. "It's wise to stick to what's been proven scientifically and what's right for you."

In fact, ergogenic aids might be likened to spouses—what's right for one person might be incompatible with another. There's no single path to athletic success.

A case in point: Husband and wife Lon and Susan Haldeman have both won cycling's grueling Race Across America (RAAM). Susan credits her efforts in part to a commercial carbohydrate and nutrient loader that gave her highly concentrated amounts of calories in a neat package. When husband Lon won the race, he did so by less tidy means—wolfing down a steady stream of Pizza Hut pizzas, Cokes, Quarter Pounders, Chun King chow mein, milk shakes and Spaghetti-O's.

See Also: *Amino Acid Supplements, Amphetamines, Anabolic Steroids, Aspirin and Its Cousins, Blood Doping*

Fartlek Training
Speed training with a twist

*F*artlek (Swedish for "speed play") is one way to add more fun to your exercise routine. It's simply switching gears, alternating hard and easy efforts over a specific distance or time.

Using this hard/easy premise, fartlek can take almost any form—from one-minute hard bursts of running with a 30-second recovery to two-mile bursts on a bike interspersed with ½ mile of easy riding. Not only does fartlek add more interest to your workout, it also adds decidedly more effort. It's a great way for busy athletes to get a terrific workout in a short amount of time.

"You warm up, throw in some fartlek work, and in 35 minutes you've gotten a better workout than just going out and running for the same amount of time," says long-time California track coach Vince O'Boyle.

Fartlek training enhances both long-distance strength and power and the athlete's sense of pace. It also conditions the body to quickly recover from the relatively short bursts of fast pace encountered in competition. And the ability to switch pace and change gait during training runs can certainly come in handy in races.

Perhaps most important, fartlek is a great way to revitalize a workout. The late Barry Brown, a standout Masters runner, was known to toss 20-second fartlek accelerations into his run. He surged, then settled back into a steady pace for a few minutes before surging again. Not only will five or six of these bursts snap you back to life, they can also trick your body into a better workout.

"By the time you get back into a comfortable pace, it's much faster than you were going, and you're farther along in your run than you realized," Brown once said.

In fact, for some people, fartlek is all the speed training they want. Serious competitive endurance athletes go further—they maximize their aerobic potential by incorporating both interval workouts *and* fartlek into their training.

See Also: *Interval Training*

Fitness Testing
Know thyself, and train better

T here are two good reasons to start your endurance training program with a full fitness evaluation. The first is common sense—especially if you're over age 35 and have recently entered the world of the exercise aficionado. But even if you already consider yourself an athlete, a complete fitness test is a terrific idea. A thorough evaluation by a trained sportsmedicine professional will give you a base on which to build your training program and gauge your progress.

Actually, this is a frequent practice among experienced competitive athletes. Their fitness is regularly monitored—before, during and after their competitive season. You don't need to go quite that far, but a fitness evaluation before setting up an exercise program offers you a baseline measure, plus another terrific benefit.

"Time management is so important to so many people," says Stephen Black, a physical therapist and athletic trainer in Springfield, Massachusetts. "A fitness analysis and a workout schedule set up by a professional takes the guesswork out of training. You know just where to place your emphasis."

Testing, testing—what to expect

The sportsmedicine business has begun to attract more and more health-care facilities, offering training centers, fitness testing facilities and diagnostic services. Private sportsmedicine clinics have also sprung up over the past 15 years to treat the growing number of sports-related injuries suffered by recreational athletes.

But if finding a facility isn't a problem, finding a good one can be. The best bet, whenever possible, is a word-of-mouth recommendation. Barring that, find out where the best athletes in your area go for testing and treatment. Be sure the facility is certified by the American College of Sports Medicine.

Then check the range of services available. Be sure the facility offers testing equipment in your chosen sport. If you're a runner, hop on the treadmill. If you cycle, ask if you can bring in your own bike for testing on a wind-trainer, rather than using a standard stationary bike. Triathletes should take an off-site swim test if no pool is available.

Once you get the results, you'll be able to fine-tune your workouts. The assessment should reveal an aerobic capacity and anaerobic threshold that varies from one activity to the next, with the highest and most relevant scores coming from your chosen specialty.

Cost-wise, be prepared. The fees for testing vary widely. If you're lucky, you work for a large corporation with its own fitness center and testing program. If not, expect to pay from $100 to $1,000, depending on whether the center has its own attending physician, how sophisticated its testing procedures are, how many services are offered and how many of these you'll want to use.

Whatever the cost, you should receive a printout of your test results and have a one-on-one session with the attending physician or certified athletic trainer to discuss your results. Finally, you should receive a personalized training schedule in writing.

Get a good fitness evaluation

All athletes, from world champs to weekend warriors, are assessed by the same criteria. Therefore, the following should appear on your fitness test.

Anaerobic threshold. Your anaerobic threshold is the point at which fatigue begins. It's the upper limit of your endurance. From this point on, the accumulation of lactic acid in your muscles will drag at your efforts to work your body.

The more aerobic work your heart can do, the higher its anaerobic threshold. By checking your maximum heart rate (MHR) during aerobic exercise, you can establish how high, or low, your anaerobic threshold is.

Champion athletes can function at high percentages of their MHR while exercising aerobically, or below the anaerobic threshold. Alas, sedentary folks start gasping for air at heart rates slightly above the normal resting rate. Endurance training is all about getting that anaerobic threshold up, up, up.

Body fat. While this isn't necessarily an indicator of aerobic fitness, most facilities include body fat percentage in their basic package. Optimal body fat levels for endurance athletes are around 10 percent for men and 13 to 18 percent for women.

The body fat you're lugging around is more of a starting point than anything, although it can serve a cautionary role as well. Body fat values are of special interest to runners when body weight is a factor.

Conversely, concern can mount when there's too little body fat, especially in the case of female endurance athletes with body fat below 12 percent. If these women are taking in too few calories to support their exercise levels, they can be risking amenorrhea, stress injuries and exercise-induced osteoporosis.

To find your percentage of body fat, visit a clinic for an official assessment. In most cases, you'll be offered a simple and usually inexpensive test called the "skin-fold caliper technique." Using calipers, which resemble large pincers, the clinician will measure the amount of pinched skin at various points on your body, including the hips, arms and back. These findings are then inserted into a formula, which turns out a pretty clear picture of your body fat composition.

If nothing but the best will do, you can get a precise readout on body fat by opting for the "whole-body immersion/displacement method." First you'll be asked to exhale all the air in your lungs. Then you'll be lowered into a tank, where your weight and volume, shown by the amount of water displaced, will be measured. (This is only accurate if you've expelled all the air in your lungs.) The result: an accurate measure of your body's fatty quotient.

Maximum oxygen uptake (VO_2 max). This is the maximum amount of oxygen your body can take in and use during high-intensity exercise. It's also known as maximum aerobic capacity and is expressed in milliliters of oxygen used per kilogram of body weight per minute of exercise (ml/kg/min).

VO_2 max measurements can vary dramatically. An older, inactive person might score in the 20s. An active female coed might take in 43 ml/kg/min. A world-class male marathoner might have a VO_2 max in the mid 80s.

Since your ability to use oxygen governs your aerobic potential and is influenced by genetics, your VO_2 max is a sort of fitness I.Q. But it's by no means etched in stone. Endurance training can raise your aerobic capacity substantially—perhaps by as much as 30 percent of your initial reading—over the first few months of your training program.

For this reason, an initial VO_2 max value can be one important yardstick by which you can measure how effective your training program has been.

Maximum heart rate. The maximum number of times per minute that your heart can beat is called your maximum heart rate, or MHR. MHR is a valuable fitness constant that's linked more to age than to natural ability or level of conditioning. A 40-year-old marathoner is likely to have pretty much the same MHR as a 40-year-old couch potato.

What separates the two on the field of play is the marathoner's ability to exercise continuously at an effort close to MHR. Pity the poor couch potato, whose efforts to push close to MHR may bring gasps of torment. The difference lies in which athlete can speed up the heartbeat while continuing to work efficiently.

Though a lab will provide a far more accurate measure, you can roughly calculate your MHR by subtracting your age from 220. Using this rough estimate, you can use MHR while training to gauge the intensity of your workout. If you're a 35-year-old athlete, your MHR is roughly 185, or 185 beats per minute.

Say you take your pulse immediately after you exercise, or even during exercise, and your pulse rate is 150 beats per minute. That's 82 percent of your 185 maximum, a pretty accurate gauge of your effort. Experts agree that the greatest aerobic benefits are gained when you keep your heart rate at 70 to 85 percent of your maximum.

Resting heart rate. Since your heart grows stronger and more efficient as your aerobic fitness increases, your resting heart rate can be used to figure out your level of overall fitness. An "average" person's heart beats 70 to 80 times a minute; the heart of a well-conditioned endurance athlete might beat only 40 to 55 times a minute to circulate the same amount of blood.

Measuring your resting heart rate in the lab, or at home, is a simple and important fitness gauge. Just take your pulse for a minute after you've been at rest for a long time—the best time is upon awakening. As your training progresses, you'll be able to see how effective it is by checking your daily resting heart rate.

As the weeks pass and you become fitter, your resting heart rate will drop as your cardiovascular system becomes more efficient. Your pulse rate will also tell you how to approach each day's training.

"If your resting heart rate goes up five or ten beats per minute, that means you had a hard workout the day before and you ought to go easy today," says Herman Falsetti, M.D., a cardiologist and sportsmedicine specialist from Irvine, California. "If it's up more than ten beats, you're starting to overtrain and maybe get sick." At this point, he advises, you should *definitely* take it easy.

Measuring cautionary factors. At most comprehensive testing centers, a supervising physician will take your medical history before beginning testing. Some sportsmedicine firms require that clients 35 and over with inactive lifestyles have an electrocardiogram (EKG) before they will conduct an evaluation. Smaller operations run by physical therapists and trainers may not do this themselves but will recommend a cardiologist who can take an EKG tracing.

Cholesterol levels. Another component generally included in these tests is a blood sample to determine cholesterol levels. This is for safety's sake, as high cholesterol levels are a sure-fire danger signal.

Cholesterol levels can also serve as a fitness baseline. Regular exercise increases the amount of cholesterol transported in the blood by the "good" HDLs (high-density lipoproteins) and lowers the levels of cholesterol carried by the "bad" LDLs (low-density lipoproteins). As you exercise, your HDL levels should increase and your LDL levels should fall.

For that reason, your blood test should differentiate between the two types of cholesterol, giving you a measure of each. It's also important to understand that total cholesterol might be fairly high in a trained athlete because regular exercise has raised the HDL levels.

Where should your cholesterol levels be? An important indicator of heart disease risk is your ratio of HDL cholesterol to your total cholesterol. Experts recommend that at least 25 percent of your total blood cholesterol be HDL. Let's say your ratio of cholesterol is 3. That's a total cholesterol reading of 180 divided by your HDL reading of 60. Congratulations! You're blessed with a nice, low ratio, which lowers your risk of heart disease. As the ratio climbs above 4, your risk increases. When the ratio exceeds 6, the risk becomes serious.

See Also: *Anaerobic Threshold, Cholesterol, Maximum Heart Rate, Maximum Oxygen Uptake*

Goal Setting
Where are you going?

T he cameras were rolling when swimmer Mike Barrowman captured the Olympic gold on July 29, 1992, setting a new world record for the 200-meter breaststroke with a two-minute, 10.16-second effort. The world exulted with 27-year-old Barrowman in his moment of glory: arms thrust over head at the finish, tears welling up during the national anthem.

What viewers didn't see was the effort *behind* the effort. Four years earlier, at the 1988 Games in Seoul, Korea, Barrowman had been the favorite in the same event. He finished fourth. As soon as he exited the pool in Seoul, his goal was clear: Gold in 1992. Barrowman kept a daily training diary and set precise, incremental goals in his four-year march. His focus never wavered. "July 29 is all I've been thinking about for a very long time," he said softly after his Olympic win.

Now, four years down the line is longer than most athletes care to look, but Olympic efforts demand an Olympian focus. The point, though, is clear. Barrowman achieved success because his effort didn't waver, largely because he knew precisely what he wanted.

In sport, and in life, defining your goals helps you focus your efforts more clearly.

"People who set goals for themselves tend to do better than people who don't," says coauthor Scott Tinley. "Goals give you an opportunity to better understand your intentions, your actions and, in some ways, even your existence."

No stranger to setting and achieving his endurance goals, Tinley sets out a six-point plan for creating your own.

1. Make your goal achievable. "The idea," Tinley points out, "is to be able to reach your goal, not just shoot for it." Too many athletes set goals that are far too lofty. Inevitably, they fall short of those goals.

2. Be realistic. Setting achievable goals means objectively assessing your age, your natural ability, your lifestyle and your level of fitness. A 45-year-old chain smoker new to fitness shouldn't vow to tackle the Ironman within the year.

That doesn't mean, however, that you shouldn't make your goal something that will require solid effort. If you don't stretch, you'll never know how far you can reach.

3. Make your goals definable. "Keep 'em short and simple," says Tinley. Setting too vague a goal makes it difficult to pinpoint exactly when you've accomplished it. If you set yourself a goal to "do really well" in a race, you're apt to feel unfulfilled at the finish.

What's "really well"? A better, more definable goal might be something like finishing in the top 10 percent in your age group, or better yet, finishing under a specific time. (Since you can't control how your competitors do, setting yourself up against them can often be a frustrating goal.)

If you set a definable goal, success, or failure, will be obvious. If you reach the goal, you can go on to the next step with satisfaction and enthusiasm. If you don't, it's time for some honest self-assessment. Did you just have a bad day? Is your goal possibly too high? Well-defined goals allow you to learn from your achievements *and* your mistakes.

4. Make your goals renewable. Whenever possible, leave yourself an out. Don't etch goals in stone. If you find an early goal might have been too unrealistic, revise it. It's important to set difficult standards for yourself, but you don't want to be banging your head against a brick wall. If you never achieve your goals, you're apt to lose interest fast.

5. Make your goals incremental. You should have one long-range, pie-in-the-sky goal. As poet Robert Browning once said, "Ah, but a man's reach should exceed his grasp, or what's a heaven for?" Still, to reach that ultimate goal, you'll need smaller goals that will lead you to that pie in the sky.

Good goal setting requires serious thought. The plan of attack for a sub-three-hour marathon, for instance, may involve a year or so of specific workout goals and shorter competitive runs in order to reach that ultimate goal.

Always have your next goal in mind and be ready to strike out for it as soon as your most recent goal has been achieved. This may sound obvious until you think of all those champions who had difficulty adjusting to life after sport.

6. Give yourself a break. Quitting isn't good, but sometimes it's necessary. Some goals are simply not achievable. Nagging doubts are one thing—you need to learn to take those in stride—but when something is all wrong, don't be afraid to let it go. There's a fine line in the endurance arena between courage and thick-headed stupidity. Quit when you know it's the right thing to do.

Now that we've examined the value of goal setting, one final word. Take your goals seriously, but don't become compulsive about them.

"The downside for athletes who are constantly goal conscious is they can tend to be obsessive about them," says Tinley. "Remember, fun's the reason you're in this. Goals are important—they help you develop a training program and an important framework—but all they are is a means to an end."

Heart Rate Monitors
Technology's gift to daily training

With the plethora of athletic gimmickry available today, it's easy to turn your back on the whole lot. When it comes to heart rate monitors, however, this would be a mistake. There's no more invaluable training and racing tool.

"I'd be lost without it," admits John Howard, a member of three Olympic cycling teams and winner of the 1981 Hawaii Ironman Triathlon.

"I use a heart rate monitor religiously for all my speedwork and virtually all my races. It gives me a precise and accurate reading of my human horsepower."

Athletes and coaches have long recognized that heart rate will accurately reflect human effort. Before the advent of heart rate monitors, pulse was measured by placing the fingers on the wrist or on the carotid pulse in the neck.

This is still a good measure of heart rate and effort, but it has its drawbacks. When the heart's racing, it's difficult get a precise reading. And try to accomplish this maneuver at 25 miles an hour on a bike!

The best heart rate monitors consist of a watch and a belt you strap around your chest. The belt measures your heart rate and the watch displays the information in a neat and continuous readout. Some monitors will measure your pulse through a sensor attached to your finger or earlobe. These are usually cheaper but tend to be less accurate.

Monitors can offer a wide variety of other features. Some will give you a readout showing you the amount of time you've spent in your target heart rate zone. Others have a beeper that goes off when you stray from that zone. You can find models that display your maximum heart rate during your workout, along with your ongoing heart rate. Some models are even water resistant. A reliable monitor may cost over $100, with extras pushing the price even higher.

A multipurpose training tool

A heart rate monitor can be used in lots of different ways. It's a great way to keep tabs on your race effort and ensure that you're not overextending (or underextending) yourself. Some athletes even set the monitor to sound a warning beep if the heart rate strays above a designated point, which would indicate that they're burning valuable reserves too early.

In workouts, a monitor can be an immediate and unerring measure of both effort and recovery. If you're doing intervals—say, five 440's on the track—you can use the monitor to determine precisely when you should start the next effort. This might be at a predetermined point where you've recovered just enough, but not so much that you're getting too much rest. Heart rate monitors can also be used in the water, so you can apply them similarly to intervals in the pool.

A monitor can even come in handy when you're sedentary. Taking your heart rate each morning before you get out of bed can give you a clear view of how your fitness program is progressing. With time you'll see your resting heart rate fall as your cardiovascular system becomes more efficient.

Noting your resting heart rate in the morning can also help you tell if you might be overtraining—if your resting heart rate is five to ten beats higher than it was the day before, take it easy that day. Or better yet, take the day off.

Perhaps most important, a heart rate monitor can help you become very attuned to your body's signals. Pay close attention to how you feel. Look at the monitor. Chances are, from workout to workout the same physical sensations will signal an identical level of effort.

Experienced athletes who have worked with monitors for a long time can guess their heart rates—and more important, their effort—almost to a beat. This can be especially invaluable for the endurance athlete who needs to pay out energy carefully.

A word of caution: As we mentioned, not all heart rate monitors are accurate. An easy way to test for accuracy is to check it against your pulse.

See Also: *Maximum Heart Rate, Pacing, Second Wind*

Hill Training
Winning the uphill fight

*T*he great New Zealand distance-running coach, Arthur Lydiard, was an avid proponent of hill training. He appreciated not only its aerobic benefits but also the way it improved leg strength and power. Cyclists, runners, cross-country skiers and other endurance aficionados all train on hills for precisely these reasons.

If you're a runner or skier, a climb of 100 to 200 yards is about right. Pick a hill with a 10 to 15 percent grade; you don't want something so steep that your form deteriorates on the way up. Work at a pace that allows you to get to the top without breaking stride yet pushes you enough to wish you'd taken up duckpin bowling instead.

Start with as few as three repeats and work up from there. As you get into better shape, you can increase the number of repeats and the speed of your climbs. Use the downhills to recover. Make sure you run down easily. Pounding downhill like a runaway chicken, arms flapping and hair flying, will lead you straight to injury.

Cyclists usually incorporate hills into fartlek-type rides, the riders hammering hard up each hill, then spinning easy on the flats. Of course, this presupposes a route with a fair number of evenly spaced hills.

Cyclists can also make like runners and just tackle a single hill. Mountain bike star Ned Overend lives and trains in Durango, Colorado, where there's no shortage of hefty climbs. Overend makes good use of them.

A favorite workout is a series of intervals on a long climb not far from his home. Overend warms up for 20 minutes. Then he starts climbing, riding easy for 5 minutes, then hard for 5 minutes; easy for 5 minutes, then hard for 10 minutes; and finally, easy for 5 minutes and hard for 5 minutes. This makes for a grueling and effective workout.

"Because it's all on the hill, you're forced to recover while you're still climbing," says Overend. "A half hour of intervals like this is more than enough."

A final cycling option is to repeat a single loop that contains one or two big hills. This is a great choice if you want to measure your progress—you can time yourself over the course again and again.

No matter what the discipline—cycling, running, cross-country skiing—hill training forces your muscles to work hard. This isn't the sort of workout you want to tackle when you first start training. Your muscles need to be well conditioned to meet the challenge. If they aren't, powering uphill is a surefire invitation to muscle pulls and strains.

See Also: *Fartlek Training*

Interval Training
To improve, you need to move

Whatever your sport of choice, eventually you'll reach the point when you'll no longer wonder "Can I do it?" but "Can I do it faster?"

One thing is certain. You won't get faster by training on the same course at the same speed every day. You'll stay fit, but your performance will plateau. Then, depending on your outlook, you'll either become bored or self-satisfied, neither of which will improve your performance.

If you want to continue improving, you'll eventually have to add speed to the equation. Happily, there are several speed-training techniques that can be adapted to almost any activity.

Rehearse with reps

Without doubt, interval training is the most versatile and effective way to build speed and fine-tune your endurance. It's also one of the most neglected aspects of many athletes' training programs. Intervals mean work—which is precisely why some of us avoid them.

Typically, interval training involves multiple repetitions (reps) of high-intensity exercise, alternating with rest or mild exercise. It's a terrific way to improve overall performance by forcing your body to gradually accept higher levels of stress. Intervals allow you to train harder during brief periods than you would in one long session.

During the rest period between intervals, your body can flush lactic acid from the muscles. This prevents exhaustion and takes your body to a whole new level of aerobic fitness—as if it were working continuously at a faster rate. The high level of aerobic fitness you'll achieve would be impossible to attain solely through long, steady training.

Intervals also help your body learn how to go fast—how to fire off the right number of muscle fibers, in the right order, in response to the correct neurological commands. They're especially helpful for highly trained athletes who've been out of the saddle for long periods and have "forgotten" how to train fast. Not until they've reestablished motor pathways and feedback systems can they return to truly effective training and racing.

Are you a runner? How does a six-minute mile feel? What about an eight-minute mile? Does your form deteriorate over the last mile of a 10-K?

Interval workouts can enhance your sense of pacing and your ability to maintain proper form even when you're zonked. They'll also prepare you to move on to the next level of performance.

"Any kind of training where you run repetitions and then rest briefly between them will acquaint you with what it's like to be in oxygen debt, and to recover," says 1972 Olympic marathon gold medalist Frank Shorter. "You have to condition your body to run fast, and cope with that, if you want to improve."

Put your imagination to work

Intervals can be mixed and matched in an endless variety of combinations. They're limited only by your imagination and your willingness to work.

You can do intervals over a specific distance or time. In swimming, for example, intervals are broken down into time increments—say, ten 100-meter repeats at 90-second intervals. If you swim each 100-meter repeat in 80 seconds, you'll have 10 seconds to rest before the next one.

On the running track, distance usually replaces time. A runner might run ten 440-yard repeats with a 110-, 220-, or 440-yard recovery jog after each.

Heart rate monitors have introduced a new element to interval use, enabling athletes to precisely measure how much effort they're expending.

Using a heart rate monitor as a guide, try a set of ten 440-yard runs, keeping your heart rate close to maximum. After each interval, let your heart rate determine how much rest you'll need. When it's dropped to a certain "recovered" level, say 110 beats per minute, you're off again.

Let your goals guide your intervals

Your training goals will decide the distance, speed and rest periods in your interval workout. Endurance athletes planning to push through a long haul should choose longer intervals. These should be at a pace that hovers at, or just above, their anaerobic thresholds, with short periods of rest in between.

This type of training increases your aerobic efficiency, refines the body's ability to mobilize stored glucose and clarifies your sense of pacing and timing.

How fast should your intervals be? Use your race goal as a guide. Let's say you want to break 40 minutes for a 10-K. That translates roughly into a 6:30-mile pace. Let's establish our 10-K runner's ideal interval distance at 440 yards (one lap on a standard track). A good starting pace would be about 7 percent faster than that of your race goal—in this case, six minutes per mile, or one minute, 31 seconds per 440.

Here's the math:

6:30 mile = 390 seconds; 390 seconds × 0.07 = 27.3 seconds; 390 seconds – 27.3 seconds = 363 seconds; 363 seconds = 6:03 mile.

A 6:03 mile divided by four comes to roughly one minute, 31 seconds per 440 yards. Presto, that's what you'll want to run for each 440-yard interval.

Experiment to find your pace

The beauty of intervals is their infinite variety, making interval training more productive than your daily six-mile plod and a lot more interesting. However, you'll want to know some rules of thumb before you start your interval training.

Since intervals are intended to build aerobic endurance, be sure to keep

Tinley's Training Dos and Don'ts

Over years of swimming, cycling and running intervals, coauthor Scott Tinley has made his mistakes. To prevent you from repeating them, he offers these five simple tips.

1. Warm up and cool down thoroughly.

2. Don't blast through the first half of an interval, then struggle home to finish. Build gradually to speed, then concentrate on maintaining a steady pace and smooth technique through the entire distance.

3. Train with a group. You'll work harder *and* have more fun.

4. Set firm goals before you start, then stick to them. Training is *supposed* to be difficult.

5. Keep a record of your interval workouts so you can evaluate your progress.

your rest periods between intervals brief. And keep moving between efforts. If you're running 440 intervals, try to jog between 110 and 220 yards after each interval.

Most runners do sets of ten repeats. Fewer reps won't tax you enough unless you're running them exceptionally quickly.

On the flip side, more aren't necessarily better. If you can do 20 repeats without much difficulty, you're either running too slowly or taking too much rest in between. Trial and error will help you find the correct pace and rest intervals.

If you're running longer intervals—880's and miles—slow down a bit. Run 5 percent faster than race goal pace for the 880's and 3 percent faster for the mile intervals. Longer intervals require fewer reps. Even the swiftest marathon runners steer clear of doing ten one-mile repeats. Remember, your objective is quality, not quantity.

There's one other important caution: Start slowly. Runners in particular should be careful not to overdo interval training.

"If you go straight into quality without caution, you're very prone to tendon or ligament injury," cautions Mark Plaatjes, a physical therapist and 2:08 marathoner from Boulder, Colorado.

Gain cycling speed with reps

Though we've addressed running, the rudiments of interval training can be applied to almost any endurance activity. Cyclists use interval training, too. Some actually do it on a track, although cycling tracks are few and far between in the United States.

A track is nice but by no means essential. Intervals can be easily incorporated into road rides, and the variations are limitless. You can do fartlek work, alternating easy ½-mile recovery spins with hard 1½-mile efforts. Or you can pick a short, looped course of about a mile, alternating hard and easy loops.

Liz Downing, the long-reigning female duathlete, honed her formidable cycling speed and stamina by riding hard for a minute, then easy for a minute. That particular ride was only 12 miles, but Downing usually finished exhausted.

"It doesn't sound that hard, but it is," says Downing. "Interval work hurts, and that's what makes it effective. The only way to get faster is to ride faster than race pace."

As for indoor bike training, choose rollers or windtrainers that let you stay on your own bike. Even subtle changes in body positioning and pedaling mechanics can hurt the efficiency of your workouts, or even lead to injury. For less serious cyclists, though, the average gym-variety stationary bike will work just fine.

To recap the points for maximum interval effectiveness:

For short intervals (one to two minutes): Do ten repetitions at 7 percent faster than race pace goal. Rest 20 to 45 seconds between reps.

For medium-distance intervals (two to four minutes): Do five repetitions at 5 percent faster than race pace goal. Rest 45 to 60 seconds between reps.

For long-distance intervals (four to six minutes): Do three to five repetitions at 3 percent faster than race pace goal. Rest one to two minutes between reps.

One interval day goes a long way

How often should you do intervals? One interval workout a week is all you'll need, as too much of this relatively high-intensity training can lead to injury. The day after a hard workout, it's a good idea to schedule a day of light training, or even complete rest.

Never follow an interval day with another hard day in the same sport. Your body needs time to recover. Ever since former University of Oregon coach Bill Bowerman introduced the hard/easy concept in the early 1950s, athletes the world over have been reaping its benefits.

"Train hard when you're supposed to be training hard, and go easy when you're supposed to be going easy," says Bowerman. "Not only will the easy days be more pleasurable, they'll help you get the most from your hard training."

Exercise physiologists also emphasize the importance of a good warm-up before a hard interval workout. A mile or two of slow jogging should do the trick, followed by several fast-paced 100-yard runs to work yourself up to your chosen speed.

Ease into each run, make the middle 50 yards your fastest, then ease back. Take a full recovery after each. When you're done with your intervals, end your workout with a slow one-mile cool-down.

Some experts recommend that interval training be used only periodically—for several months to sharpen up for racing season. However, the endurance-type intervals we've mentioned here can be integrated with your year-round training program. They'll boost your overall aerobic conditioning and add variety to your weekly regimen.

There's one exception to the frequency rule, and that's swimming. When floating free of gravity's effects, swimmers experience little, if any, of the pounding and stress of terra firma sports. Thus, interval training in the pool can be done, and should be done, on a daily basis. The non-weight-bearing nature of the sport forces swimmers to work harder than other athletes to gain high-end aerobic benefits.

If you're at all serious about improving your swimming, consider joining a Masters swimming program. This will provide you with a coach, a comprehensive workout routine, guaranteed time in the water and perhaps most important, pool buddies who'll prod your efforts. Check your local Y, community center, high school or college for organized programs in your area.

See Also: *Anaerobic Exercise, Cooling Down, Heart Rate Monitors, Lactic Acid, Warming Up*

Junk Miles
More valuable than you think

*E*xercise physiologists are fond of playing with numbers. According to their calculations, in order to benefit from exercise, you should be working at 50 percent or more of your maximum heart rate. This implies that anything slower is wasted effort.

Not necessarily. Actually, there's a time and place for exercise bouts of supreme casualness.

Coauthor Scott Tinley is the first to admit that he's logged his share of junk miles—slow, almost slothlike mileage that requires minor effort and garners little physical gain. Tinley calls it "sightseeing," and that's exactly what he means. He might go for a run where his heart rate never strays over 100 beats a minute, an effort level for Tinley that falls somewhere between that of clearing the dinner table and shuffling a deck of cards.

Why bother with junk miles? "Several reasons," says Tinley. "First, these casual sessions are an ideal time to work on your technique. Casual spins on the bike allow you to hone your pedaling technique—instead of hammering the pedal down and ignoring the upstroke, you can focus on making each revolution of the pedal a complete, fluid circle, applying effort throughout the circle.

"Easy runs are a great time to concentrate on your form and stride. Easy swims might give you the chance to focus on pulling completely through the water with each stroke."

Technique nuances, points out Tinley, are often missed during hard training sessions, as your heart hammers away in your skull. Junk miles also allow for a mental break, a chance to simply relax and contemplate life's finer things. Plus, there's a matter that concerns all fitness buffs. Tinley's heart rate may be less than 100 beats a minute, but he's still burning fat.

"I'm burning excess calories, I'm outside in the fresh air and I'm maintaining a base of muscular adaptation and aerobic conditioning," says Tinley. "If you're out doing it, and enjoying the activity, what's junky about it?"

Long, Slow Distance Training
A steady pace has its place

T om Warren goes all-out when it comes to training. He's taken two weeks
to bicycle from his San Diego home to the tip of Baja, California, a distance of 1,100 miles. He's popped off six-hour ocean swims. And he once
celebrated his birthday by running nonstop for 18 hours from his San Diego
doorstep to Ensenada, Mexico.

Warren, winner of the 1979 Hawaii Ironman Triathlon, isn't particularly
keen on racing—he says it interrupts his training. But when he does race, the
results can be spectacular. Warren finished the 1989 Ironman in nine hours,
42 minutes, a time that would have won the event outright nine years earlier.
Not bad for someone 46 years old.

There's an obvious lesson here. LSD (short for long, slow distance) training
is the foundation of any successful endurance program.

Creating your aerobic base

The ideal endurance training program combines LSD workouts with
speedwork. Your LSD workouts will provide a solid aerobic base; interval
and fartlek training will hone your high-end aerobic potential.

Before we get started, it's important to understand that *slow* is a relative
term. Plodding along at 40 percent of your maximum heart rate is fine if
you're a mall-walker, but it's hardly adequate if you intend to do more than
scuff Formica.

For serious endurance athletes, 65 to 75 percent of maximum heart rate is
the range to aim for—a relaxed but challenging pace that keeps your level of
aerobic fitness inching up with each workout.

About 75 percent of your training should be done at this "easy" pace. This
daily, bread-and-butter homework maintains your aerobic capacity and fills
the gap between hard workouts. If this seems like a high percentage of easy
mileage, take comfort in the fact that even top athletes don't go hard all the
time. They're too smart for that.

"I don't think anyone needs any more than three hard workouts a week to
achieve top condition," says 1972 Olympic marathon gold medalist Frank
Shorter. "That's the most I've ever been able to do, and that gets me as fit as I
can be. The rest of your training has a different cardiovascular purpose. How
it's accomplished isn't that important."

Design your own program

Long, slow distance can take any number of forms. LSD training consist-
ing of a five-mile daily run is probably enough to keep you fit. If you're

planning on tackling a serious endurance event, however, you'll have to go harder than this.

A three-year study of 323 Hawaii Ironman Triathlon participants showed they logged an average training week of 7 miles of swimming, 227 miles of cycling and 45 miles of running. Eighty percent of this mileage was LSD training.

That's just an example. Don't concern yourself with other athletes' mileage totals. Odds are, they're exaggerated anyway. The mileage you log will reflect your commitment to training and your ability to juggle the other personal responsibilities in your life.

It's more important to remember the basics. Keep about 75 percent of your training at LSD pace, and maintain that pace at 65 to 75 percent effort.

Overdistance: prepping yourself for the long haul

No matter what your mileage totals, if you're preparing for a long event, it *is* important to get in some overdistance training. Tackling longer distances than you're accustomed to helps you physically and mentally. Physically, you teach your body to burn fat as fuel—fat being your most efficient energy source for the long haul. Mentally, you hone your mind to cope with events that can be as long and as wearing as a Congressional budget hearing.

Schooling the body to effectively use fat is critical for any endurance athlete competing in events that last at least 90 minutes. Your body can never metabolize fat quickly enough to provide all the energy you'll need for high-intensity exercise. But the more fat you burn, the less of your precious glucose and glycogen you'll need to use.

Long, slow-paced workouts burn body fat more efficiently and convert it into energy for your muscle fibers. For maximum performance, you'll need to access all your body's fuels—stored glucose from the liver and muscles and fatty acids from adipose tissue. LSD training teaches your body to do just that.

Remember, speed is *not* the issue. The point is to burn fat—not glycogen—and that means going relatively slowly. Pace yourself, enjoy the scenery and consider your long workout an adventure.

Long training sessions also give you the opportunity to rehearse mental strategies like dissociation and positive imagery, also known as "mind games." These often come into play when the miles begin to stack up like bricks. Our ability to reason is what separates us from zucchini; late in a race your ability to cope mentally may keep you from becoming one.

How long, how often?

Coauthor Scott Tinley recommends penciling in one long training session per week. If you're training for a short event, say a 10-K, he suggests making the long session twice that distance. If you're training for a longer event, say a marathon, you'll want to approach the full distance, between 20 and 24 miles.

Remember, too, says Tinley, that although the pace of the workout will be easy, going twice as far as usual still puts considerable strain on your body. Plan your schedule so you can take a fairly easy day before your overdistance workout and another easy day afterward.

If you're a multisport athlete, you'll be facing a unique challenge. Tinley recommends that triathletes try to get in one long swim, one long run and one long bike ride each week. This may sound daunting, but it isn't really that strenuous if you're training for the standard distance triathlon of a 1.2-mile swim, 25-mile bike ride and 6-mile run. Just double each distance for your overtraining workout—one day, a 2-mile swim; another day, a 50-mile bike ride; a third day, a 12-mile run.

Of course, if you're preparing for an Ironman (2.4-mile swim, 112-mile bike ride, 26.2-mile run), you can toss the doubling premise out the window—double those distances and you'll need a week to complete a single workout. When Tinley trains for the Ironman, he might use a Saturday morning for a 100-mile ride, then toss in an evening "get through it any way I can" 6-mile run. Sunday morning might mean a long run of 20 to 25 miles, followed in the afternoon by a 3,000-yard swim.

Ultimately, how far you go on your overdistance days depends on your goals and your level of fitness. Tinley recommends you start with a distance 1½ to 2 times longer than your normal training distance. Stay there until you're comfortable, then slowly bump up your mileage.

As a measuring stick, the standard long run for a marathoner is between 20 and 28 miles. For cyclists, a century ride—100 miles—is generally considered a healthy dab of overdistance.

However, the dictates of overdistance training can vary widely. A former Race Across America (RAAM) cyclist included a 24-hour spin on his windtrainer as part of his preparation. Leave that sort of lunacy to the professionals and the fanatics. The important point is to acclimate mind and body to the long haul.

Steady, consistent training at a moderate pace forces your body to make minor physiological changes. They may not be noticeable tomorrow or next week, but they'll make a huge difference over time. High-level aerobic fitness is something that comes with years, not months, of effort.

Supreme fitness can have its practical applications. On vacation in the Bahamas, Tom Warren and a group of fellow tourists were rudely hustled aboard a ferry for a short trip between two islands. Warren protested. The ferry boat operator told him to pipe down. Warren told him what he could do with his ferry, hopped overboard and swam off. He beat the ferry across.

See Also: *Fartlek Training, Glucose and Glycogen, Interval Training, Mind Games*

Massage
Positive strokes for sporting folks

*I*n 1992, Francie Larrieu-Smith made the U.S. Olympic marathon team, a noteworthy accomplishment for anyone, but particularly so for Larrieu-Smith, who was 39 years old at the time. Her accomplishment might have shocked the running establishment except that the year before, she'd set an American record at 10,000 meters.

While Larrieu-Smith is something of a physiological marvel, she's no iron maiden. She readily admits to suffering from a number of age-related maladies—tight hamstrings, back pain, a nagging hip problem—all aggravated by training.

Like many older athletes, she confronts age by making ample use of all the sportsmedicine she can find. High on that list is massage. During intense marathon training, Larrieu-Smith indulges in as many as three massages a week, each of them 60 to 90 minutes long.

"I truly believe massage lets me recover faster, helps me prevent injuries and lets me handle more work," she says. "Three massages a week may seem a bit excessive, but I really believe preventive medicine is probably the reason I'm still around."

As you might suspect, Larrieu-Smith isn't the only proponent of massage. Athletes in every sport, from three-time Tour de France champion Greg LeMond to horseshoe pitcher George Bush, rely on massage. (And speaking of the former president, Bush received a massage just before his second presidential debate with Michael Dukakis in the fall of 1988.)

The rub on sports massage

Therapeutic massage goes back as far as Hippocrates, but even the Greek father of medicine couldn't have predicted the myriad uses for massage today. Deep-tissue massage has been used to promote healing in whiplash-injured necks. Scalp massage is used for relief from chronic headaches. Jaw massage is used to reduce severe jaw joint pain.

At least one study, conducted by researchers in Norway, suggests that massage may even put the body's own anesthetics to work by promoting the release of endorphins.

Many endurance athletes view massage as a critical part of their training. The list of elite athletes who regularly stretch out on a massage table reads like a *Who's Who* of endurance sport. Larrieu-Smith and LeMond are joined by four-time Boston Marathon champ Bill Rodgers, three-time Olympic marathoner Rob de Castella, five-time Ironman champion Paula Newby-Fraser and coauthor Scott Tinley, a three-time Ironman winner.

"Massage can be an incredible advantage to an athlete who's training hard daily," says Tinley. During hard training, he averages one to two 60- to 90-minute massages a week. "It would be difficult for me to maintain the level of training that I do without massage."

You don't need to log gargantuan amounts of training time to benefit from massage. Anyone who trains regularly subjects muscle and mind to substantial strain. Mentally, the soothing salve of massage eases tension— and where a soothed mind leads, rigid muscles often follow.

Physically, massage reduces muscle tightness. It also eases the strain of training by aiding blood circulation. This flushes accumulated lactic acid and other metabolic wastes away from the muscles. Muscle soreness and damaged muscles are soothed and healed. What more could a hard-working athlete ask?

Invaluable R&R

"Massage is a real important recovery method," says Bob McAtee, a Colorado Springs massage therapist who works extensively with athletes. "Muscles don't get strong while you're working out, they get strong during rest between workouts. Massage can be used to enhance the recovery phase between workouts so that athletes are better able to train at higher levels."

The trained hands of a certified sports massage therapist can bring two other important advantages for endurance athletes. First, they can often ferret out muscles at risk for injury, tight and tender spots that might indicate potential problems, and major layoffs, down the line. Discovering these problems early can keep them from sidelining you entirely.

Equally important, they can bring much-needed mental relaxation. Thousands of Americans use massage for its most popular therapeutic benefit—stress release. Since mental tension quickly becomes muscle tension (through the release of hormones from the adrenal glands), massage can counteract that tension by soothing rigid muscles. According to McAtee, this relaxation can have a profound effect on performance.

"On the massage table, you learn how it feels to be relaxed," he says. "If you carry that feeling of relaxation over into a race or training—remember what it's like for your shoulders to be relaxed, your legs to be relaxed— you're much more likely to perform better."

Heal thyself

As an athlete, you have two options—getting a massage from a certified massage therapist or learning self-massage.

Self-massage can be a valuable addition to your training routine. As little as 10 to 15 minutes of self-massage a day can help your muscles recover quickly from training, says McAtee. He goes on to offer the following pointers on technique for the neophyte masseur or masseuse.

First, use large, vigorous strokes involving the entire muscle. Then work your way into smaller, more specific techniques to target especially tight spots. To help circulation, direct the strokes toward the heart. Large strokes might include rolling, kneading or long, gliding strokes down the length of the muscle. Follow these with smaller strokes, working across the grain of the muscle to help separate and relax the muscle fibers. You can alleviate sore spots with moderate thumb pressure, but if you encounter pain, leave it be.

"Pain generally means you're working too deeply or you're working on something that shouldn't be massaged. If it's painful, don't do it," advises McAtee, who recommends talking to a certified therapist before trying self-massage.

Self-massage has obvious drawbacks. Unless you're a contortionist, you won't be able to reach everywhere. Plus, when you're massaging one area, you're tensing another. If you don't know what you're doing, you can cause more harm than good. Although massage can be used to help reduce swelling associated with injury, this should be done only by a competent professional.

In the case of severe muscle strains and tears, leave them alone for at least 72 hours, then see a professional.

Exercise your options

McAtee, a long-time massage therapist and member of the American Massage Therapy Association (AMTA) national sports massage team, recommends a mix of both professional and self-massage.

It would be nice to follow in Larrieu-Smith's footsteps and hie ourselves down to the masseur three times a week. In most cases, however, your frequency of massage will probably be dictated by your budget and your proximity to a good pair of hands.

McAtee likes to see runners get tuned up with a massage every 70 miles, cyclists every 200 to 300 miles and serious triathletes once a week.

"If you're going to get a massage and you want to get the most out of it, it should be done after your hardest training day," McAtee advises. "That way you can get the muscles recovered, relaxed and ready to go."

Ready to hop on the table? You'll find a licensed sports massage therapist by contacting the AMTA in Chicago. In states that license massage therapists, try the Yellow Pages. Some states don't require licensing; in those cases, be sure to ask for credentials or references. Then lie back and show your muscles how much you appreciate them.

See Also: *Lactic Acid, Muscles and Muscular Endurance*

Mind Games
Leading the body with the mind

The mind is capable of remarkable feats. Take the experience of Derrick Crass. One of the United States' premier weight lifters, Crass was competing in the clean and jerk at the U.S. Olympic Sports Festival when his rear foot slipped and 411 pounds of metal drove him to the stage, knocking him unconscious.

As he was being carried toward the door on a stretcher, Crass regained consciousness. To everyone's amazement, he announced that he wanted another try at lifting. Getting off the stretcher, he stepped to the stage, hefted the weight to his chest, huffed once and jerked the mass over his head. The crowd went wild.

Crass, however, wasn't finished. Breaking into a smile, he leaned ever so slightly to one side and lifted one foot off the platform. Crass the Stork stood and beamed at the crowd, balancing twice his body weight on one leg.

Such feats are rare, but they do illustrate how powerful the mind can be when it comes to athletic performance. In fact, many experienced athletes believe it's the mind that separates the best from the rest.

"Athletes need to learn to use the mind to control the body," says John Howard, a member of three Olympic cycling teams and winner of the 1981 Hawaii Ironman Triathlon. "Most of us do just the opposite. We let the body control the mind."

Choose a mental strategy

The psychological ploys athletes use to keep going are as varied as those who employ them. Seven-time World Professional Marathon Swimming champion Paul Asmuth, the world's top marathon swimmer during the 1980s, sometimes imagined he had something attached to his head pulling him through the water.

Tom Johnson, twice winner of the Western States 100, often gets himself through long races by chasing from one reward to the next—here, I'll take a drink; here, I'll get something to eat and take a rest.

On a baser note, one female marathoner admits to imagining the faces of two detested co-workers. She then visualized them under her feet on the blacktop and alternately ran over each face for 26 miles.

For simplicity's sake, we'll divide mental strategies like the examples above into two camps—association and dissociation. Each strategy has its place, especially in events of long duration.

Dissociation is similar to daydreaming—it's offering the mind a respite from the task at hand. It can take any form, limited only by the athlete's imagination. By simply focusing on something other than what you're doing, you try to ignore discomfort and keep negative thoughts from streaming into your mind.

Association is just the opposite. Here you focus intently on the task at hand, concentrating on your body's signals, painful though they may be.

Focus on the physical

When six-time Ironman winner Dave Scott raced, he'd regularly run through what he called "a physical inventory," a mental checklist to ensure that he was relaxed from head to toe. Were his ankles loose? His legs? His lower back? Were his shoulders bobbing loose and low, or were they bunched up and tense? When things got really tough, like running neck-and-neck with Mark Allen near the end of the race, Scott would repeat his checklist continuously.

"It was the same reel," says Scott, "over and over and over again. I used all those clues to remind me that I was still performing at an optimum level."

Experienced athletes and sports psychologists agree that you have to closely monitor your body's signals—breath rate, temperature, heaviness in the calves and thighs.

"It's crucial to stay focused," agrees cyclist John Howard. "So many people try to get through events by externalizing. They think about tomorrow's dinner, or how great it'll be to finish. The real athletes are able to draw deeper power by going in, by focusing very closely on what the body is doing. When you don't pay attention, you lose touch. And when you lose touch, you lose control."

You don't necessarily have to focus on the pain sweeping through your body, however. Instead, focus on your technique. Keep your stride long, turn your pedals in a circle, pull all the way through with your swimming stroke, keep your breathing even. You'll find those niggling doubts and fears melting away as you concentrate on the mechanics of your efforts.

Steve Scott, three-time Olympian and for years America's top miler, uses a myopic focus to survive tough races. He often tackles a race lap by lap. By the third lap, when things really start to hurt, he might focus exclusively on keeping up with those in the lead.

Scott also uses this technique during particularly grueling interval workouts. He'll focus intently on each repeat, trying to ignore the big picture. "I take each rep at a time, and all of a sudden I'm at the eighth interval with only two to go," says Scott.

Let fantasies take flight

Of course, concentrating (associating) for an extended period can be overdone. Dissociation, on the other hand, allows you to mentally relax, offering crucial distraction during long events.

When dissociating, athletes may figure out complex mathematical formulas, relive pleasant experiences or repeat a mantra—relax, relax, relax—over and over again in their mind.

Fantasy's a good distraction, too. Why not turn the second half of a hard ten-mile run into the final five miles of the Boston Marathon, with you gaining on the leaders?

The most effective mental approach combines dissociation and association, alternating spans of intense focus with respites of mental meandering.

"You can't analyze every step," points out Dave Scott. "Allow yourself pulses where you relax, look around, notice that airplane flying overhead. Then come back to what you're doing."

This was precisely the strategy that Howard employed during the inaugural 3,000-mile Race Across America (RAAM) bicycle race. In fact, Howard preplanned a schedule that alternated dissociation with association.

"I went constantly in and out of periods of internalizing and externalizing," he recalls. "Sometimes I found myself wanting to listen to my Sony Walkman, and sometimes I didn't want to be in contact with anything but the raw elements. All I wanted to do was bury myself in what I was doing."

Sometimes dissociation and association can be used effectively at the same time. Dave Scott combines the two to face down moments when "your legs are screaming, your lungs are jumping and your heart rate's coming out of your skull." When that happens, Scott goes into mental overdrive.

"I'll focus on the body's signals and the pain, but at the same time I'll dissociate from it, telling myself that it's really not that bad," he says. "I'll tell myself I'm still in control. I know I'm not going to die."

Developing these mental skills takes practice. Unfortunately, many people view them in the same light as onion dip—something they can whip up at a moment's notice. This just isn't so.

It's crucial to practice focusing and relaxing during training. Then, come race day, you'll arrive with your mental plans firmly in place. Arriving at a moment of reckoning, and finding you aren't prepared to handle it, simply won't work.

Quiet your mind

Some athletes practice a form of meditation to improve their performance. Given that the human mind is about as predictable as a Third World government, meditation's effects on performance are hard to pin down. Clinical studies have shown, however, that meditating for as little as 20 minutes twice a day can be remarkably effective in improving general well-being.

"This phenomenon shuts off the distracting, stressful, anxiety-producing aspects of what is commonly called fight-or-flight response," writes Herbert Benson, M.D., associate professor of medicine at Harvard Medical School, in his book, *Your Maximum Mind.* "In primitive situations, where dangers from wild animals might have been the order of the day, this sort of response was quite useful. In our own time, however, the fight-or-flight response tends to make us more nervous, uncomfortable and even unhealthy."

If you're not one for meditation, coauthor Scott Tinley recommends a practical alternative. Before a race or difficult training session, find a spot where you can be alone, close your eyes briefly and see yourself moving through the event. Remind yourself to stay calm.

Let's say you're only moments from the start of a triathlon, and swimming isn't your strong suit. Visualize yourself breathing evenly during the swim and not getting caught up in the mass hysteria at the start. Observe how you avoid pushing hard until you reach the first buoy. Then take yourself through the rest of the race, seeing it unfold as you wish it to.

With meditation or visualization—whatever you want to call it—the point is to focus on what's important and exclude what isn't.

"The idea is to calm yourself," says Tinley. "Consider the guidelines *you'll* need to follow in the race, not the ones set by your frenzied competitors."

Tinley offers a final word on the value of mind games. "If we're out of shape and attempt something that's beyond us, it's going to hurt, whether we visualize, associate, dissociate, affirm or hum the tune from *Rocky.*"

See Also: **Prerace Jitters, The Wall**

Open-Water Swimming
Giving Flipper a run for his money

Open-water swimming can be a joy. Unfortunately, many athletes approach open-water swims with a relish reserved for tax audits and root canals. Granted, oceans and lakes present several challenges, including waves, currents and goose-pimple–provoking temperatures. Look at these challenges as precisely that. Your real opponent in open-water swimming is your own insecurity.

First, realize your anxiety is not unusual. Seven-time World Professional Marathon Swimming champion Paul Asmuth remembers his first ocean swim succinctly. Quoth Asmuth: "I was petrified."

If open-water swimming makes you uneasy, Asmuth recommends acclimatizing slowly. Start in fresh water. Lakes are calmer, plus you'll be less apt to worry about waves tossing you off-course.

Find a straight stretch of shoreline where you can swim yet still touch bottom. Swim parallel to shore. You may feel silly navigating between wrestling teens and preschoolers in water wings, but it's nice to know you can stand at any time.

As you get more comfortable, move into deeper water. Once you're comfortable with lake swimming, move to the ocean. Ocean swims are part of many triathlons, plus they're fun and challenging events in themselves.

For those who like to stretch their limits, a word of warning. Once you're in over your head, don't swim alone. Asmuth doesn't, and he's navigated more open water than most cruise ships. Experienced waterfolk offer constant respect to what is, after all, a foreign element. Take their lead, and don't take chances.

Chart your own course

Navigating in open water is more complicated than it sounds. As any open-water swimmer will tell you, things look appreciably different when you're bobbing in the surf than they do when you're standing on the beach. A dolphin's-eye view of the world is very limited.

When it comes to open water, swimming fast means swimming straight, which can be difficult in moving water. And if you're competing in an open-water swim, odds are that most of your fellow competitors will blithely churn off in myriad directions.

Keep your head and chart your own course. Swimming straight, says Asmuth, is easier than you think. Before getting into the water, pick some kind of landmark—a house, a clump of trees, a rock formation—on the opposite side that you can head for. Although they're perfect for lake swims, these kinds of landmarks aren't an option in ocean swims; most well-organized ocean swims use bright buoys the size of mobile homes to mark the course.

Once in the water, check your position at frequent intervals, since a small navigational error early in the swim can put you way off-course. Even if you swim a straight line naturally (and few of us do), waves and currents can push you off-course.

Asmuth sight-breathes every seven to ten strokes, lifting his head up out of the water to check his surroundings. He lifts his head for one stroke only—swimming with one's head out of the water is tiring. If he doesn't get a good look, he drops his head back in the water, takes a few strokes, then lifts his head again.

Master your sight-breathing

Sight-breathing takes practice. Michael Collins, an accomplished open-water swimmer who coaches the Davis (California) Aquatic Masters, has his swimmers practice sight-breathing in the pool. His swimmers prepare for open-water season by doing swims of 1,000 to 3,000 meters, lifting their heads out of the water twice each lap.

With practice, you can learn to see what you're looking for quickly and easily. Until you've mastered sight-breathing, there's no shame in slowing or even stopping to get your bearings. Use the breaststroke for a few strokes or simply tread water for a few minutes to make sure you're heading in the right direction.

Sight-breathing doesn't always mean looking forward. You can also check your course using landmarks behind you. If you just passed a buoy, key off it by exaggerating the roll in your stroke when you breathe and sight back under your armpit, keeping the buoy directly behind you. It's tricky yet simple, and it saves you the effort of lifting your head.

Both Asmuth and Collins warn that rough-water swimming also requires a few stroke adjustments. Your arm recovery, the point in the stroke where you pull your arm out of the water and bring it forward, has to be higher, lest your arms be slapped down by waves and chop.

They also stress the importance of bilateral breathing, breathing every third armstroke. Most inexperienced swimmers prefer to breathe every other stroke, always on the same side. Breathing every third stroke provides fewer opportunities to suck down air, but it makes it much easier to swim straight.

"When you always breathe to one side, you usually have one arm pulling water in a motion that's quite different," Collins says. "You end up with a lopsided, inefficient stroke. And that sends you off-course."

A final word on bilateral breathing. At first it'll seem impossibly difficult because you're getting less air. Stick with it. With time, breathing every third stroke will become as natural as swimming straight.

Stay warm

The best way to stay warm when the water is cold is to stay out of it.

"Why practice being miserable?" asks Chicago resident Bob Bright, a veteran of the Iditarod sled dog race in Alaska. Bright, who runs and bikes to stay fit, passionately avoids swimming in chilly Lake Michigan.

Like other athletes, Bright's aware of the risk of hypothermia, or loss of heat from the body. It's a threat to be taken seriously, striking quickly and without warning. When you're immersed in the water, heat is rapidly sucked from your body, mostly from your head and torso.

If you do decide to tackle cold-water swims, wear a couple of swim caps to cut off some of the heat loss from your head. If the water temperature drops below 70°, a neoprene wetsuit cap is more effective.

Even better, if swim organizers allow wetsuits, use one. Not only will a wetsuit keep you warmer, it also provides quite a bit of buoyancy, helping you swim faster.

Make it pay off

Swimming provides terrific aerobic exercise. As a cardiovascular workout, it has few equals. So many muscle groups are called into play that the heart and lungs must work double-time to supply oxygen.

Plus, swimming's virtually stress free. All you have to do is propel your weight, not support it. Swimming injuries are few and far between—short of backstroking into a wall if you're in a pool, it's difficult to get hurt.

Swimming's biggest drawback is a familiar one to anyone with more than a passing acquaintance with chlorine. Boredom. Open-water swimming provides an enticing alternative. Your early fears will be replaced with a sense of liberation.

"There's a real freedom to open-water swimming," says marathoner Asmuth. "No walls, no coaches, no pace clock, no interruptions—just the sound of your own breathing and the water rushing over your ears."

See Also: *Aerobic Exercise, Hypothermia, Water Exercise*

Pacing
A measured approach to winning

*P*erhaps one of the most stunning examples of pacing took place at the 1990 Ironman Canada Triathlon. As with any Ironman event, Canadians didn't scrimp on distances—first was a 2.4-mile swim, followed by a 112-mile bike ride and a 26.2-mile run.

The women's race was the focus of the day, a head-to-head duel between Paula Newby-Fraser and Erin Baker. The match-up between the top two women in the sport had been hyped with much gusto. But it quickly collapsed when Newby-Fraser dusted Baker in the swim and bike events, mounting an impenetrable lead going into the run.

Or so everyone thought, until Baker, running at a 2:30 clip, whipped past an astonished Newby-Fraser 11 miles into the run. Baker would eventually fall off the pace, but not by much. After swimming 2.4 miles and riding 112, she would run a 2:49:53 marathon.

Asked about this remarkable feat later, Baker smiled and attributed her run to a simple premise: well-paced swim and bike events.

"A little bit saved adds up to a lot more reserves than you think," she grinned.

Save now, star later

Correct pacing has laid the foundation for many a stellar endurance performance. And, as many of us know, poor pacing has often led to a stupendous fizzle. The facts are simple. We have a limited amount of energy. The secret to racing well, especially in endurance sport, is parceling that energy out in controlled amounts so that the last dollop is spooned up just as we cross the finish.

Proper pacing, a precise equation with little margin for error, is a tough act to get together.

"Developing a good sense of pace is something that's very difficult to do without lots of experience," says coauthor Scott Tinley. "It takes many athletes years to develop a proper sense of pace."

The first step to proper pacing is to give the matter conscious thought. Many endurance athletes go into an event with, at best, sketchy plans for pacing. Those few ideas often dissolve as soon as the gun goes off. The athlete steps to the line and wings it, spending energy reserves like unlimited credit. Suddenly, with plenty of race remaining, there's nothing left.

This is precisely why the final haul at most endurance races looks like Bourbon Street at closing time, a conga line of weary bodies staggering toward the finish. It's a sad scenario, made even more so by the fact that most of us can relate to it.

Your heart does the rumba. Your lungs strain to suck air that seems to be siphoned through a clogged straw. And you're still a long way from the finish.

"When your heart rate's going sky high and it's early in the race, that's a bad sign," sums up John Howard, a member of three Olympic cycling teams and winner of the 1981 Hawaii Ironman Triathlon. "Racing well comes down to conserving your energy for the proper moment."

A case for slow but steady

Experienced athletes are miserly with their energy reserves, portioning them out with the reluctance of grade-schoolers sharing candy.

"I'm always assessing exactly where I am in the race, where I need to go, and how I can get there with less energy," says Tom Johnson, two-time winner of the Western States 100. "I always start a race well within my capabilities, then accelerate through it. If you overdo it early, you're finished, and there's still a long way to go."

Faced with 100 miles of trail-running, Johnson has farther to go than most. But he believes his "start slow" premise is applicable regardless of distance.

"You should always start with caution," he says. "You have to respect the distance you're going, even if it's just a mile. Any race demands a lot of your body. If you're not careful, it's really easy to run yourself into oblivion."

Nor is there any shame in backing off when the pace becomes too difficult. Many recreational athletes resist admitting they need to slow down, fearing they'll be cast in the Wimp's Hall of Fame.

Nonsense, say elite athletes, who throttle back all the time. When your heart starts to feel as if it might burst and your legs threaten to turn to cement, the best thing to do is give your body what it's screaming for: *relief.*

"Very often when you're beginning to slow down, you fight it," says 1972 Olympic marathon gold medalist Frank Shorter. "What you really should do is relax and go with it. Slow down until you level off at the effort at which you're going to be able to recover. Backing off allows you to continue the fight."

Though it's often hard to see, many elite athletes race in "pulses," hard efforts interspersed with brief time-outs for recovery.

"Unless you're right at the finish, you should never push to the extreme where you think, 'Gee, I hope I can hang on,' " says six-time Ironman champ Dave Scott. "I've always raced where I back off, then build up again, then back off, then build up again. You should always be refilling the tank while you're racing."

Scott also means this literally. Proper hydration and food intake are a crucial part of any successful pacing effort, especially in races that stretch past 90 minutes. At this point, your body's limited glycogen reserves are depleted.

The joy of fat

There's a good physiological reason you should parcel out your efforts. During exercise, muscles burn carbohydrate (in the form of glycogen) and fat (in the form of fatty acids) to produce energy. Your body's total glycogen stores—the quick-burning carbohydrate that fuels hard efforts—amount to only 2,000 calories, a reserve that's expended after about 90 minutes' work.

Fat, on the other hand, is an inexhaustible energy supply. A single pound of fat contains 3,500 calories. Fat is so calorie rich that even the leanest athletes cart around tremendous energy reserves—in theory, a 150-pound cyclist with Gandhi-like body fat of 4 percent has enough fat stores to pedal across the country without ever taking a bite of food.

Since most of us are far less reedlike, the conclusion is obvious. When it comes to energy reserves, visit Fat City.

If we're so amply endowed with fat reserves, why can't we blaze away on them forever? Alas, our muscles can't burn fat quickly enough to fuel high-intensity effort. Effort greater than 60 percent of our aerobic capacity generally demands glycogen. Carbohydrates are also needed to properly use our fat stores.

The secret to thriving over the long haul is simple: combine the staying power of fat with the flash of carbohydrate, a tortoise-and-hare amalgam where both critters piggyback you over the finish line.

"Competing successfully in any kind of endurance event boils down to being able to burn fat and spare glycogen," says Ellen Coleman, R.D., a Riverside, California, sports nutritionist and two-time Ironman finisher. "Making your glycogen last as long as you can, that's the secret to endurance.

Coleman suggests you work out for at least an hour, and preferably more. As your exercise time increases, so does the amount of fat being burned. Fat is also your muscles' fuel of choice to keep a slow, steady pace of 60 to 70 percent of your maximum effort.

Remember these three words: long, slow distance.

There's more good news. Your ability to use fat as fuel will improve as you become more fit. The more oxygen you can deliver to the muscles, the more fat you'll be able to burn.

"Feeling" your pace

Developing a sense of your pace, on the other hand, can be a challenge. It requires trial and error, keen attention and sometimes years of experience.

"The trick," says Tinley, "is to learn what pace you are capable of, know that pace and then be able to apply it perfectly under race conditions."

This is done by using interval training. If you want to hone your sense of pace for the long haul, intersperse longer-distance intervals with fairly short periods of rest. Use your race goal to determine the difficulty of these intervals and keep your effort slightly higher than the race pace.

Let's say you're training for a marathon and hope to come in at just under three hours. That works out to a 6:50-mile pace. You'll get solid conditioning by running a series of four to six one-mile repeats. Keep your pace about 3 percent faster than your goal pace on race day. Then rest one to two minutes between intervals, jogging (or walking) to keep your muscles warm.

Intervals are also helpful to gauge how different efforts feel. This is best done with a heart rate monitor, or you can take your pulse. Subtract your age from 220 to estimate your maximum heart rate. Then experiment with intervals at 60, 70, 80 and 90 percent effort, concentrating on how you feel during each effort.

You can also run a six-minute mile, a seven-minute mile and an eight-minute mile, paying close attention to how you feel. In time, you'll learn to recognize the physical sensations that accompany different levels of effort.

The consummate high-wire act

Endowed with years of such experience, many elite athletes can gauge precisely how hard they're pushing by the physical sensations they experience. If they're going too hard, they back off. If it's too easy, they up the ante. Pacing, by definition, means maintaining control.

"Since you've practiced it in training, you'll be able to sense when it's time to go harder and when it's time to ease off," says Frank Shorter. "You'll develop a sense for exactly where you should be."

Ultimately, racing at your optimum pace is a razor's-edge dance. You want to be at the high end of aerobic effort—pushing up against discomfiting, lactic-acid–building anaerobic effort—but you don't want to push too far.

"Treading that fine line between aerobic and anaerobic, that's the way you go fast over the long haul," confirms John Howard. "Keep the anaerobic efforts to a minimum. Then, when the end's in sight, really throw the coals on. Ideally, you should cross the finish with nothing left."

See Also: *Anaerobic Exercise; Bonking; Fat; Interval Training; Long, Slow Distance Training; Maximum Heart Rate*

Peaking
Tip-top and ready to go

P eaking is the art of arriving at the starting line of an important event in absolutely top condition—trained, rested and eager to perform at your very best. Unfortunately, your chances of predicting the next earthquake are probably better than your estimation of whether or not you're in peak condition. Because every athlete is different, peaking is a nebulous art, at best.

"What works for one person doesn't necessarily work for another," says coauthor Scott Tinley. "Reaching a peak is quite specific to the individual."

In fact, for the experienced athlete, peaking can even be specific to an event. Tinley varies his taper, or rest period, and his training according to the importance of the event, the level of competition he'll face, the type of training he's been doing and the length of the coming event.

If you're preparing for an Ironman, for example, you'll cut back on training mileage and increase your rest for a much longer period than for a 100-yard dash. While you'd start tapering for the Ironman three weeks before race day, your taper for the dash might begin just a week before the meet. Whatever the length of the taper, the idea behind peaking is the same. If you give your body more rest, it will, hopefully, rebound to a higher level of performance.

In general, peaking is done in two basic phases.

1. The high end. This is the speed and power base of your training program that brings your aerobic conditioning to its highest level. This final phase of training generally lasts from two to four weeks and is characterized by a steady increase in the intensity of your workouts. Long, slow distance training is faster paced, with faster intervals. Rest periods are longer to emphasize the quality of each repetition.

2. The taper. This is a gradual reduction in the amount and intensity of your training that allows your body to recover without losing its well-honed competitive edge. The goal with tapering is to rest enough, but not too much. You want to stay sharp but not get stale.

Admittedly this can be a delicate balance. Back to Tinley's advice: If you're preparing for an Ironman, think about beginning your taper three weeks before the event. If your focus is a 10-K run, a week will do.

Tinley recommends using a "sliding scale" to reduce your efforts, a frequent suggestion from experienced coaches and athletes. "Cut back mileage and intensity gradually," says Tinley. "Don't just stop working out four days before the event."

Keep in mind that peaking isn't something you can do effectively over and over again. First, there's the practical reality. If you're constantly peaking, you're not training enough. Plus, the body responds to peaking the way we respond to first loves—the first one is special, and the effects taper off rapidly from there.

Putting peaking into practice

Physiologically, your body needs the long conditioning buildup for an optimum peak. When the rest period comes, these reserves will be bubbling just below the surface, eager to help. When you reach for them, they'll drive you to new heights. This is why experienced athletes peak for only one or two events per season. They simply "train through" other races, altering their training mileage not a whit.

Let's say you have ten races in a season, and you taper five to seven days for each one. Tinley points out that this is well over a month of easy training—hardly the groundwork for a successful season.

Realize, too, that peaking isn't just physical. You also need peace of mind, knowing, for example, that your equipment is fine-tuned and ready. You should be familiar with the race course as well, and have a strategy mapped out.

When John Howard is serious about an event, the three-time member of Olympic cycling teams and winner of the 1981 Hawaii Ironman Triathlon actually rides the course beforehand, mapping out strategy as he wheels along. "Here, along this flat section, I'll conserve; here, midway up this climb, I'll make my break."

An experienced athlete won't just step to the line and wing it. You shouldn't, either.

"You have to go into a race with a preconceived plan," says Howard. "Success is often the result of a well-planned effort. You have to prepare yourself physically *and* mentally."

Finally, successful peaking is a very personal matter. You'll probably have to experiment to find the program that works best. Hence, it's a good idea to choose an event of minor significance to you, then practice peaking.

See Also: **Detraining, Interval Training, Goal Setting, Overtraining**

Prioritizing
Finding time for fitness

*T*he benefits of exercise have been breathlessly documented by everyone from exercise physiologists to reformed rock stars, newly minted converts urging us to huff, puff and gyrate. Too bad this advice is often effectively smothered by a more pertinent question: Where do you find the time?

Finding time to exercise is a matter of discipline and organization. Brent Knudsen is a triathlete. He's also vice-president of a Fortune 500 company, a job that absorbs about 60 hours of Knudsen's week. Still, he manages to work out daily.

How? He maps out an exercise schedule at the beginning of each month, then does his utmost to stick to it. Knudsen admits planning a month in advance may be a bit much, but a schedule, he says, is essential to any successful exercise program.

"You have to schedule exercise into your day just like you'd schedule in a business meeting, and—just like a business meeting—make it a priority. Schedule exercise, and then commit to it."

When to work out is a matter of personal preference. Knudsen swims at noon. At night he cycles on a stationary bike while reading reports he set aside during the day.

Others swear by early-morning workouts—they point out that fewer conflicts are apt to pop up at 6 A.M. Some prefer the regenerative boost of a noon sweat. Others like to wind down with training at the end of the day. When you choose to exercise is not as important as settling into a routine. Once you establish a pattern, you're less likely to miss a workout.

Get creative with your workouts

Variety can also go a long way toward ensuring that you'll stick with your program, especially if your lifestyle contains a degree of uncertainty. Frequent travel, for instance, can wreak potential havoc on an exercise routine.

Here's where creativity comes in. Planning a trip to New York? Running can take on a real sense of urgency in certain urban areas. But if you also lift weights and swim, you're apt to find something a bit more convenient and user friendly—like a health spa at the hotel.

Calisthenics are always a good on-the-road option. Tom Sullivan, a Hollywood actor, producer and lecturer, spends about 220 days on the road each year, but he rarely misses a workout. This is all the more impressive because Sullivan is blind. He starts each day by rolling out of bed and right onto the floor for a bout of calisthenics.

Remember, too, that exercise, sex and tax refunds have something in common—a little is better than none at all. You won't always have three-hour blocks of free time in your day, but don't despair. Take that 20 minutes of exercise—and feel virtuous about it. You'll have earned it!

In the end, though, self-discipline is the key, and of course, that's up to you. Put your mind to it and almost anything is possible. As a young San Francisco laborer, 1981 Hawaii Ironman finisher Walt Stack got up at 2:40 A.M., allowing him time to swim, bike and run before he reported to work at 7:30. Retired, and with a few more hours on his hands, 83-year-old Stack was still running back and forth across the Golden Gate Bridge and swimming in San Francisco Bay.

"The difficult things in this world are solved through motivation," says Stack. "No matter how tired you are, no matter how busy you are, if you're determined, you can always make the time. It's completely up to you."

See Also: *Goal Setting*

Stretching
The Cinderella of sports endurance

Stretching is one of those neglected, oft-spurned activities most endurance athletes feel guilty about. After all, stretching is good for you. And yes, it certainly can prevent injuries. It can also improve performance; a wider range of motion makes you more agile. Why, then, do athletes shun stretching, or, if they do stretch, get it over with as quickly as possible?

Bob Anderson, a long-time runner and cyclist who literally wrote the book on the subject, has concluded that most people strain when they stretch. It's not a pleasant experience, so they avoid repeating it.

That's too bad, because stretching should play a significant role in your overall conditioning. In fact, your increased fitness makes it necessary. Exercise, you see, makes your muscles stronger, and at the same time shorter. (The individual muscle fibers tend to twist and tighten almost the same way a rubber band does when you twist it from both ends.) Not only does this limit your flexibility, it also increases the likelihood of muscle tears and strains.

Tight muscles also lead to biomechanical irregularities that can quickly snowball into injury. For example, if you're a runner and develop tight hamstrings, you'll have poor leg extension that slows you down. It'll also put undue stress on your ankles, knees and hips.

Experienced athletes know how valuable stretching can be to prevent tight muscles. They generally recommend stretching as a year-round activity, whether you're training or not. Mark Plaatjes, a physical therapist and 2:08 marathoner from Boulder, Colorado, takes four weeks off each year from training, but he continues to stretch during that time off.

"Your flexibility is something you have to work at most of the time," says Plaatjes. "If you take time off, your flexibility is probably the first thing to go."

The joy of stretching

To prevent loss of flexibility, we return to the inevitable—stretching. Anderson contends that stretching would be more pleasant if we weren't so uptight about it.

"Most people don't relax when they stretch," he points out. "And the key to enjoyment is relaxation."

Anderson's book, *Stretching,* has virtually become the bible on the subject. Its approach is refreshingly practical, offering pointers to make stretching safer and more enjoyable and thus more effective.

First and foremost, Anderson encourages athletes to stretch by "feel." Flexibility, he says, is unpredictable. The runner who can touch palms to the floor one day might not be able to reach his shoes after a particularly demanding workout. Stretching by feel eliminates that possibility.

"It's really easy to stretch correctly as long as you go by feel," he promises. "If you feel it, but it doesn't hurt, you've created the right kind of stretch. Many people think mild stretching doesn't work, but it's very effective."

Nor does successful stretching have to entail lengthy bouts of full-body contortions from tendon to toenail. Anderson recommends at least five minutes of stretching before exercise. He doesn't hold any particular variation sacred but advises you to pick a series of stretches that include standing, prone and sitting stretches.

"Pick six to eight stretches that you like," he says. "If you want to add more, fine. But don't burn out. If you do 32 a day, you're bound to get tired of it."

Actually, the whole business of stretching is pretty simple. Your body will be the best judge of how long and when to stretch. Even specific stretching techniques should be geared to what you can comfortably perform now.

Mastering the mechanics

When it comes to actually doing the stretch, go the slow-and-gentle route. Ease into it, stopping when you feel tightness. Then relax. Never stretch to pain and *never, ever* bounce during a stretch. This could produce muscle strains and tears.

Current wisdom also decrees that you avoid using your body weight to force a stretch, as with the old standard toe touch. Throwing your body weight behind a stretch may force you to go beyond your natural limit, and presto, you're injured.

As to how long you should hold a stretch, it varies according to whom you ask. In fact, a dozen experts will give you a dozen different answers. Anderson, for example, recommends 15 to 30 seconds to allow time for the body to relax. But he admits that this is a general answer to an oft-asked question.

Even more relevant is keeping the stretch mild. You'll know it's working when you return to it later and find it easier to do the second time around.

Anderson agrees with many experts who feel that the best time to stretch is after the muscles have been briefly warmed up. Five to ten minutes of easy jogging or pedaling in a low gear will do the job. Blood will have begun moving through your muscles, loosening them for more flexibility when stretched. And, experts argue, stretching warm muscles cuts down the risk of injury.

However, Anderson points out that stretching after mild exercise only applies if you plan to stretch past the point of comfort, but before the point of actual pain. And most athletes, he says, once warmed up, won't be likely to plop back down to stretch. They'll want to get going. Thus, the ever-practical Anderson proposes stretching whenever it's most convenient.

"If I thought I had to be warmed up before I could stretch, then there would only be a few times during the week when I could stretch," he says.

Anderson himself stretches anyplace, anytime. One favorite is a simple neck stretch before he even gets out of bed. Or, if he's stiff first thing in the morning, he'll lie on the floor on his back, gently pulling his knee to his chest with his other leg flat.

Many athletes complain that they just don't have time for a long stretch before a workout. Fine, says Anderson. Do your longer bout of stretching when you do have the time, maybe at night while watching TV. By making stretching convenient, you're apt to do more of it. And regularity, not timing, is what brings real benefits. You'll be surprised how much regular stretching can improve your performance.

"Every athlete performs better when relaxed," states Anderson. "If you're stretching regularly and stretching relaxed, with the right kind of tension, you'll get a lot more out of yourself when it's time to perform."

Selecting a routine

Although you'll find books filled with specific routines for specific sports, these two are good, all-purpose stretches.

1. Knee pull for thighs and trunk: Lie on your back with one leg straight. Lock your hands over your other knee and pull it gently back to your chest. Hold, relaxed. Do this with both legs.

2. Seated toe touch for back and hamstrings: Hold your legs out straight, with the toes pointed away. Slide your hands down your legs until you feel your muscles stretch. Hold that position. Now try to reach your ankles. Don't force it. If you can, grab your ankles and slowly pull your head down toward your legs. Finally, if you can do it without pushing, reach out slowly and touch your toes. Hold them briefly, relax, then repeat the toe touch again.

If you're pressed for time, move through these stretches in order, giving two minutes to each exercise.

The real beauty of stretching is its simplicity.

"Stretching doesn't take a lot of talent, a lot of fitness or a lot of flexibility," says Anderson. "It just takes sensitivity toward the way you feel, and that's something any athlete can understand."

See Also: *Cooling Down, Detraining, Muscles and Muscular Endurance, Warming Up*

Time Trials
Befriending the clock

F or the serious endurance athlete, there's no escaping the clock. And a time trial, woven into your training every month or so, is a great way to gauge the success of your training program.

How does a time trial work? Simple. Pick any distance; the important thing is to choose a standard you can return to again and again for comparison.

For swimmers, a 500- or 1,000-yard pool swim will do nicely. Runners often get together to run a regular neighborhood 5-K or 10-K course. Cycling clubs often hold weekly time trials during the summer, marking off a precise distance on the road—10 to 20 miles—then sending riders off one at a time (to eliminate the advantage of pack drafting). Though cycling clubs might have someone taking times at the finish, all you really need is your own watch.

A time trial should reflect your maximum effort. Once you know your capability, you'll want to see if you can improve on it as your training continues. If you're a cyclist or a runner, your time trial could encompass your entire workout, from warm-up to cool-down.

Not surprisingly, time trials are terrific conditioners. These hard efforts expose you to the honest pain you'll experience when you race, making you that much tougher physically and mentally.

Three-time Tour de France champion Greg LeMond rose to the top of the cycling world largely through his superb time-trialing abilities. Cut loose from the draft of the pack, few cyclists could ride as hard or as long. If it worked for LeMond, it could work for you.

Don't duck these tests—they're an important measure of your abilities. If you choose to time trial with others, stick to your own pace. The trial's supposed to measure your progress, not your attempts to keep up with the fastest runner in town until you keel over. Even if you don't keep a regular training log, record these time trials. Looking back over the previous six months will give you a clear idea of how far you've come.

See Also: *Anaerobic Exercise, Anaerobic Threshold, Heart Rate Monitors, Marathon, Peaking*

Warming Up
Getting your engine going

See the runners arrive at the marathon two hours early. See them spend most of that time searching out a toilet and jawing with friends. See them do a few jumping jacks and toe touches seconds before the starting gun. See them bolt off the line. See their muscles seize up like rusty gate hinges. See their race end before it starts.

With the possible exception of the national debt, fewer things are more universally ignored than a proper warm-up. This doesn't make sense, since launching into hard exercise without warming up is like getting married after the first date—your odds of success are slim and your risks are great. Yet, for every expert who patiently explains the benefits of a proper warm-up, there are legions of athletes who turn a deaf ear.

Coauthor Scott Tinley sighs. "People are impatient. They're pushed for time. They want to go hard right away so they can get something from their exercise," he says. "What they usually get is compromised performance, or worse yet, injuries."

Jump-start with a warm-up

When you understand what a warm-up accomplishes, you'll be more apt to give it the careful attention it deserves. Warm-ups, as the name implies, are designed to raise your internal temperature. This alerts your body that some form of effort is in the offing.

Once warm, your muscles will contract more forcefully and relax more quickly, enhancing your ability to produce speed and strength. You'll also be at lower risk for muscle strains and tears.

A warm muscle is also a better-coordinated muscle, because nerve impulses travel faster when warmer. It happens thus: As you move your muscles during warm-up, they generate heat. The blood moving through the muscles picks up that heat, encouraging blood vessels to open. This increases your body's ability to transport oxygen. The more oxygen available to the working muscles, the greater your endurance and performance potential.

Warming up is also good for the joints, giving them a wider range of motion. And, finally, your warmed-up body will begin to create more of the hormones that help produce energy. In a nutshell, during a proper warm-up, your body is juicing itself up for effort.

"Warm-ups will aid you in the transition from rest to exercise," says Edmund R. Burke, Ph.D., associate professor at the University of Colorado. "If you get the blood flowing and your body temperature up a little bit, you'll transition into hard effort far easier and with less risk of injury."

"Take 15"

Dr. Burke knows athletes. He works extensively with swimmers and cyclists at the U.S. Olympic Training Center in Colorado Springs and was staff coach for the 1980 and 1984 Olympic cycling teams. A proper warm-up, he points out, is usually highly individualized, varying with the sport, the athlete, the type of event and the conditions that day. For example, a warm-up for a 35-mile cross-country ski race will differ from a warm-up for a 100-meter dash on a hot, muggy day.

Still, Dr. Burke offers some useful guidelines. He recommends at least 10 to 15 minutes per warm-up, although 15 to 30 minutes is even better. The ideal warm-up would include some stretching. If you're preparing for an event or a workout calling for an immediate hard, anaerobic effort—say, intervals on the track—expend a few short, hard efforts to get your heart rate up and your body ready for serious effort.

The effects of a good warm-up may last up to 45 minutes, but Dr. Burke advises starting to taper off your warm-up 10 to 15 minutes prior to the starting gun. Ideally, your warm-up should be complete 5 to 10 minutes before the start.

If you're warming up for a workout, Dr. Burke recommends as much of a warm-up as you can afford. Again, 10 to 15 minutes is ideal, but if you only have an hour to run, it's hardly practical.

Instead, use the early part of your run as a warm-up, building gradually into the run over the first mile or two. Or, on a 25-mile bike ride, use the first 4 miles or so to prepare your muscles.

Use common sense

Knowing that endurance athletes can be overzealous, Dr. Burke cautions against warming up too much. "You don't want to waste energy reserves and dehydrate yourself before the event starts. It's better to be a little bit under-warmed-up than over-warmed-up."

How do you know when you're warmed up? "As a general rule, you know your muscles are warmed up once you start to break into a sweat," says Dr. Burke.

Remember, these are simply guidelines. You'll need to experiment to see what works for you, both physically and psychologically. Though coauthor Scott Tinley advises 10 to 20 minutes of warm-up, he's taken as long as 45 minutes to prepare for as little as 15 minutes of hard effort.

"I don't want to risk injury by doing that maximum effort without being fully warmed up, maybe even overly warmed up," he says. "When it comes to preventing injury, I usually tend to err on the side of caution."

See Also: *Cooling Down*

Water Exercise
No pain, plenty of gain

W hat kind of workout can you get in the water? Six weeks before the 1989 World Cross-Country Championships, Margaret Groos, one of America's top runners and a 1988 Olympian, got a stress fracture. Unable to run but unwilling to quit, Groos started running in the pool. Immersed in deep water without a flotation device, Groos would run from one end of the pool to the other, pumping her arms and legs. With the benefit of her water training, Groos placed a solid 16th at the World Championships.

Most athletes come to water exercise after an injury. Water resistance therapy has been used to help rehabilitate such famous athletes as Carl Lewis, Mike Powell, Florence Griffith Joyner and Wilt Chamberlain.

One of the few sports to escape gravity's effects, water exercise is a haven for the dented and the damaged athlete with nowhere to turn. Water's buoyancy cushions the body's weight-bearing joints from trauma; its resistance acts as an instantly variable weight-training machine. It also provides a terrific aerobic workout.

For these same reasons, some athletes have made water training a regular part of their routines. Larry Almberg, a top Masters runner, came to water exercise after winding up on the short end of a picnic wrestling match with a pulled groin muscle. Unable to run on dry land, Almberg headed down to the local lake, where he waded out into deep water to run intervals—running hard for two minutes, then easy for a minute.

After he healed, Almberg continued to make deep-water pool running a regular part of his routine. Later that year, at age 42, he ran an astonishing 4:09:21 mile, one second faster than his collegiate best.

Almberg believes the water workouts helped him ease the incessant pounding of running yet stay remarkably fit. He also believes running in the water gave him another advantage.

"There's a tendency for a lot of runners to get real tight hamstrings and lose some of their flexibility," he says. "Running in deep water seems to really help me stretch out and lengthen my stride."

Wade in and work out

How does one "run" in water? For optimum results, visit your local sports outfitter and ask to see a lightweight flotation belt or vest. Without one, you'll have a hard time maintaining proper running form. Two popular models are the Wet Vest and the AquaJogger. Flotation devices sell for between $40 and $140. They're light, float you high and allow you to freely swing your arms for a maximum workout. Some experienced runners prefer to work without their buoys once they get the hang of it; without them, they're forced to work harder.

When you're settled into the pool or lake of your choice, be sure the water line is at shoulder level. Your mouth should be comfortably out of the water without your having to tilt your head. Now you're ready to take off, aquatically speaking.

To begin, simply run in water the same way you would on land, using the same motions. Keep your feet on the floor of the pool, your arms close to your body and your hands lightly clenched. While running, keep your eyes forward and maintain a position as close to vertical as possible.

You'll find that water workouts lend themselves to variety; you can alternate easy and hard days. A general rule is to run for at least 30 minutes, regardless of intensity. Many athletes find water the perfect medium for marathon training.

If you're reluctant to run in deep water, head for the shallows. Or try water walking, recommended by Linda Huey, a former sprinter and now a Santa Monica, California, water therapist.

Locking your arms and legs straight and then moving through the water, says Huey, creates tremendous resistance and a terrific workout. If you feel you have to run, Huey still recommends you keep your arms straight as you drive them back and forth in the water.

Whether you're fit or injured, water exercise, says Huey, can be a real benefit.

"Running and walking in deep and shallow water foster strength, speed and endurance," says Huey. "It's a great way to heal injuries and fight day-to-day training fatigue."

See Also: *Aerobic Exercise, Cross-Training, Interval Training*

Weight Training
A new image for an old sport

Many endurance athletes tend to view weight training in one of two lights. At best, it's a waste of valuable training time. At worst, it's a conceit practiced by egomaniacs with mountainous muscle mass and minds of mud whose fitness goals rarely stretch past the mirror.

Yet, given weight training's recently discovered benefits, both are short-sighted views. Researchers, weight lifters and the bagger at Safeway have long known that lifting gives you bigger, stronger muscles. In recent years, however, that picture has expanded. A host of studies has credited weight training with lowering cholesterol, reducing blood pressure, improving glucose metabolism, strengthening bones, burning body fat and, yes, even improving heart rate and endurance.

Not all of the studies are in agreement, but there's been enough of a consensus that even the august American College of Sports Medicine (ACSM) revamped their decade-old exercise guidelines. In 1991, they added weight training to their recommended fitness program.

"A lot of people are concerned that they'll become bulky and have big muscles, which is true if you do nothing but heavy weight lifting," says Kerry Stewart, Ph.D., assistant professor of medicine and clinical exercise physiology at Johns Hopkins University School of Medicine in Baltimore. "But if you use weights in a moderate way, you can gain a wider range of health benefits than we ever believed, without the bulk and heavy muscle."

Taking weight training to heart

Dr. Stewart is a leading researcher on weight training's effects on the heart. Much of his work has led to the debunking of old weight-training myths. Previously, studies showed little cardiovascular gain and plenty of cardiovascular risk—skyrocketing blood pressure often accompanied bouts of heavy lifting.

While working with high-risk heart patients, Dr. Stewart found that circuit weight training—light-weight, fast-paced, high-rep lifting—could be both safe and beneficial for the heart. In fact, with the exception of patients with severe damage, the vast majority of recovering heart attack patients were able to benefit from these sessions.

Dr. Stewart's studies, seconded by other research work, revealed that circuit weight training reduced cholesterol levels and lowered blood pressure. It also produced marked gains in cardiovascular endurance. Aerobic exercise is still the winner in providing these benefits, but weight training is a strong contender.

"We've been hearing for years that aerobic sports were the only way to go," says Dr. Stewart. "But we've learned that moderate levels of weight training can be done by almost anybody and that this training can improve cardiovascular health."

He emphasizes that most healthy folks can gain a trio of benefits from aerobic circuit weight training. Not only does it build strength and flexibility, it enhances aerobic fitness as well.

Going for the fat burn

Seekers of a svelte body will be heartened to learn that weight training packs a powerful fat-burning punch. Muscle cells are the body's most efficient fat burners. This explains why, at age 30 or so, one's unattended body begins to take on soft edges.

What's happening is simple. When you're less active, you lose muscle mass. Your fat-hungry muscle cells are now faced with a veritable all-you-can-eat buffet. Adding muscle helps restore the balance.

Linn Goldberg, Ph.D., a researcher at Oregon Health Sciences University in Portland, believes the fat-burning potential of weight training and aerobic exercise are actually fairly close, if you engage in aerobic-type weight training.

Go for light-weight, high-repetition (10 to 15 reps) lifting, with little rest between weight stations.

Fit athletes interested in burning fat (and garnering aerobic benefits) can increase the number of reps, Dr. Goldberg advises. The lighter the weight you lift and the more times you lift it, the more calories you'll burn. It's also crucial to move quickly from one exercise to the next, thus keeping your heart rate up in the same manner you would during a run.

"Remember that the number of calories you burn depends on your rest breaks," says Dr. Goldberg. "The less rest you take, the more calories you'll burn."

Adding muscle and metabolically active muscle cells may also help the body gobble up excess glucose in the bloodstream. Some studies have indicated that weight training can deflate diabetes by improving the body's ability to metabolize sugar. If you're not diabetic, you still shouldn't ignore this information. Inefficient metabolism of sugar can also contribute to coronary artery disease.

Incidentally, you're unlikely to see agreement on weight training's benefits. Much of the research is less than ten years old, and scientists are still picking over it like bargain-hunters at a garage sale.

Researchers do agree on one point. Weight training offers one important advantage that endurance training can't—it strengthens bone and muscle.

Fortifying your frame

There's a tendency among endurance disciples to view the heart and lungs as the centerpiece of their fitness universe. But even if you have a heart the size of Maine and the lung capacity of a Hoover vacuum, you still have to drag your musculoskeletal system along.

Marathons, long bike rides and triathlons put substantial stress on bone and muscle. For some endurance athletes, this can be the weak link. Supremely fit aerobically and woefully weak structurally, they push their bodies to the point where muscles snap and tear and bones bruise and crack. It's hardly surprising, then, that niggling injuries like tendon strains and shin splints put many a training program on hold.

"Your musculoskeletal system has to be strong to withstand the abuse that you're going to put yourself through," advises professional triathlete Ray Browning, who understands abuse better than most. Browning has completed more than 25 Ironman distance triathlons.

"You don't have to be heavily muscled, but by doing one or two days a week of basic upper- and lower-body strength training, you can train and race harder with far less risk of injury," he says.

Setting up a routine

For basic overall fitness, the ACSM recommends a minimum of two days of strength training a week. These should include a minimum of eight to ten different lifts involving the major muscle groups. Each lift should comprise 8 to 12 reps with a weight heavy enough to drive you to near exhaustion by the final heft.

The ACSM bases these guidelines on two sound premises: first, that more lifting will produce greater strength gains, and second, that these benefits taper off fairly rapidly. Studies have shown that subjects who weight train three days a week garner only slightly more benefits than folks who lift twice a week. This premise fits in nicely with what is probably, for most people, an already crowded training schedule.

The ACSM members also noted that people who weight trained more than two days a week often got sick of it and quit.

How much time you devote to weight training is up to you. Many endurance athletes tend to concentrate more on weight training early in the season, strengthening their bodies for the stress to come. As the season progresses, weight training becomes geared to maintaining those early strength gains as they focus more on their sport of choice.

If you find you enjoy weight training and you'd like to do more of it, well and good. Just remember that to build strength, your muscles need rest. Weight lifting produces tiny tears in the muscle, and these tears need time to heal. Take a day or two off between sessions or, if you lift on consecutive days, work different muscles during different sessions—chest, shoulders and triceps one day; back, biceps, forearms and legs the next.

Your personal goals will dictate the type of weight training you do. If you want to build strength and muscle mass, cut back on repetitions and lift heavier weights. If a well-rounded strength base incorporating cardiovascular and strength gains is your goal, follow the program that's recommended by the ACSM, using lighter weights, more reps and less rest between sets.

Focusing on form

To get the most from your weight-training time, keep one word in your mind each time you lift: *form*. It's better to lift a light weight properly than to jerk about trying to lift a weight that's far too heavy .

"We don't stress how *much* we lift, we stress *how* we lift," says Dave McKay, head strength and conditioning coach for the Oakland Athletics baseball team. "It takes a person with an idea of what he's doing to back off, lift a lighter weight and stay with perfect form. If you don't lift correctly, you won't get nearly as much out of it. Plus, there's a good chance you'll injure yourself."

When Oakland's players are lifting, McKay hovers over them like a mother hen, cackling the same word over and over—form, form, form. McKay admits that form is difficult to remember when your muscles are bursting during your final lifts. And that's precisely when you should call it to mind.

"When you get fatigued, that's the time to tell yourself, 'This is going to be my most perfect lift,' " says McKay. "Sure, you're tired. But if you cheat on form, it defeats the whole purpose."

Free weights or machines?

Though it inevitably opens up a can of worms, we can't ignore the debate about free weights versus machines. Over the years, proponents of each have fervently defended their choice, sniping at each other in scientific journals, trade publications and mainstream books and magazines. Once you've hacked through all the literature, you'll emerge with several claims for each method.

Proponents of free weights attest to their versatility. With one set of dumbbells, you can exercise muscles in your back, chest, arms and shoulders. Because they often work large muscle groups, free weights develop balance and muscular coordination. By working large muscle groups, free weights also ensure that few muscles are missed. And, used correctly, free weights can also target the smallest of muscles.

It sounds terrific, until you hear from the machine lovers. They claim that weight machines can do all of the above and more. Machines, they explain, offer maximum resistance throughout a lift, stressing muscles to the utmost. Machines also provide a greater range of motion. Machines target muscles more effectively, with motion directed by cams and pulleys. Even the most misguided lifter can't goof up by bringing the wrong muscles into play. As to injury, can you imagine someone dropping a machine on their head?

This debate, alas, is one of those rare cases when objective science can't provide you with a solution.

"There is no clear-cut answer," says John Garhammer, Ph.D., associate professor of physical education at California State University in Long Beach. "Both methods have their benefits."

Dr. Garhammer has looked closely at both free weights and machines. He does have his preferences.

"In terms of objective scientific literature, free weights offer the most advantages," Dr. Garhammer says. "I'm not saying machines aren't useful, because they are. But if you look at the whole picture, free weights offer quite a number of advantages."

Small efforts, big gains

As an athlete, your best bet is to listen to the arguments and make your own decision. Above all, choose a strength-training program you like, so you'll stick with it. If you're adamantly opposed to any sort of weight training—or don't have access to a club or the money to create a home gym—consider calisthenics. Though they aren't as effective as a good weight-training program, calisthenics—gym-class standards like sit-ups, push-ups and pull-ups—are still surprisingly good at strengthening your muscles.

Some athletes make calisthenics a regular part of their training routine, especially early in the season when they're concentrating on a building a firm musculoskeletal base. At the beginning of each season, you'll find physical therapist Mark Plaatjes charging about the backyard of his Boulder, Colorado, home, enjoying a makeshift exercise circuit of 10 to 12 stations. Plaatjes jogs from one station to the next, doing sit-ups, pull-ups, lunges and hops. This might sound overly tame, but if it's good enough for a 2:08 marathoner, it should be good enough for you.

Plaatjes also jumps rope every day. "Skipping rope is a wonderful general conditioner," he beams. "You get a really good cardiovascular workout, plus a terrific workout for your arms and legs."

Not surprisingly, the same rules that apply to weight lifting apply to calisthenics. Low-resistance, high-rep calisthenics build muscular endurance, while muscle strength is best gained through higher resistance and fewer reps.

According to Brian Sharkey, Ph.D., an exercise physiologist at the University of Montana in Missoula and a past president of the American College of Sports Medicine, doing more than ten reps of a calisthenic exercise suggests that you're not developing strength effectively. Dr. Sharkey advises increasing the resistance, not the reps, to make the exercise more difficult.

For push-ups, have someone put a hand on your back and push against you. Or put your feet up on a chair. For tougher pull-ups, extend your legs perpendicular to your body in a pike position.

Like many experienced endurance athletes, coauthor Scott Tinley sees weight training as an important supplement to training.

"A lot of endurance athletes don't give much thought to weight training, but I think it plays a key role in performance," says Tinley. "I'm not going to replace a swim or bike or run workout with a weight-training workout, but if you have the time, I think it's an important supplement."

Don't let all the hubbub surrounding weight training confuse you. Though they may choose different mechanisms, most everyone agrees on the foundation of a successful strength program. Decide what you want to accomplish—weight loss, strength gains, cardiovascular training—then design a program with your goal in mind.

A final bit of encouragement. If you've never done any strength training before, the results might surprise you. Peter Lemon, Ph.D., professor of exercise physiology at Kent State University in Ohio, has noted substantial increases in muscle strength and size with as little as a few seconds of muscle stimulation three times a week.

"The average person will realize tremendous improvements, because most of us are sorely unfit from a strength standpoint," says Dr. Lemon. "It actually requires very little time to reap benefits."

See Also: *Aerobic Exercise, Cross-Training, Muscles and Muscular Endurance*

Part

3

Nutrition for Maximum Endurance

*I*t's strange that the same athletes who glom onto each new training fad as if it were issued by the Oracle at Delphi ignore basic nutrition guidelines that would help them a lot more. What applies to the general populace often applies threefold to endurance athletes. Sound nutrition can often mean the difference between failure and success, health and sickness and, in extreme cases, life and death.

Even if you do have a sound grasp of nutrition and apply it to your training, there are some twists that might surprise you. Did you know that fat, universally chastised by fashion magazines and manufacturers of powdered weight-loss aids, can be an invaluable endurance ally? Did you know that protein can play an important role in fueling the muscles? Did you know that 2 percent milk can actually contain 32 percent fat? Did you know that amino acid supplements offer about as much of a performance boost as liquefied blacktop?

To perform at your full potential, you need the facts. We've covered the basics—carbohydrate, fat, protein, hydration—and tacked on entries of specific concern to endurance athletes: electrolytes, caffeine, fruit as a carbohydrate replenisher and more. Some of this information will be familiar. Some of it will surprise you. All of it will help you.

Amino Acid Supplements
Forget the pills and powders

Amino acid supplements have been touted as an absolute necessity for athletes—and nearly all that touting has been done by supplement manufacturers hoping to ransack your wallet.

Do you need amino acid supplements?

"No," states Boston-based sports nutritionist Nancy Clark, R.D., author of *The Athlete's Kitchen* and *Nancy Clark's Sports Nutrition Guidebook.* "You get plenty of amino acids just by drinking a glass of milk or eating a cup of yogurt. If you compare the amount of amino acids you get in food with the amount you get in supplements, you'll discover there's very little value in supplements. You spend a lot of money unnecessarily when you'd be fine with another can of tuna fish."

Fellow sports nutritionist Ellen Coleman, R.D., of Riverside, California, is more succinct. "Amino acid supplementation is at best wasteful," says Coleman. "At worst, it can actually hurt your performance.

Facts and fallacies

The keen interest in amino acid supplements is not unwarranted. Amino acids are important. In various combinations, they make up your body's proteins, and without proteins your body functions would grind to a halt.

Proteins are an important constituent in your body's cells; they're also part of various hormones and enzymes. And without protein, your body tissue can't undergo growth or repair, crucial elements when it comes to training.

Unfortunately, supplement manufacturers have latched onto these salient facts, tossed in a bucketful of misconceptions and run with them all the way to the bank.

Here's a sampling of the fallacies you may be fed about supplements.

Amino acid supplements are absorbed far more readily than the amino acids in protein-rich foods. Not true. Your body absorbs 85 to 99 percent of the protein in animal food and about 90 percent of the protein from vegetable sources. Granted, amino acid supplements are completely absorbed, but there's more to consider than absorption.

Let's talk quantity. Most amino acid supplements provide between 200 and 500 milligrams of amino acids per capsule. But only one ounce of chicken or beef provides 7,000 milligrams of amino acids.

Amino acid supplements replenish your body's protein stores more quickly. Fine, but there's no evidence that faster absorption is beneficial. It actually takes hours, not minutes, to rebuild muscle tissue damaged during exercise.

Amino acid supplements build bigger muscles. Exercise, not protein, builds bigger muscles. You'll get better results from pouring that protein powder down the sink than from drinking it.

Amino acid supplements stimulate the secretion of growth hormone, increasing muscle mass and decreasing body fat. Exercise, not protein, increases muscle mass.

There are facts the supplement-makers neglect to tell you. Supplements contain no other nutrients. So just shoveling down specific supplements could contribute to nutritional deficiencies—of niacin, thiamine and iron, to name a few.

Then there's the cost. Three ounces of chicken breast costs about 30 cents. A single serving of an amino acid powder, providing fewer amino acids, can cost five times as much.

Laying on the leucine

Researchers have found that once carbohydrate energy stores are exhausted, the body does turn to protein—specifically the amino acid leucine—to provide energy. Leucine may supply as much as 10 percent of your body's energy once your glycogen reserves have been exhausted. Because of this, says Clark, endurance athletes need more protein, but no more than they're probably already getting.

"We get plenty of leucine in the foods we eat," says Clark. "It's highly unlikely that you'd come up with a leucine deficiency. Most endurance athletes are probably getting more than enough."

Animal proteins, including meats, fish, poultry, dairy products and eggs, contain reasonable amounts of the nine "essential" amino acids your body can't produce, including leucine.

Combining vegetable proteins, such as cornbread and chili beans, and peanut butter on whole wheat bread, will also ensure that you get enough leucine.

Clark raises another interesting point. Research indicates that amino acids may help buffer the effects of lactic acid, helping you exercise longer. Again, there's no need to supplement a sound diet, which provides plenty of amino acids.

And finally, excess protein won't help you, and it may hurt you. Extra amino acids are either used for energy or converted to fat. This conversion produces an excess of nitrogen, which your body flushes out through urination. This could lead to dehydration.

Coleman points out that there may be other risks, as yet unknown, from amino acid supplementation. She asks the question you should be asking yourself: "Why take a supplement that hasn't been proven safe or effective?"

See Also: *Protein*

Antioxidants
As easy as A, C, E

T ell the truth now—if someone were to offer you a magical potion to boost your endurance levels, improve your performance and enhance your immune system, would you casually saunter over for a look-see? We suspect not. Chances are, the Road Runner would eat your dust as you raced to the nearest supplier of the stuff.

But hey, no need to panic. There's plenty to go around. In fact, although there's been lots of media hype lately about the wonders of "antioxidants," they're hardly exotic. You'll find them on the shelves of your local market and in supplement form at your favorite pharmacy. Antioxidants are simply the latest buzzword for that well-known trio, vitamins A, C and E.

Let's explore, for a moment, why everyone, and particularly athletes, can benefit from antioxidants. Researchers now know that the more energy we use during an activity, the more free radicals we create. Exercise, particularly long-term endurance activity, generates even more of these as our metabolism increases.

Free radicals are toxic oxygen molecules released during the process of metabolism, which is heightened during exercise. The thing about free radicals is that they don't really like to be free, so they look for another molecule to combine with. When this occurs, the host molecule—usually a cell membrane or fat molecule—is severely damaged.

In practical terms, this activity can weaken the immune system, cause degenerative illness, sap energy and accelerate aging. Free radicals can also impair the body's ability to repair itself. So when you sprain your knee or need to recover quickly for that last mile, you want to prevent those radical little devils from doing you in.

To protect you from the ravages of free radicals, your body produces scavengers in the form of enzymes. These search and destroy as many of the errant oxygen molecules as they can find. Coming to their assistance are antioxidants, some of which can be found in the foods we eat. Enter our super-trio, vitamins A, C and E.

Of rats and men

More than ten years ago, researchers studying the effects of vitamin E on rats found that those with insufficient vitamin E steadily lost the ability to produce energy in their cells.

More recently, researchers in Australia confirmed in human tests that vitamins C and E may, in fact, protect muscles from free radical activity during a heavy workout. Cyclists and runners who participated in the study took one gram each of vitamin C and vitamin E for four weeks. This was followed by another month on a placebo. When the results of both four-week sessions were compared, the findings were clear: The antioxidants had worked!

While on the vitamin regimen, the athletes had 25 percent less evidence of muscle damage than they did while on the placebo. And, to the researchers' surprise, an unexpected benefit showed up. Levels of testosterone, a hormone in men and women that helps muscles repair themselves, shot up significantly while vitamins C and E were being taken.

"The results indicate that supplementary antioxidants reduce muscle damage associated with exercise and may enhance muscle regeneration," concluded the researchers.

How much is safe to take? The study participants took 16 times the Recommended Dietary Allowance (RDA) of vitamin C (60 milligrams for both sexes) and 100 times the RDA for vitamin E (15 international units for men, 12 for women). However, you might want to start with 500 milligrams of vitamin C and 100 international units of vitamin E.

And while it's easier to pop a capsule, why not go directly to the source? Make room for an orange or two daily, toss some red and green peppers in your salad, keep some juicy strawberries in your fridge (all five-star sources of vitamin C). You'll get your vitamin E in whole-grain bread and vegetable oils.

Carrots get an "A"

While we're on the subject of a punchout at the free-radical corral, we can't ignore beta-carotene, the natural form of vitamin A. This potent neutralizer of free radicals should be included in everyone's diet. In fact, one group of researchers called beta-carotene "the most efficient quencher of singlet oxygen thus far discovered." Singlet oxygen is a form of free radical that can cause degeneration and aging of the body.

Is it any wonder, then, that you'll often see endurance athletes happily chomping away on a carrot? It makes sense when you learn that one average carrot gives you 3,000 international units of beta-carotene. This is one-third the minimum RDA, which is currently 15,000 to 25,000 international units. Other rich sources of this vitamin are sweet potatoes (10,000 international units), papayas, apricots, tomatoes, squash, cantaloupe and broccoli. Green vegetables boasting bunches of beta-carotene include spinach, collard greens, kale, mustard greens and lettuce.

You should be aware, however, that there's a difference between natural and animal-based versions of vitamin A. Natural forms of beta-carotene, and beta-carotene supplements, are rarely toxic in high amounts. But animal-based versions of vitamin A, or retinol, can cause problems in doses over 15,000 international units daily.

Caffeine
Pros and cons for athletes

Robert Voy, M.D., former director of sportsmedicine and science for the U.S. Olympic Committee, once called caffeine "the world's most popular drug."

Dr. Voy might be right. He sure hits the nail on the head when it comes to endurance athletes. And if you doubt that, spend an early weekend morning counting customers at a 7-Eleven convenience store near the starting line of a marathon or triathlon. Almost every customer will be wearing Lycra running or biking tights and a neon warm-up jacket, with both hands wrapped around a jumbo-sized cup of java.

Of course, most people don't think of caffeine as a drug—not *really*. Sure, it can get your eyes open in the morning, but can it actually help you perform better?

In fact, caffeine is a highly effective central nervous system stimulant—so effective, in fact, that its use as a performance-enhancing substance is restricted by the International Olympic Committee. It's pretty rare in a drug test, however, to find the amount of caffeine that's punishable—12 micrograms per milliliter—in a competitor's urine. You'd have to drink eight cups of coffee at one sitting, then donate a urine sample within two hours.

Researchers have evidence that caffeine intake can improve endurance. David Costill, Ph.D., director of Ball State University's Human Performance Laboratory in Muncie, Indiana, for example, has documented caffeine's ability to burn fatty acids more quickly. And the more fat you burn, the longer your stores of muscle glycogen will last.

More caffeine isn't necessarily better, however. Dr. Costill's studies indicate that one to two cups of coffee, or 100 to 200 milligrams of caffeine,

How High the Caffeine?

How does the kick in coffee compare with that found in other sources?
Check the table below: you may be in for a surprise!

Coffee	Caffeine (mg/6-oz. cup)
Maxwell House, instant	23
Melitta X-Fine, drip	61
Folger's, instant	64
Savarin, drip	98
Chock Full O'Nuts, drip	105

Soda	Caffeine (mg/12-oz. can)
Diet Sprite	0
Coca-Cola	33.0
Coca-Cola Classic	33.6
Diet Pepsi	36.0
Pepsi, regular	36.2
Pepsi Light	36.9
Diet Coke	46.0
Dr. Pepper	50.6
Mountain Dew	56.6

Chocolate-Based Products	Caffeine (mg/serving)
Cocoa drink, 5 oz.	4
Chocolate syrup, 1 oz.	5
Chocolate milk, 8 oz.	8
Baker's German sweet chocolate, 1 oz.	8

taken an hour before competing, provide all the benefits and none of the drawbacks of larger amounts. At least one study showed that even when caffeine was ingested immediately before exercise, there was an increase in performance.

Research on caffeine's effects has left many questions unanswered. And there are no across-the-board rules for its use, either. The timing of the dose, the amount consumed, the athlete's history of caffeine use and individual sensitivity to the drug can affect its impact.

On the plus side, caffeine travels through your system quickly. Because

Dark semisweet chocolate, 1 oz.	13
Milk chocolate, 1 oz.	15

Tea	Caffeine (mg/6 oz. cup)
Celestial Seasonings, decaffeinated	0
Lipton, decaffeinated	5
Tetley, decaffeinated	6
Salada, "naturally caffeine reduced"	22
Tetley	38
Lipton	46
Salada	47

Drugs	Caffeine (mg/tablet or capsule)
Darvon (pain relief)	32
Vanquish (pain relief)	33
Anacin, maximum strength (pain relief)	35
Fiorinal (headaches)	40
Norgesic Forte (muscle relaxant)	60
Excedrin (pain relief)	65
NoDoz (alertness)	100
Vivarin (alertness)	200

it's processed by the liver and excreted by the kidneys, it's out of your body three hours after it's consumed.

The downside of the drug

However, there are a number of concerns about caffeine intake. Chronic use has been linked as a factor in heart disease, cancer and birth defects. And caffeine clearly has one obvious drawback—it's a diuretic. Obviously, having to run to the john during a race is a disadvantage. But even more serious, increased urination can lead to dehydration.

High doses of caffeine (300 to 750 milligrams) can also cause irritability, anxiety, depression, bowel irritation and irregular heartbeat. Probably the worst-case scenario for use of caffeine by an athlete would be a cranky, recently divorced 40-year-old marathoner with a family history of heart disease drinking three cups of coffee on an empty stomach before a hard 20-mile run in a city like Atlanta, Georgia, on a steamy Sunday morning in August.

Regular coffee drinkers may experience less of a diuretic effect, but even hardened coffee quaffers should concentrate on getting enough water, especially if exercising in hot weather.

"It seems that whatever diuretic effect caffeine does have, a regular coffee drinker is adapted to it," says Lawrence Spriet, Ph.D., associate professor at the University of Guelph in Canada. "But if you're not a regular caffeine user and you're not clear on how to rehydrate, drinking coffee before you exercise isn't a good idea."

Dr. Spriet, who's studied the effects of caffeine on exercise performance, suggests that a cup or two of coffee before an event or workout won't hurt, and it might help. But don't expect miracles.

If you choose to use beverages or medications containing large amounts of caffeine, watch your body's reactions when conditions get tough. Keep some food in your stomach, drink lots of fluids and don't get carried away with a too-fast pace early in the game. Your caffeine rush may run out before you do.

Calories
The athlete's fuel

C alories, calories, calories. Diet gurus have made fortunes teaching people to watch, count, ignore, worship, despise, visualize and vaporize them. Yet most folks aren't entirely sure what they are and whether or not to be wary of them.

Dedicated endurance athletes tend to regard calories with less suspicion than most—primarily because they have a hard time stuffing enough food into their mouths to keep their pants up. When you're training five hours a day and burning 5,000 to 8,000 calories in the process, trying to count the darn things is futile, to say the least.

There's no more wondrous sight in all of sport than a pretty and seemingly delicate 100-pound female triathlete wolfing down a breakfast that would embarrass a lumberjack. "You want *more* pancakes?" asks the waitress in amazement.

"Please," answers the triathlete sweetly. "And another orange juice."

Like octane, kilotons and megawatts, calories are simply units of energy. Mostly, they measure the energy potential of food.

In a slice of whole-wheat bread, for instance, the molecules of protein, carbohydrate and fat together contain around 100 calories' worth of biochemical energy. When you eat the bread, the food can go in one or all of three different directions.

- Protein gets used to build and repair muscles, ligaments and other tissues.
- Fats and carbohydrates release energy as molecules of fatty acids and glucose are broken down within the cells. These enable your brain to think, your eyes to blink and your legs to run marathons.
- Food energy is stored for later use, predominantly as adipose tissue throughout the body and as glycogen in the liver and muscles.

As unique as your fingertips

Every individual burns calories at his or her own rate. A number of factors will influence how fast they'll burn—sex, age and level of activity are among them. Because women have less muscle mass than men, they generally burn calories more slowly. A man on a hard run might burn 12.5 calories or more each minute; a woman might burn only 9.5 calories.

Notice any "love handles" lately? For the answer to "where did that come from?" look to two factors. First, our bodies become less efficient calorie burners as years go by. Second, we tend to ignore the first factor and continue eating as we did when we were younger.

We all need a certain number of calories to support our minimal activity. We're talking survival level here—supplying the energy needed for breathing, circulation and cell regeneration. This minimum daily caloric requirement is known as a person's "basal metabolism."

Although there's individual variation possible, science has given us a rough guideline to gauge our bottom-line caloric needs.

The average person burns one calorie for every 2.2 pounds of body weight every hour. A 120-pound woman will burn roughly 1,300 calories daily just to survive. A 150-pound man will burn roughly 1,600 calories in a day.

Going for the big burn

Caloric consumption goes up when you exercise, and the more and harder you exercise, the more calories you burn. An endurance athlete in heavy training can burn Mr. Couch Potato's 1,600 calories in a single workout and may need to take in 6,000 calories a day and more—that's 40,000 calories a week—simply to maintain body weight. Triathletes in the Hawaii Ironman Triathlon can burn more than 10,000 calories during the competition itself, *not counting* prerace and postrace energy consumption.

Of course, there are exceptional circumstances. Most of us are more concerned with how much we retain than with how much we burn. Boston-based sports nutritionist Nancy Clark, R.D., author of *The Athlete's Kitchen* and *Nancy Clark's Sports Nutrition Guidebook,* offers an easy and practical calorie counter. You can roughly estimate how many calories daily will maintain your weight by multiplying your weight by 13 if you're sedentary or 15 if you're moderately active.

You can also keep a record of your caloric intake for several days, logging everything you eat and drink, then comparing it with the calories you burn. Most nutrition books can supply you with the caloric content of foods and drinks, as well as an estimate of the calories you'll burn with specific exercises. Comparing the two could be an illuminating experience.

While the challenge for the serious endurance athlete is to eat enough food to get the required number of calories, the challenge for most of us is to strike a healthy balance.

Unfortunately, it doesn't take much to skew that balance. Eat a mere 200 calories (one cupcake) more than you need each day, and over a year, you've gained over 12 pounds. On the bright side, roughly ten minutes of walking up stairs is enough to wipe out that 200-calorie excess. The beauty of exercise is, you can have your cake and eat it, too.

See Also: *Anorexia Nervosa, Fat, Fitness Testing*

Carbohydrate
Energy to burn

*T*riathlete Dave Scott has founded a career on excess—he has won the daunting Hawaii Ironman Triathlon a record six times. Before he became the Ironman's king, however, Scott was famous for excesses of a different sort: he once ate 8½ pounds of ice cream and a bucket of gooey toppings in a single sitting. Shortly after, Scott reached two conclusions. First, his stomach hurt. Second, his nutritional habits were awful.

Within a year, he went from a diet heavy on meats and sugars to a diet comprised of over 70 percent carbohydrate. The change was almost immediate. Both on and off the field, he had decidedly more energy.

It would be presumptuous to attribute Scott's athletic success to a change in diet. But Scott won't write it off, either.

"To compete at an optimum level, you have to provide your body with optimal fuel," says Scott. "Athletes who adhere to the notion that all calories are created equal are really short-changing themselves."

Carbos—your ideal energy food

Sports nutritionists have long held that 70 percent of your calories should come from carbohydrates. For an athlete expending between 3,000 and 4,000 calories daily, it's recommended that 10 to 14 portions of carbohydrate be eaten daily.

Why all the fuss about carbos? Simple. They provide the fuel you'll need to work your body.

Here's a brief review of how it all happens. Once digested, carbohydrates break down into glucose molecules. These are whisked off through the bloodstream to either the liver (where they are recombined and stored as glycogen) or directly to the cells, where they await the body's call for fuel. As soon as you need energy to contract those muscles, glucose molecules break down quickly to create ATP (adenisone triphosphate), your body's driving energy source.

Endurance athletes generally combine carbohydrate and fat for maximum exercise fuel. But when it comes to high-performance situations, carbohydrate is far and away the best energy bang for your buck. Because fat converts to energy slowly, it can't supply enough energy to keep you working at more than 50 percent of your maximum aerobic potential. Carbohydrate, on the other hand, provides energy in a flash.

Unfortunately, your body can store only so much glycogen. When the cupboard is bare, you'll know it—your energy levels will drop like a falling piano.

A well-trained athlete has enough glycogen stored in the liver and muscles and enough glucose floating free in the blood to maintain a fast-paced aerobic effort for 90 to 120 minutes. About half the energy during that period is supplied by fat. Pass that point without replenishing carbohydrate stores, and crash! your energy will suddenly dissolve.

How quickly you can burn your carbos varies tremendously. A hiker on a recreational jaunt can walk all day and keep glycogen stores largely intact; body fat and carbohydrate stores contain ample fuel to keep the hiker going. But a Tour de France cyclist laboring through the Alps is breaking down glycogen and burning up glucose at a furious rate. Unless there's a good supply of food and carbohydrate replacement drinks on hand, that cyclist will be pedaled-out in no time.

Avoiding carbo depletion

Since carbohydrates are vital to solid endurance performance, you'll want to stockpile them for added energy while training and racing. An endurance athlete in heavy training is constantly exhausting energy supplies, then—hopefully—replenishing them for the next day's effort by shoveling in more carbos.

In fact, sports scientists recommend that athletes eat at least 50 grams of carbohydrate after intense training to replace glycogen. After that, another 50 grams should be eaten every two hours until mealtime.

The alternative is a dismal one. Neglect your carbohydrates and the specter of exhaustion will quickly loom up before you. You'll feel listless. You'll struggle with chronic fatigue. Your performances will tailspin. Basically, you'll wish you were back in bed.

What sort of carbohydrates should you eat? Fueling your body isn't much different from fueling your car—ideally, you want something that will burn efficiently and won't leave any ugly residue.

Candy bars and sugary soft drinks supply energy, but they also supply a lot of empty calories. Some or all of these calories will convert to fat if they're not burned off quickly enough. Even some high-carbohydrate foods contain unexpected fats. That "healthful" granola is 35 percent fat; creamy macaroni and cheese is 40 percent fat; a buttery croissant is 60 percent fat.

Few endurance athletes need to worry about excess weight gain. Yet they're concerned about getting the right *kind* of calories.

The good news is, there are reams of clean-burning, ruthlessly energy-efficient carbohydrate—spaghetti and tomato sauce, baked potatoes (hold the sour cream), pancakes (easy on the butter), whole-wheat bread, raisins and bananas, to name a few.

Fruit is a particularly rich source of carbohydrate. Every morning, 10,000-meter world record holder Arturo Barrios hustles out the door for his morning run, carting a bag of fruit and a bottle of fruit juice. As soon as he finishes running, he polishes them both off.

"You have to replace the fluids and carbohydrates you've lost right away," says Barrios. "That way you avoid getting tired from dehydration and carbohydrate depletion."

Carbos on the run

After water, carbohydrates are the most important supplement you'll need while exercising.

Next time you're watching a competition, observe which foods athletes take along. Dave Scott likes dried figs. During his six Hawaii Ironman Triathlon victories, along with more traditional food and drink, he shoveled down a healthy supply of the fruit. High in calories (and energy), dried figs are also high in fiber.

Scott apparently could handle the roughage, but figs might move through your system with a vengeance. During competition, there are also certain logistical concerns to factor in. Although melons are a great source of energy and fluid, running with a cantaloupe could be awkward.

Choose the carbohydrate source that meets your needs, but remember: While in the throes of exercise, you'll require energy quickly. The faster you digest your food, the sooner that glucose you need for energy will appear in your bloodstream. Thus the popularity of carbohydrate replacement drinks, which rush energy directly to your system.

Solid food, on the other hand, takes longer to digest. It can also increase your risk of dehydration, as digestion tends to suck water into the stomach.

In a shorter endurance event, like a marathon, you can probably get by on energy replacement drinks alone. However, during longer endurance events, say a century bike ride, food is crucial. Find a carbohydrate-rich food you can stomach on the go.

A quick word on carbohydrate replacement drinks: Their actual carbohydrate content can vary dramatically. A drink high in carbohydrate might supply you with more energy, but it could also have you bent double in the bushes. Experiment with these drinks before you race.

Timing your carbo intake

It's also important to get some carbohydrate into your system immediately after exercise. Remember Barrios and his bag of fruit? Carbohydrate eaten shortly after your training session will be absorbed more quickly by your carbohydrate-starved system. Studies have shown that in the first hour after exercise, your body can absorb up to 80 percent of the carbohydrate eaten. That drops to 60 percent in the second hour and falls off even more after that.

Properly timing your postexercise carbo intake is especially important if you're training several times a day. It's also a good idea to concentrate on simple carbohydrates—fruits, fruit juices or honey—rather than complex carbos such as bread, pasta and potatoes.

Your body breaks down simple carbohydrates into glucose and glycogen more quickly than the complex variety. A study in Denmark showed that athletes who ate foods high in simple carbohydrates stored 65 percent more glycogen than their colleagues in the first six hours after exercise. Good postworkout replenishers include low-fat fruit yogurt, dried fruit, commercial energy bars (avoid those with high fat content), graham crackers and wholegrain cereals.

A final bit of good news. Studies have shown that endurance training improves your body's ability to burn fat, thus sparing carbohydrate. As you become more fit, your muscles receive more oxygen. This enables them to break down fat into energy. The more oxygen your muscles receive, the more fat they can use up. The result—your energy is being supplied by both fat and carbohydrate sources, keeping you on the go longer.

Carbohydrate Loading
The downside of a popular practice

Almost anyone even remotely involved with distance running or triathlons is familiar with the practice of "carbo-loading" at prerace pasta dinners—those mass feedings where athletes pay $10 to $15 for some overcooked pasta, a side order of iceberg lettuce and a hunk of garlic bread. The feast is generally topped off with a can or two of light beer.

The meal is great for race sponsors whose banners hang in the dining room and for the media, which is always pleased to portray runners and their ilk as a strange breed with strange habits. Unfortunately, carbo-loading probably does the runners themselves more harm than good.

You certainly can't make up for poor dietary habits in a single evening, and a heavy meal the night before a long race will accompany you to the starting line. You'll probably be bloated in the morning; the amount of glycogen in your body is normally associated with three times its volume in water.

The practice of carbohydrate loading arrived at about the time of the running boom of the early 1970s. The original scenario called for a long, hard workout the week before a big race, followed by two or three days of hard training. This was combined with a diet high in fat and protein but low in carbohydrate. The next three days were marked by high carbohydrate consumption and a sharply reduced workout schedule. Theoretically, at least, prerace "carbo parties" were intended to represent the culinary climax of a stressful week-long regimen.

The theory behind carbo-loading

The ability of your muscles to store glycogen is at the heart of the carbo-loading theory. Glycogen, of course, is the stored form of glucose, your body's basic endurance fuel. As glycogen stores run low, your body falls back on fat for energy. However, fat can't be mobilized and used quickly enough in the muscles to support vigorous endurance exercise.

Runners refer to "hitting the Wall," the point in the race at which their muscles' glycogen stores are exhausted. The theory behind carbohydrate loading is that, when muscles are deprived of glycogen for long periods, they'll store extra amounts when carbohydrates are reintroduced.

Laboratory findings have confirmed this loading theory, but in practice the depletion stage of the regimen is crippling. Athletes who tried carbo-loading complained of excessive fatigue, irritability, lack of motivation to train and susceptibility to colds and flu.

Indeed, considering the tough, glycogen-depleting training schedules of competitive endurance athletes today, intentional glycogen starvation seems ludicrous. Experts now agree that your most productive prerace diet is your regular training diet. You may perform better by eating higher-calorie foods, increasing caloric intake from 60 to 70 percent three days before your competition. However, there's no need to increase the amount of food you eat. Concentrate instead on drinking enough water and you'll be in good shape.

Carbos before . . .

What you eat on race morning can be as important as what you've eaten several days prior. "New dietary practices should never be instituted on the day of an important competition," says Keith Wheeler, Ph.D., manager of education and research for Exceed Sports Nutritionals.

Dr. Wheeler suggests that precompetition meals be consumed at least two hours before the race. Eating too close to start time can result in low blood sugar, caused when insulin is released after glucose levels rise in the blood. The insulin does its job and lowers glucose levels and then stops fatty acids and glucose from being mobilized. This will, in turn, "cause a premature use of muscle glycogen stores, leading to a decreased performance capacity," says Dr. Wheeler.

Before chowing down on your preendurance meal, consider Dr. Wheeler's list of the five important qualities it should have.

1. High carbohydrate content. Carbohydrate as 60 to 70 percent of total calories supports blood glucose levels during competition.

2. Low fat and low protein content. Fat slows gastric emptying, and protein can aggravate dehydration.

3. Low salt content. High salt levels can cause greater fluid loss.

4. Minimal bulk foods. Bulk foods increase gastrointestinal residue, which in an anxious athlete can lead to vomiting or diarrhea.

5. Adequate fluid availability. One or two eight-ounce glasses of water or juice will help ensure adequate hydration.

Carbos after . . .

Though you may not feel like eating shortly after a hard race or workout, you should. Studies have shown that the two hours following hard exercise are an important "glycogen window." This is the period when your body will suck up glycogen like a sponge. This will speed your recovery from your efforts and enable you to stockpile carbo reserves quickly for your next activity.

Immediately after a hard effort, think "fluid replacement." But don't ignore carbohydrate-rich foods. Dr. Wheeler suggests that athletes eat at least 1½ grams of carbohydrate per kilogram of body weight (figure about 100 grams of carbohydrate for a 150-pound man). This will maximize glycogen rebound.

It's actually easier than it sounds, especially at races where sponsors offer spreads of high-carb goodies, from bananas (25 grams of carbohydrate) to yogurt (50 grams). You can even kill two birds with one stone—many of the free drinks available contain healthy amounts of carbohydrate (eight ounces of apple juice contain about 30 grams of carbohydrate).

If you're reluctant to go elbow-to-elbow with your fellow competitors after the race, too, treat yourself to a few slices of cheese pizza (21 grams of carbohydrate per slice) or an ice cream cone (35 grams of carbohydrate per scoop). Indulge yourself. You've earned it, and you need it.

See Also: *Bonking, Carbohydrate, Glucose and Glycogen, Pacing, The Wall*

Cholesterol
Knowing the good from the bad

In recent years, cholesterol has become fitness's most popular whipping boy. Few terms raise more fear; part of it is well founded. Along with smoking and high blood pressure, excessive levels of cholesterol in the blood are a major risk factor for heart disease, the number one killer in America. It's small wonder that the mere hint of this fatty substance causes otherwise rational souls to graze in the vegetable section like starving rabbits.

However, you should be aware of some simple cholesterol distinctions. Cholesterol comes in two varieties: LDL and HDL.

The cholesterol you ingest from animal products ends up floating around in your bloodstream in particles called LDLs, or low-density lipoproteins.

These particles are important for several reasons. They're the main means of transport for fat in the blood, carrying from 60 to 80 percent of all cholesterol present in your system.

The body can get rid of a certain amount of this LDL cholesterol, removing it through the liver. However, excessive amounts of LDL can end up settling out in your arteries. LDL cholesterol is the "bad" cholesterol—the fatty deposits linked with the onset of coronary artery disease.

HDL to the rescue

Enter the good guys: HDLs, or high-density lipoproteins, will cart cholesterol away from your body's tissues and out of the blood to be removed by the liver.

Until the mid-1970s, researchers believed that diet, weight loss and drugs were the best means to reduce the cholesterol threat. More recently, however, they have become convinced that exercise can play a large role in preventing heart disease.

Regular exercise not only lowers the levels of LDL cholesterol, it raises the levels of HDL cholesterol. This combination is a positive one—there's less fatty material to clog up your arteries and more workers to haul off the gunk that remains.

For this reason, measures of total cholesterol (HDL plus LDL) aren't the best indicator of your health. As an athlete, your total cholesterol may be high because you have elevated levels of "good" HDL cholesterol. A trip to your doctor will tell you precisely what you need to know, through a blood test that measures your HDL and LDL levels separately.

One final point. Though proper diet and regular exercise can go a long way toward reducing the dangerous cholesterol that leads to heart disease, don't take any chances.

Not only must you be vigilant against too much cholesterol and fat intake, but your body is constantly producing its own cholesterol and may be genetically programmed to produce more than is desirable. If so, your efforts to stick to a low-fat, high-carbohydrate diet and an exercise regimen may not do the trick. Don't take a chance: Get those cholesterol levels checked.

See Also: *Fat*

Electrolytes
Don't sweat the small stuff

*I*t's common knowledge that sweat is mostly water (98 to 99 percent). What you may not know is that the rest of your sweat is made up of electrolytes, tiny ions of sodium, potassium and chloride.

These minerals play important roles in a variety of body functions, from helping muscles contract to metabolizing fuel and transporting it where it's needed. As an athlete, there's one important thing you should know—you probably don't need to be overly concerned about the electrolytes lost during exercise.

Fortunately, most of us get more than enough sodium, potassium and chloride in our diets. The American Dietetic Association (ADA) recommends a daily minimum of 500 milligrams of sodium, 750 milligrams of chloride and 2,000 milligrams of potassium for the average 150-pound person. Americans generally consume about 5,000 milligrams of sodium and 2,500 milligrams of potassium each day. In fact, most of us have enough sodium chloride or salt in our bodies to fill a small shaker.

"Typically, any athlete really receives adequate sodium, potassium and chloride to replenish any losses associated with exercise," says Annie Prince, R.D., Ph.D., associate professor and researcher at Oregon Health Sciences University in Portland. "You really don't need to worry about losing electrolytes. You'd have to be on a really bizarre diet not to get enough sodium, chloride and potassium."

Staving off hyponatremia

Prolonged exercise in extreme conditions can, however, deplete electrolyte reserves, especially sodium and chloride. A case in point was the 1984 Hawaii Ironman Triathlon. Competing in ferocious heat, nearly 900 athletes finished the race in the medical tent. Of those, roughly 25 percent were suffering from hyponatremia—bouts of dizziness, vomiting and muscle cramps caused by an acute loss of sodium. This is a condition high on the list of those to be avoided. Acute deficiencies can cause coma, seizures and even death.

Subsequent studies between 1985 and 1989 showed that, during 12 hours of Ironman competition, a triathlete could lose 36 grams of sodium almost effortlessly. This is almost 30 percent of the body's sodium storage capacity.

Based on these and other studies, experts linked the occurrence and severity of hyponatremia to how long an event was and how hot and how humid the environment was. The more one sweats, and the longer the time, the higher the risk of hyponatremia.

The Ironman, of course, represents the extreme. Most experts agree that a well-balanced diet will keep your salt levels where they should be, keeping plenty of reserves available.

However, if you're planning on tackling an endurance event that threatens a long haul and sweltering conditions, it might be a good idea to check in with a sports dietitian, says exercise physiologist Mary O'Toole, Ph.D., director of the University of Tennessee's Human Performance Laboratory in Memphis.

Dr. O'Toole, who has worked extensively with triathletes at the Hawaii Ironman, recommends that serious endurance athletes have their diets analyzed for potential electrolyte (and other) deficiencies.

Common sense on salt loss

What about those athletes you've seen popping salt tablets like jelly beans? Is theirs an example you should follow? The experts unanimously echo, "No."

Salt tablets can irritate the stomach lining and make you vomit. Dehydration could be next, since tossing up breakfast draws water into the stomach and away from the tissues.

"If there's one sports nutrition myth that needs to be put to rest, it's that athletes need to take salt tablets to replace their losses," states Dr. Prince.

If you're concerned about salt loss, take a saner approach. First, you can bolster your salt supplies by upping your salt intake before exercising. And, thanks to fast food, it's ridiculously easy to supplement your salt intake. Try pizza, spaghetti sauce or virtually any type of fast food (but avoid the real greasy stuff).

Other sources include low-fat cheese, salted crackers, pretzels, pickles and sauerkraut. And don't forget condiments like catsup, mustard, relish and garlic salt. Loosen up a bit with the salt—one small packet of salt contains 500 milligrams of sodium.

Note, too, that the body of a conditioned athlete produces its own buffer. The sodium content in the sweat of a conditioned, acclimatized athlete decreases with time. In as little as 12 days of training in the heat, your body will produce less-concentrated sweat. The less salt in your sweat, the less you'll lose.

Electrolytes on the run

Is it necessary to gulp down electrolyte replacement drinks during long bouts of training or racing? Not at all, says Dr. Prince. Most commercial electrolyte drinks contain only token amounts of sodium, chloride and potassium.

These drinks are needed for some of the other things they provide—namely carbohydrate and fluid—but not for the minute amounts of electrolytes they supply.

"If you want only to replace electrolytes, you'd really have to drink large quantities of these electrolyte replacement beverages to equal what you could easily get through food," Dr. Prince explains. After all, she continues, when you're sweating liberally, losing electrolytes isn't the problem. The nutrient you should be most vigilant about replacing is water.

If you're concerned about electrolyte loss, all three of them—sodium, potassium and chloride—can easily be ingested during exercise. In fact, the ADA offers a simple concoction to restore your sodium and chloride. Simply add ⅓ teaspoon of table salt to a quart of water and drink that mixture throughout the race.

Fruits are also a terrific and easy way to bolster your electrolyte reserves. Orange juice, for example, contains a whopping supply of potassium. So does pineapple juice.

Nor is it a sin to eat on the run. Again, fruit is good, providing fluid, carbohydrate *and* electrolytes. One banana contains about ⅓ teaspoon of potassium.

When it comes to salt, shoveling down saltine crackers, pretzels and potato chips is fine. Just make sure that you can handle whatever you eat.

Most important, supplement your food with large doses of water to keep water in the cells during digestion, thus foiling the dehydration demon.

After the race, the body often takes care of itself, craving precisely what it needs. Ever seen athletes shoveling down anything and everything with all the restraint of sailors on shore leave? Go ahead, just this once, and binge. You've earned it.

And although the topic here is electrolytes, Dr. Prince offers a gentle reminder on nutrition that applies across the board: "Athletes should remember that the best way to prevent potential imbalances of any kind is through a balanced diet."

See Also: *Carbohydrate, Ergogenic Aids, Fat, Fruit, Protein*

Fat
There's a plus side, too

*F*rank Burnham has taken on an unpopular cause: He defends fat. In a trade magazine called *Render*, which Burnham edits and publishes, he contends that fat gets a bad rap. Cynics might point out that the Los Angeles–based magazine is funded by the meat industry, but Burnham doesn't waver. Fat is energy, he says. We need fat. We use fat. We've gotta have fat.

He has a point, especially when it comes to endurance sport. Fat is just as important in the endurance diet as carbohydrate—even more so when it comes to just plain enduring. One gram of fat contains more than twice as much energy as the same amount of carbohydrate, and enough can be stored to keep you alive for several weeks.

Even a highly trained endurance athlete can pack away only enough carbohydrates to continue exercising at high intensity for a period of 90 to 120 minutes. Ultradistance events like the Western States 100, the Hawaii Ironman Triathlon and the Race Across America (RAAM) bicycle race require that participants' bodies use fat as their primary source of energy.

As a case in point, look at Lon Haldeman. One year he won the RAAM by spinning across the country while consuming a health harpy's nightmare—fast-food pizzas, burgers, milk shakes and Spaghetti-O's.

Fat's bad reputation stems mostly from human overindulgence. Excessive fat in your diet and a sedentary lifestyle are a dangerous combination that's been linked to a wide variety of illnesses, including heart disease and colon and rectal cancer.

On the other hand, endurance athletes who shun necessary amounts of fat in search of perfect nutrition are simply misinformed—and probably not racing and training at anywhere near their potential.

Fat—friend or foe?

A certain amount of dietary fat—20 to 25 percent of your total daily calories—is necessary. Not only does it act as an energy source, it also contributes to your ability to use fat-soluble vitamins (A, D, E and K) and other nutrients. Fat is involved in building cell walls and is a component of certain essential hormones.

Fats—or lipids, as science dubs them—are found in almost every food source, from meat and fish to nuts, grains and milk products.

There are several different kinds of fats, but as an athlete you need concern yourself with only one distinction—the difference between saturated (bad) and unsaturated (good) fats.

Thankfully, you don't need a degree in food chemistry to tell the difference between the two. As a general rule, saturated fats—like those in red meat and butter, for example—are solid at room temperature. Unsaturated fats are liquid at room temperature and are often referred to as oils—olive oil and corn oil are unsaturated fats. Be careful, though—some oils are high in saturated fats. When in doubt, read the labels.

What makes saturated fats bad? There's mounting evidence that they can be linked to a number of health problems, including cancer and heart and arterial disease.

If you exercise regularly and watch your fat intake, you'll be doing your body a favor. Exercise has been shown to increase the level of high-density lipoproteins (HDL) in the blood. These fat-protein bubbles whisk cholesterol out of the bloodstream and off to the liver, keeping it from collecting on blood vessel walls and eventually blocking the vessels off.

Don't be overly smug, though. Because your body produces all the cholesterol it needs, you'll need to watch your fat intake carefully. Otherwise, no matter how much you exercise, your HDL will be fighting a losing battle.

Fat as energy for exercise

As fat advocate Burnham reminds us, fat is energy. In fact, it's your most abundant source of energy. And when you've used up all your stores of glycogen, fat is your only source of energy.

When you eat fat, it's broken down into two basic components—fatty acids and glycerol. It's then recombined and carted off for storage, primarily in fat cells. When it comes time to plumb fat for energy, the fat cells are broken down and free fatty acids are carried to the muscle cells. There they contribute to the release of energy.

If fat's such a great source of energy, why all the fuss about carbohydrate being the ultimate high-performance fuel? Why aren't our, ahem, overly abundant fat supplies our consummate energy source?

The answer, in a word, is oxygen. To break down fat into energy, you need a whopping supply of oxygen. And, as anyone who has ever gone beyond a brisk walk knows, if you're exercising hard, oxygen is often in short supply. If it's short on oxygen, your body can't burn fat. It *can* burn carbohydrate, so it does.

Think of your body's energy production as a fire. If the fire starts to die, your body reaches for the carbohydrate. Woompf—as if you added gasoline, the fire burns brightly, but not for long, and then you need more carbohydrate.

Fat, by contrast, is like adding wood to the fire. It requires more oxygen and takes longer to come to a full burn, but it lasts far longer. When you're exercising hard and not getting enough oxygen, your body is burning some fat. For the most part, though, it's madly tossing on carbohydrate to keep the flames high.

To keep your exercise fire burning efficiently, you need to go heavy on the wood and spare the gas to sustain the flame as long as possible. Experienced endurance athletes have honed this to an art, burning as much fat as they can so they can conserve their limited carbohydrate supplies.

Fat may not be a flashy energy source, but at a slower pace—where the body provides enough oxygen to break down fat—you can outlast a Congressional hearing. That's precisely why, when it comes to events like the RAAM and the Western States 100, fat is one terrific endurance fuel.

Focus on fat-burning

Most endurance training fails to encourage the body to break down and use fat as energy. Speed training, fast-paced medium-distance runs, weekend 10-K's and one-hour bike rides are terrific for pushing the body's aerobic capacity. But the fuel of choice during these efforts is usually carbohydrate.

It's the long or overdistance run or bike ride that teaches your body to burn fat more efficiently. Speed isn't the issue. A slow, steady pace is what counts. Fifty to 60 percent of your maximum heart rate is ideal.

If measuring your heart rate is too scientific, a simpler test will do—you should be able to talk comfortably while exercising. When you can, you'll know that you're keeping a good fat-burning pace.

How long should these long, slow efforts be? It depends on your current level of conditioning. A good general rule of thumb is to double the distance of your average daily workout. And remember, go slow. Smell the flowers. Admire the view. Enjoy yourself.

See Also: *Carbohydrate, Cholesterol, Glucose and Glycogen, Long, Slow Distance Training*

Fruit
The perfect endurance food

O f all possible foods, why have we singled out the modest fruit for special accolades? Nutritionist and Oregon State University professor Jim Leklem, Ph.D., explains, "There's no one food out there that will provide athletes with a magical edge. But fruit comes close."

Loaded with carbohydrate, fluids and essential vitamins and minerals, fruit is the near-perfect food for endurance athletes. It can be used to improve nutrition on every athletic front—before, during and after racing and training.

Athletes know the benefits of eating a training diet high in carbohydrates. When you bolster your glycogen supplies before exercising, you'll have more energy reserves. Because most fruits are high in carbohydrate and are easily digestible, they're an ideal way to shore up energy reserves before a race. An apple, an orange or a glass of pure juice 30 minutes before a run will provide the carbohydrate and fluids you'll need later. "Carbo-loading" with fruit also helps you avoid a common trap.

"Instead of just carbohydrate-loading, most people end up carbohydrate-loading and fat-loading," says Annie Prince, R.D., Ph.D., associate professor and researcher at Oregon Health Sciences University in Portland. This is because people have a tendency to lace their carbohydrates with fat, such as sour cream on the potato or thick sauce on the pasta.

Fruit, incidentally, possesses another highly prized quality for athletes watching their fat intake: It hasn't any.

The original fluid replacer

During a race or while training, athletes turn to fruit as a handy way to replace fluids and carbohydrate. Because fluid loss is always a concern (and running with a cantaloupe can be awkward), fruit juice offers a good on-the-move option.

In fact, fruit juice is better than many commercial fluid-replacement drinks. It offers a high sugar content that puts glucose right into your system, where it can be used for energy.

If you do use fruit juice, though, be sure to dilute it with about 50 percent water. Juices, on the average, are about 10 percent carbohydrate—too much for athletes to absorb without compromising their water absorption. If you take in too many carbos, your stomach is forced to concentrate on digesting them. This slows the release of water from the stomach to the tissues. Since dehydration should be your number one concern when exercising, be generous when mixing water into your fruit juice.

Dried fruit works extremely well for some athletes, bolstering calories and carbohydrates during competition. During his record six Ironman victories, Dave Scott could often be seen chewing on figs while biking and running. Like prunes, dates and apricots, figs offer a convenient and concentrated carbohydrate snack.

Caution is in order, however. Don't audition dried fruit at the event itself; see how your system handles this snack while training. Because they're high in fiber, these fruits can move through your system with alarming speed. "A lot of people can't handle the bulk," cautions Scott.

Fruit also makes an ideal postworkout snack. Immediately after exercise, the body is low on both fluid and carbohydrate. Fruit, which provides lots of both, is welcomed by the body like a long-lost friend.

Bump up your fruit intake

The fact is, fruit's good for you anytime, and odds are you're not getting as much as you need. According to Boston dietitian Susan Luke, who numbers many athletes among her clients, the average female athlete needs about 10 fruit servings a day; the average male athlete, 12 to 15. This isn't as daunting as it sounds—one banana, for example, equals two fruit servings, and a quart of fruit juice equals about six servings.

A word of caution. Although fruit has comparatively few calories, they can add up rapidly. Fruit juice, for example, is particularly high in calories.

The solution? Substitution.

"What you need to do is substitute fruit for some of the other things you're eating," says Dr. Prince. "Rather than have two bowls of cereal, have one bowl and add a banana. If you add fruit without adjusting the rest of your diet, you'll be adding more calories. Don't overdo."

Finally, here's a caution for those who may be fructose intolerant. Some folks just can't stomach the high concentrations of fructose (fruit sugar) contained in fruit. If your system rebels, you'll likely experience abdominal pain and diarrhea. To avoid having this happen during a race, check to see how much fruit you can handle *before* the big day.

See Also: *Calories, Carbohydrate, Carbohydrate Loading, Dehydration, Glucose and Glycogen*

Protein
Food for muscles and stamina

It's a scenario that's almost as old as sport itself: Athletes, hoping to build muscle, sitting around a training table stuffing down steak and eggs at a rate that has the beef industry doing backflips. It seems possible that any minute now, someone's going to moo.

Not you? Well, here's a second scenario that might strike closer to home. The fat-free fiend, wolfing down bagels, pasta and bananas like there's no tomorrow, avoiding any source of fat, be it meat or chicken or dairy products. If you fit that bill, you might be protein deficient.

Boston-based sports nutritionist Nancy Clark, R.D., author of *The Athlete's Kitchen* and *Nancy Clark's Sports Nutrition Guidebook,* sees most athletes falling into one of two categories—they're getting either too much protein or not enough.

"I see a lot of athletes who scrimp on protein by eating too many carbohydrates, and I see others who eat too much protein and not enough carbohydrates," says Clark.

How do you find out which camp you're in? "It's a good idea to have a nutrition checkup to see if you're getting what you need," says Clark. "It rules out any potential problems and gets you started on the road to success."

Assess your protein needs

What is protein, and what does it have to do with endurance? Proteins are chains of amino acids of varying lengths. They're an important structural element in all your body's cells and help grow and repair tissues. For the athlete, protein plays its starring role as the primary component of muscle tissue. Without protein, your body wouldn't be able to build and repair the muscles you've stressed from exercise.

How much protein do you need? As a general rule, nutritionists recommend that men and women get 10 to 15 percent of their total calories from protein. The problem is, this isn't an entirely accurate gauge. If you're a woman who's dieting and eating only 1,200 calories a day, with 10 to 15 percent of those calories from protein, your total caloric intake is too low to provide enough protein.

On the flip side, if you're an ultramarathoner gulping down 5,000 calories a day, 10 to 15 percent of that amount will give you far more protein than you need. And that protein will be stored as fat.

Clark, whose books were written expressly for athletes, has a more practical measure. She suggests determining your protein needs in terms of grams of protein per pound of body weight. She lays it out simply. To meet daily protein needs, a sedentary adult needs 0.4 gram of protein per pound of body weight. A 120-pound woman who doesn't exercise needs about 48 grams of protein a day (120 × 0.4). That's really not much. A single 6½-ounce can of tuna fish contains about 50 grams of protein.

Of course, athletes need more protein than inactive folks, primarily to build and repair muscle tissue. Active adults, who exercise moderately several times a week, need about 0.6 gram of protein per pound of body weight, says Clark.

Using her formula, an active 120-pound woman needs about 72 grams of protein daily. Adults hoping to build muscle mass or youths who are just plain growing need even more protein—about 0.9 gram per pound of body weight. Endurance athletes training hard also fit into this category.

Figure your category, pick the appropriate figure and multiply it by your body weight. But remember, these are only guidelines. The needs of athletes vary. See a sports nutritionist for your specific protein needs.

Keep up your protein reserves

Endurance athletes, says Clark, need more protein because it can serve as a primary source of energy. Exercise physiologists once believed protein was used as energy only as a last resort—after glycogen reserves were depleted and a big chunk had been taken from your stores of fat. Your body would then break down the proteins in your muscle tissue, round up those amino acids and hustle them off to the liver, where they'd be used to produce glucose.

Of course, you'd want to avoid breakdown (or catabolism) of your muscles. After all, why would an endurance athlete want those muscles that were so laboriously cultivated to turn into scrap? But recent studies suggest an amino acid known as leucine might provide up to 10 percent of your energy when your carbohydrate reserves are shot.

This doesn't mean, however, that endurance athletes should begin shoveling down forkfuls of tuna.

"Because protein is a more important energy source than we thought, endurance athletes need more protein than, say, body builders, but the additional amount isn't phenomenal," says Clark. "Because they generally consume a lot of calories, most endurance athletes are probably already getting more than enough protein."

Most foods common to a good endurance diet—milk and grains, tuna, beans and lean chicken—are rich sources of protein.

Vegetarians in particular need to keep up protein intake. Why? Back to amino acids for a second. There are 22 amino acids, which are the building blocks of protein. Your body can make most of them. However, 9 amino acids can't be produced by your body; they have to be taken in through food and hence are labeled "essential" amino acids. Animal protein contains all of these essential amino acids. Vegetables and other sources do not.

This is precisely why vegetarians must eat a variety of plant sources to ensure that they get all the essential amino acids. Examples of good combinations are pasta and cheese, cereal and milk, rice and beans, cornbread and chili beans.

Watch your fat intake

What's the danger of excess protein? A diet high in protein is usually also high in fat. Chowing down with a thick steak too often will overshoot your protein needs and drive your cholesterol levels to the moon, increasing heart disease risk. Plus, excess protein is converted to fat. With the possible exception of Sumo wrestlers, most athletes find this counterproductive.

Cautions Clark, "If you're filling up on proteins and you aren't filling up on carbohydrates, you're probably going to have a higher cholesterol and fat intake, and that's just not a healthy choice."

See Also: *Carbohydrate, Cholesterol*

Part 4

Injuries, Obstacles and Perils

Blisters, bonking, frostbite, hyperthermia, hypoglycemia, shin splints, snowblindness, stress fractures. Not the sort of sales pitch you'd use to promote endurance sport. But endurance by definition entails challenge. And challenge, stripped of its public relations gloss, means that all sorts of things can go very wrong.

Let's face it—there's a decidedly dark side to the endurance drama. While this can lead to all manner of legendary mishaps, our aim is to make sure these stories don't involve you. In fact, with minor preparation and common sense, many of the maladies suffered by endurance athletes are quite easily avoided.

Managing other endurance obstacles takes a bit more doing, but with sufficient knowledge, even these can be avoided. Experienced athletes will tell you there's no such thing as the Wall.

Indulging in endurance sport means taking some risks. For many, this is precisely endurance sport's appeal. But jousting with the bull doesn't mean you have to let yourself be impaled to enjoy the experience to its fullest. Endurance athletes have enough challenges without making things harder. Become familiar with the information in this section, and you may never have to return to it again.

Air Pollution
Training in the not-so-fresh air

*I*f you live in New York, Los Angeles and almost certainly in the world's most polluted urban area, Mexico City, you have a real dilemma. Chances are you'd find more than one sensible physician who would argue that you'd probably live longer as a couch potato than as an athlete. The reason? Lousy air.

Ozone, carbon monoxide, dust, smoke and other forms of air pollution can have strikingly negative effects on athletic performance. They may even pose serious health risks to endurance athletes who live and train in heavily polluted environments.

Indeed, athletes are considered to be at much greater risk from air pollution than the general public because they breathe more often and more deeply. They also tend to breathe through their mouths, not their noses, where hair and mucous membranes can trap pollutants before they reach the lungs.

Itchy eyes, sore throats, coughing and shallow, painful breathing can by themselves make strenuous physical activity unpleasant. But the less obvious effects on performance are even more damaging. Air pollution can greatly reduce the amount of air your lungs can take in, due to irritation and swelling in the upper respiratory tract.

It has also been found to temporarily lower maximum heart rate, maximum oxygen uptake (VO_2 max) and anaerobic threshold—all of which are critical elements in aerobic performance.

Fortunately, these parameters bounce back fairly quickly; much of the recovery occurs within a few hours. But it's also sobering to note that it doesn't take much exposure to experience these negative effects. Studies have shown that the exercise performance of trained athletes has been impaired after only one hour of moderately heavy exercise at ozone concentrations as low as 0.18 parts per million—levels that are frequently exceeded in cities like Los Angeles and Mexico City.

In addition, combinations of pollutants in the air have been shown to act *synergistically*. That is, their total effect on the body is greater than the effect of each pollutant individually.

Carbon monoxide and ozone: the deadly duo

The two most common air pollutants you'll likely encounter during inner-city training are carbon monoxide and ozone.

In fact, carbon monoxide is such a heavy hitter when it comes to pollution power, we've given it an entry of its own. In brief, though, once carbon monoxide from auto fumes enters your body, it combines with red

The Air Pollution Self-Defense System

You can reduce your risks from air pollution by observing these guidelines.

- Avoid training at peak daily and seasonal pollution times.
- Save your long workouts for weekend mornings, when automobile and industrial emissions are at their lowest points.
- Avoid training vigorously when Stage I (or higher) health advisories are announced or expected. Check your newspaper for forecasts or call your local air quality control agency.
- Skip physical activity if you have heart or respiratory problems when pollution levels exceed minimum air quality standards.
- Try to stay off the main roads and as far away from heavy automobile traffic as you can.
- Stay indoors before competing on smoggy days. Breathe through your nose before the event and keep your warm-up to a bare minimum.
- Don't exercise within three hours following exposure to carbon monoxide if you have heart disease.
- Don't attempt to adapt to air pollution.

blood cells and cuts off their oxygen supply. Can it be fatal? In extreme cases, yes. But even in lesser amounts, it'll shave your aerobic capacity and endurance performance.

Although invisible, carbon monoxide can have serious consequences. To preserve your health, avoid high-traffic areas and rush-hour times when running or cycling.

Ozone is the primary component of urban smog. It is formed when emissions from automobiles, factories and other pollution sources interact with sunlight. Ozone can make your eyes water, your throat burn and your breathing uncomfortable enough to limit aerobic performance.

Also, according to William Brooks McCafferty, Ph.D., of the University of Redlands in Redlands, California, "other possible factors, such as a decline in total lung capacity or excess mucus formation, have been suggested."

Even more disturbing, some studies have shown a correlation between high levels of ozone and childhood asthma. Several researchers have noted that asthma admissions to urban hospitals increase markedly during times when levels of ozone are at their highest point.

The long-term implications of these studies for the endurance athlete are not clear, but it certainly makes sense to minimize the risks by cutting short or canceling your outdoor training schedule on smoggy days.

One other form of air pollution bears mention, though most athletes are smart enough to avoid the stuff. Though there are many forms of pollution, no single form is as deadly as the cigarette. Cigarette smoke hits hard across the board—irritating bronchial tubes, causing emphysema, making the smoker more susceptible to infection and reducing oxygen transport, not to mention causing lung cancer and heart disease. Though the smoker bears the brunt of the onslaught, studies have shown that nonsmokers are at even greater risk for some harmful effects of sidestream smoke.

Should you adapt to air pollution?

Studies have shown that your lungs and respiratory tract can indeed adapt to high levels of ozone in the air you breathe. Within just several days of your initial exposure you are likely to be free of the itchy eyes and sore chest that characterized your first two days of training in a heavily polluted city.

However, with air pollution, there is just no winning. You may adjust to the conditions to an extent—at least enough to make exercising bearable— but no matter how well you adjust, prolonged exposure to foul air leads to cancer, asthma and emphysema. Experts therefore advise against forcing your body to adapt to an air-polluted environment.

Living in a major city where pollution is a problem does not automatically consign you to the sofa, the television set and a six-pack of beer. Take precautions to minimize the effects of dirty air, including running in the early morning and late evening and after and before rush hours, when levels of carbon monoxide are at their lowest. Avoid lunchtime runs on hot summer days, since ozone levels are at their highest during that time.

See Also: *Asthma, Carbon Monoxide*

Amenorrhea
Taking diet and exercise to extremes

Women serious about endurance competition once tended to consider amenorrhea a blessing: train hard, get lean and stop having your period. The freedom of not having to deal with a menstrual cycle—not having to worry about a sometimes awkward problem at the last minute on race day—was a relief, pure and simple. And what harm could it do? Everyone, it seemed, knew someone who had been amenorrheic for years, then backed off from training, resumed their menstrual cycle and had children. Big deal.

For years, the medical and scientific community felt much the same way. If amenorrhea wasn't exactly normal, it was widely viewed as harmless and temporary, with no lasting impact on women's biggest concern—fertility.

Today, doctors and sportsmedicine experts are taking a hard look at exercise-induced amenorrhea. Its apparent link to osteoporosis, or low bone density, a potentially crippling disorder common in postmenopausal women, has given the medical community pause.

"Studies have shown a strong correlation between a decrease in bone density levels and the low estrogen state related to amenorrhea," says Vivian Turkel, M.D., of the University of California, San Diego, Medical Center Hospital.

Even in its relatively early stages, osteoporosis can increase an athlete's susceptibility to stress fractures and other bone injuries. And over the long term, the process is degenerative and largely irreversible. Thus, a career-ending series of minor injuries may be a prelude to more serious problems in the future.

Interestingly, moderate levels of weight-bearing exercise have been found to *increase* bone density. Thus, exercise is routinely recommended for postmenopausal women at increased risk for osteoporosis.

The price of pushing the limits

It's a different story, however, for women who are still menstruating. According to Dr. Turkel, "When you really push the limits, too-strenuous exercise starts doing the reverse. It's probably okay to miss one or two periods, but women shouldn't get to the point where they're not having periods at all."

Christine Wells, Ph.D., a professor of exercise science at Arizona State University in Tempe and an athlete herself, agrees. "Women shouldn't be amenorrheic," Dr. Wells says. "It's an abnormal condition. It's dangerous—to their performance and their future health."

It's significant that bone density in older women tends to decline rapidly in the early years following menopause. Physicians fear that amenorrheic endurance athletes could be in the same boat—that by the time a woman's competitive career has ended, the worst damage has already been done.

The accepted treatment for an athlete with lower-than-normal bone density is hormone therapy—usually with the female hormone estrogen in the form of birth control pills. Raising estrogen levels can improve the bones' absorption of calcium and help stave off osteoporosis.

Nutritional counseling can help head off this condition, as poor nutrition usually contributes to low bone density. In fact, inadequate calcium is the main culprit behind osteoporosis.

Obviously, it's a wise woman athlete who begins stocking up on healthy sources of calcium, such as low-fat dairy products like yogurt, milk and cheeses and green vegetables like turnip greens, collards and kale.

Finding the culprit

No one's exactly sure why some female athletes stop menstruating before menopause. An early theory linking amenorrhea to levels of body fat below 12 percent has been largely discounted. Nor does intense exercise alone seem to trigger the condition. Instead, amenorrhea is only one of many symptoms of chronically poor nutrition. Others include low body fat, chronic fatigue, low estrogen levels, osteoporosis and chronic electrolyte imbalances.

According to San Diego nutritionist Nancy Brown, amenorrhea has been noted in female endurance swimmers who have plenty of body fat but must deal on a regular basis with cold water and high training loads.

Conversely, Brown cites a case of one elite female marathoner whose body fat reached abnormally low levels (4 percent) but who never missed a period. Clearly, the causes of exercise-induced amenorrhea are complex.

"Amenorrhea is most likely a matter of too much exercise in relationship to how much food you're taking in," suggests Dr. Wells. "Almost all the amenorrheic women we see have low calorie and protein intakes. They're just eating the wrong stuff."

Boston-based sports nutritionist Nancy Clark, R.D., author of *The Athlete's Kitchen* and *Nancy Clark's Sports Nutrition Guidebook,* agrees with her colleague. "A lot of endurance athletes get so into eating carbohydrates that they forget about protein," she says.

Complicating the issue still further are the high nutritional requirements of endurance athletes. It's not all that easy, *physically,* for a 110-pound female triathlete to consume 4,000 calories' worth of healthy food per day. Dedicated endurance athletes often need to put as much focus and effort into eating as they do into their actual training and racing.

Specifically, calories from protein should comprise 12 to 15 percent of the endurance training diet. That's approximately one gram of protein per pound of body weight per day. Fortunately, that's not difficult to accomplish. Two cups of cottage cheese contain about 60 grams of protein; a cup of milk contains 12 grams; a hamburger provides about 25 grams.

Thus, a 110-pound female athlete could meet her daily protein needs with two cups of cottage cheese, two glasses of milk and a hamburger. Lean red meat is the best source of protein, but if red meat's not for you, there are plenty of alternatives—chicken, tuna, beans and peanut butter, for example.

Commitment, yes—compulsion, no

Clark also notes that many amenorrheic women have bona fide eating disorders, which make them as compulsive about their diets as they are about their exercise programs. Too often, she says, anything containing fat and/or protein is avoided as unhealthy.

The line between commitment and compulsion is often thin, and eating disorders are surprisingly common among female endurance athletes. In some cases, the evidence of a disorder is subtle and easily denied, while in others the clues are painfully obvious to all but the victim herself.

One striking case in point was a former elite distance runner who declined to eat breakfast the day after finishing the 140-mile Hawaii Ironman Triathlon. She'd drunk so much Gatorade and eaten so many bananas during the race, she said, that she'd put on weight and was afraid of getting fat. In fact, she hadn't put a pound on her 100-pound frame.

"It's the compulsiveness that's the problem," Clark says. "Many amenorrheic women have very strict rules about what they eat and what they don't." Clark and other experts agree that food compulsions or rituals are warning signs that you may be taking things too far. If you find yourself frequently using food as a motivation to train, or you find yourself training *instead* of eating, it might be time to reassess your priorities. Your body's long-term health should never suffer for the sake of your short-term athletic goals.

"It's okay to exercise," Clark says. "There are many women who do a ton of exercise and menstruate. Just make sure you're eating enough to support the activity."

See Also: *Anorexia Nervosa, Obsession*

Ankle Sprains
RICE is nice

At one time or another, most of us have been laid up with an ankle sprain, an annoying injury to a ligament that results from an awkward misstep. Given the banality of this injury, it's odd that many people still aren't sure how to treat it.

Remember four short words and one nifty acronym, says La Jolla, California, sports podiatrist Joe Ellis, D.P.M.: rest, ice, compression and elevation, or RICE. Get off the ankle, says Dr. Ellis, and elevate it. Wrap it firmly with a bandage and ice the area several times daily for about 20 minutes per session. If possible, tape the ankle to reduce the swelling.

Give a minor ankle sprain proper attention and you can bounce back quickly. Washington Redskins quarterback Mark Rypien suffered a slight ankle sprain three days before the 1992 Super Bowl. By Sunday, he was unbeatable.

Having said that, it's important to realize that not all ankle sprains are quickly healed, nor should they all be left to self-care. A minor sprain might simply stretch those ligaments. A severe strain can tear or rupture them. If your ankle's the size of an eggplant and exhibits the same color, says Dr. Ellis, there's probably a severe tear and bleeding under the skin. Don't wait—see a professional. If you continue to use the ankle without proper treatment, you could tear the ligaments again.

Once the ankle heals, it's a mistake to forget about it. Stretched ligaments rarely regain their former tightness; that first sprain can open the door for others.

Strengthen ankles with exercise

You can help prevent later sprains by fortifying the weakened area. Dr. Ellis recommends several easy exercises to strengthen your ankles.

First, you can lift light weights on the end of your foot. Sit on a table with the weight on your foot and your injured leg extended and trace the letters of the alphabet, from A to Z, in the air with your foot.

Second, try standing with your feet about 12 inches apart. Bend your knees slightly and alternately raise the inside and outside of your foot. Do this 20 to 30 times, several times daily.

Third, and simplest of all, with your shoes on, walk on your toes for several minutes. Then walk on your heels with your toes in the air, again for several minutes.

Finally, if you're a chronic ankle sprainer, try a tilt board. Walking on this device—a sort of round garbage can lid balanced on a center stay—helps improve coordination and ankle strength.

The beauty of these exercises is that you can perform them anywhere. Remember, when it comes to ankle sprains, proper foot care, including a visit to a physical therapist, if necessary, can speed recovery and prevent future problems.

Anorexia Nervosa
Diet addiction with serious consequences

There's a dark side to this business of getting fit—that murky area known as "eating disorders." Although these can be difficult to pin down in a society that venerates the diet-of-the-week, certain behavior patterns should put you on Red Alert.

Of all the aberrations connected with eating, anorexia nervosa (self-induced starvation) is the most dangerous. In severe cases, anorexics who can't overcome their aversion to food will die.

Although at the top of the heap, anorexia is but one of a number of eating disorders. Most common among athletes is "disordered eating," where laxatives, stringent diets or occasional fasts are used to attain an "ideal weight." Research has indicated that one-third of all female collegiate athletes have some type of disordered eating pattern.

Poor nutrition can lead to serious problems, such as amenorrhea (the absence of menstrual periods) and osteoporosis (loss of bone density). Though anorexia is less commonplace, athletes must be aware of the dangerous territory they'll enter if they flirt with self-starvation.

You've probably heard about the weight loss that accompanies anorexia (at least 15 percent of original body weight). But you may not be aware of its serious potential complications. These include heart rhythm irregularities, gastrointestinal problems, organ damage and seizures. Anorexia can also permanently stunt growth in adolescents.

There's an obvious connection between endurance athletes and anorexics. Although there are no concrete figures, anorexia has made its presence known among this group. Many of the qualities associated with successful endurance athletes are also found in anorexics. Both personality types are highly driven, sometimes compulsive. Both wish to control their minds and bodies. Both also deny pain and discomfort—fatigue in the case of the athlete, hunger in the case of the anorexic.

The skinny on fat

Athletes traditionally loathe putting on a few extra pounds, unless they're Sumo wrestlers or marathon swimmers. But many push far past reasonable weight-loss limits.

We all have a genetically endowed "setpoint," where our weight hovers when we're in sound working order. When athletes push past this ideal point, they jeopardize precisely what they hope to achieve.

"It's fine to be lean, but within reasonable limits," says Jack Wilmore, Ph.D., professor at the University of Texas at Austin and an expert in body composition. "Many athletes push themselves too low, and we start to see decreases in performance and general body function. This can lead to eating disorders. It's a really serious problem that can't be overstressed."

How much fat should we be toting about? Dr. Wilmore prefers to discuss ideal body fat in ranges. Successful male athletes, he says, generally have a body fat content below 15 percent; successful female athletes, under 20 percent.

Of course, everyone's body fat percentage is determined largely by genetics. Thus, you can stray above the recommended range and still be successful. In fact, Dr. Wilmore once worked with two elite women distance runners, one with 13 percent body fat and the other with only 6 percent. Both ran equally well.

"The problem is," says Dr. Wilmore, "that it's tempting for someone who doesn't understand the area to say, 'Well, the 13 percent athlete ought to get down to 6 percent for even more improvement.'"

Instead, he points out, "They reach a level where their performance starts to substantially decrease."

When thin becomes dangerous

When do you cross the border between thin and anorexic? There are plenty of potential warning signs.
- Anorexics typically lose 15 to 25 percent of their body weight.
- They have an intense fear of becoming obese and panic if they gain only a few pounds.
- They're often compulsive exercisers.
- They prefer to eat alone.
- They might lose hair.
- They become stressed, depressed and moody.
- They believe family and friends take too much interest in their eating habits and try to make them eat more than they want.
- Women may stop menstruating.
- They're often obsessed with food yet disgusted by it.
- They become increasingly isolated from family and friends.
- Most dangerous of all, they typically deny all of the above warning signals.

"Denial is very much a part of the disease," says Ellen Coleman, R.D., a Riverside, California, sports nutritionist and two-time Ironman finisher who has worked with both anorexics and athletes. "Even when people with anorexia become emaciated, they still think of themselves as fat."

Though rare, anorexia can result in death. If any of the information here sounds an alarm, don't wait to get help.

See Also: *Amenorrhea, Calories, Fat*

Asthma
Athletes with asthma can compete

J im Ryun. Danny Manning. Bill Koch. Nancy Hogshead. Jackie Joyner-Kersee. Sound familiar? In order, these are: the former world record holder in the mile; the 1987–88 NCAA basketball player of the year; America's top cross-country ski racer; swimmer and triple gold medalist at the 1984 Olympics; and heptathlete and perhaps the greatest female track and field athlete of all time. All are asthmatics, illustrating that asthma need not be the debilitating disease many believe it to be.

Stephen Rice, Ph.D., a sportsmedicine specialist at the University of Washington in Seattle and an asthmatic himself, echoes the prevailing sentiment among asthma experts today, an echo that reverberates on the field of play.

"Once upon a time, if you had asthma or exercise-induced asthma, nobody wanted you to do anything, but that's changed," says Dr. Rice. "If it's well treated and under control, there's no reason why you can't compete successfully."

This is especially good news because both asthma and exercise-induced asthma (EIA) are by no means rare. Asthma affects an estimated ten million Americans of all ages, and most people with asthma are affected by exercise. Dr. Rice estimates about 10 percent of the population has exercise-induced asthma. The American Academy of Allergy and Immunology puts the figure even higher, estimating it at 12 to 15 percent of the population.

Even more surprising, EIA often goes undetected. You may have EIA and not even be aware of it. Swimmer Nancy Hogshead is an ideal example. For years, Hogshead assumed "small lungs" were responsible for her postrace coughing and wheezing.

After she finished fourth in the 200-meter butterfly at the 1984 Olympics, a doctor noticed her coughing. Did she always cough like that after a race? he asked. He suspected that Hogshead had EIA, and indeed, after years of competitive swimming at the national and world-class level, it was confirmed that she did.

Hogshead wasn't the only Olympic athlete who was unaware of having EIA. A questionnaire prepared by the American Academy of Allergy and Immunology found that 67 of 597 Olympians on the 1984 U.S. team had experienced symptoms of EIA and never even knew they had it.

Is it asthma or EIA?

Asthma is a narrowing of the breathing tubes in the lungs. As the lining of the tubes swells and the muscles surrounding them constrict, it becomes difficult to force air in and out of the lungs—a harrowing experience for anyone familiar with the accompanying gasping, wheezing and shortness of breath.

No one knows what causes asthma, but experts have identified a wide range of triggers, from cigarette smoke, dust, pollen and strong odors to air pollutants, cold air, emotional stress and, yes, exercise.

What's the difference between asthma and EIA? Perhaps the most important difference is that EIA is far less serious. Asthma can kill, and according to figures from the National Asthma Education Program, the number of asthma-related deaths is on the rise—from 1979 to 1988, the death toll from asthma in the United States climbed from about 2,000 to 4,600 yearly.

Experts are puzzled by the rise. Some attribute it to mismanagement of the disease, but the fact remains that asthma can be deadly.

EIA, by contrast, is in most cases relatively benign. Unless you experience an EIA attack in conjunction with a severe asthma attack, says Dr. Rice, all you're likely to experience with EIA is discomfort. "Exercise asthma is a more limited problem that usually relieves itself and is not life-threatening," Dr. Rice says. "People don't die from exercise asthma. If your only problem is exercise asthma, you're at essentially little risk."

In general, the only difference between EIA attacks and regular asthma attacks is that EIA attacks generally occur shortly after an athlete stops exercising, are less severe and don't last as long. Usually, says Dr. Rice, an EIA attack lasts no longer than 30 minutes.

EIA's symptoms and signposts are usually quite predictable. If you experience shortness of breath or odd coughing spells after exercise, see a physician. Your respiratory function will be measured, you'll run on a treadmill for 10 to 15 minutes and then your respiration will be measured again at several intervals. If the air flow out of your lungs is reduced, you could have EIA.

EIA is particularly daunting for endurance athletes, who exercise strenuously for long periods of time. For them, attacks can occur during exercise, sometime between 6 and 12 minutes into the activity. There's a feeling of constriction in the airways, with tightness in the chest. A coughing spasm may follow. Sometimes EIA sufferers push through these attacks, but the experience can be decidedly uncomfortable.

Is there any danger in pushing through an EIA attack? Not unless the attack is a genuine asthma attack. In fact, says Dr. Rice, unless it's just far too uncomfortable, pushing through an EIA attack can sometimes put an end to it. The body releases chemicals during exercise that stymie EIA triggers. Airway function increases during exercise—in asthmatics and nonasthmatics alike—making it easier to breathe.

"The idea of running through an EIA attack is not a dangerous thing, because by continuing, you're blocking the negative effects," says Dr. Rice.

The severity of an attack—whether of full-blown asthma or EIA—can vary widely, depending on the person, the temperature and amount of moisture in the air, the presence of other allergic triggers and the type, intensity and duration of exercise.

Managing EIA

If you understand what causes EIA, the timing of the attacks makes sense. Most people breathe through the nose when they're not exercising. The air that passes through the nose is warmed and humidified before passing on to the lungs.

But as athletes exert themselves, they rapidly inhale air through the mouth. Air taken in through the mouth is cooler and drier. The breathing tubes of someone with EIA react to this cool, dry air by constricting. Suddenly, they're having an asthma attack.

"As long as you can exercise and continue to be a nose breather, you can warm up the cool air from the outside world before it gets to your throat and lungs, and you can minimize the water loss," Dr. Rice explains. It's when an asthmatic has to breathe through the mouth that the temperature drops, water is lost and conditions are ripe for an attack.

Unfortunately, for precisely these reasons, endurance athletes are far more likely to experience EIA. Not even a nose of Jimmy Durante proportions is efficient enough to suck down enough oxygen during hard endurance effort.

Fortunately, athletes with EIA can take the following preventive steps against asthma attacks.

- Do vigorous but gradual warm-ups before exercising.
- Avoid eating two hours prior to exercise.
- Avoid shellfish, celery and melons.
- Avoid cold, dry air.
- Use a face mask in less-than-ideal situations.
- Breathe through the nose.
- Take slow, deep breaths.
- Limit maximum effort to less than five minutes.
- Keep training consistent and vigorous.

Before exercising, it's crucial to premedicate. Several asthma medications, such as prescription mist inhalers, albuterol and cromolyn sodium, can be taken 20 minutes before exercise. These have proven very effective in reducing and eliminating asthma attacks during exercise. They open the breathing tubes in minutes, and their effects can last as long as six hours.

Still, if you plan to continue exercising for more than two hours, National Asthma Education Program guidelines recommend that you repeat the medication after two hours.

Warming up in a few five-minute exercise periods also seems to help reduce symptoms. In a strange twist, a long warm-up and purposely triggered attack may eliminate the chance of an attack during an event.

"Once you've had an attack, there seems to be this refractory period where you can't get another attack for a while," says Dr. Rice. "And if you do get an attack, it won't be as severe as the initial one.'

While athletes who suffer only from EIA can take a few chances, Dr. Rice recommends that true asthma sufferers be extremely cautious. He asks his patients to buy a peak flow meter and calculate how their lungs are faring that day before embarking on any kind of exercise. The flow meter measures the maximum amount of air you can blow out.

If you can exhale at between 80 and 100 percent of your maximum, says

Dr. Rice, consider this your green light for exercise. If you can only manage between 50 and 80 percent of your max, that's a warning that this might not be a good time for physical effort. If your peak flow is less than 50 percent of your max, take the day off.

As Dr. Rice points out, you can also avoid an EIA attack by skirting the conditions that might provoke it. If it's cool, dry or smoggy outside, move indoors where the air is warmer, cleaner and often humidified. Skip the mountain pass ride that day and assault the stationary bike instead.

Better yet, head for an indoor pool. Many physicians recommend swimming as a sport for people with EIA because the air just above the surface is warm and humidified. If you insist on venturing out into cool conditions, says Dr. Rice, you can help warm and moisten the air entering your lungs by wearing a scarf or mask over your nose and mouth.

Exercising: more good than harm?

For some reason, exercise seems to help asthmatics. Regular aerobic exercise makes the body more efficient in its use of oxygen, so you can get by on less. Without the need to suck down great gobs of air, a fit asthmatic may be able to avoid some attacks.

"Aerobically fitter people often don't experience the sort of gasping air movement that triggers an attack," observes Dr. Rice.

Still, he understands serious athletes well enough to know that no matter how fit they are, they're likely to push themselves into trouble.

"People who are competitive are going to run right to the edge of what they can do," he points out. "They're going to push right to the point where they're in an at-risk situation. They can't ignore the importance of premedicating themselves."

Blisters
Prevention is the name of the game

*F*or an endurance athlete, few problems seem so minor, yet involve so much pain and suffering, as blisters. You can train for a big race for months, pace yourself—do all the right things—only to be sidelined halfway through the event by a blister on your big toe.

Blisters occur when friction between the skin and another surface creates heat, irritating the delicate tissues beneath the surface. Fluid then leaks out of the injured tissue, forming a bubble. If the irritation continues long enough, blood will mix with the fluid—a sign of deeper, more severe tissue damage that will invariably be accompanied by greater pain.

Further complications can arise if you try to avoid aggravating the blister and strain a muscle or ligament in the process. Obviously, you'd like to sidestep (ouch!) all these nuisances if you could. But how?

Simply remember that anything that prevents friction will prevent blisters. In practical terms, this translates into buying shoes that fit your feet well. You don't want your foot to slip around inside the shoe—all that movement will raise blisters quick as a wink. Nor do you want a shoe that's tighter than a straitjacket.

Toe-wise tips for happier feet

Comfort is the key. Be sure you've got about ½ inch of space between your toes and the front of the shoe. Lack of toe room is the primary cause of toe blisters.

Sound contradictory? It's not. Just look for a shoe that's snug in the heel and across the middle of your foot. Make sure it has some room up front— after all, your feet tend to swell when you run.

Most salespeople won't let you test-drive shoes with a five-miler, so do your shopping in the afternoon. Since your feet swell during the day, you're more likely to get an accurate "running" fit.

After you've made your purchase, resist temptation. Don't go right out and run a 12-miler. No matter how ideal the fit, new shoes still need time to conform to your foot. Wear them for a day or two during your normal daily activities. When you take your first run in them, keep it short—a mile or two—then increase the distance gradually. Otherwise, you could end up with blisters the size of Maine.

Blisters can also be caused by loose-fitting socks. Like your shoes, your socks should fit snugly. Baggy socks will ball up at the end of your toes and rub up some terrific blisters. Take a look at your local sports outfitter—you'll find yourself awash in socks.

A *Runner's World* magazine survey found that socks made mostly, if not completely, of synthetic fibers were preferable because of their ability to take moisture from the foot to the surface of the sock, where it evaporates. Synthetics also retain their shape after several washings.

Still, when it comes to blister prevention, no sock will be perfect for everyone. In fact, many runners run without socks and never have a blister problem. You'll just have to experiment to see what's right for you.

Here are a few other blister-prevention tips from La Jolla, California, sports podiatrist Joe Ellis, D.P.M.

- Rub petroleum jelly on areas prone to blisters and irritations.
- Apply bandages or other adhesive strips to problem areas before, not after, a workout or competition. It's always best to give your bandage technique a test run before a race.
- Never, never break in a new pair of shoes in a race. If you feel even

the hint of a "hot spot," go back to the ugly, smelly old runners that treated you so well for so long.

To burst or not to burst

Despite your best efforts, you will probably—at some point—get a blister. If so, do you pop it or not?

Some experts advocate leaving a blister intact, but that doesn't do much good if you need to train and the thing hurts. To drain a blister, wash the area thoroughly with antiseptic soap and warm water. Then, with a pin or needle that you've sterilized in rubbing alcohol, puncture the side of the blister and drain the fluid. Swab the area with an antiseptic solution and cover with a sterile bandage. Change the dressing daily and watch closely for signs of infection—redness, swelling and pain. If signs of infection do occur, see a doctor. An infection below the skin can spread quickly and become a serious problem overnight.

Blisters may seem a trivial matter, but anyone who's experienced them knows differently. No one is immune. At the 1989 Los Angeles Marathon, Mark Plaatjes, a Boulder, Colorado, physical therapist and a 2:08 marathoner, was the favorite. Plaatjes never finished the race. He was forced to drop out after 18 miles—his shoes were filled with blood from the blisters he'd raised.

Bonking
The biker's Wall

*B*onking is the cyclists' expression for what runners call "the Wall"—that point in a marathon when muscles run out of glycogen. Triathletes use a slightly more descriptive phrase: "blow up," as in "I blew up at mile 30."

But nothing short of personal experience can describe the feeling of reaching into your carbohydrate cupboard (metaphorically speaking) and coming up empty-handed. You won't feel that localized burning pain experienced by sprinters.

Instead, you'll experience complete and almost instantaneous exhaustion. Rather than just pulling the cork on your energy supplies, the bonk smashes the bottle. Your legs will turn to rubber, while your spirit turns to Jell-O. Drained and debilitated, all you'll want to do is stop, get off your bike and thumb the first ride you can get home.

The best way to avoid the bonk in the short term is to eat a substantial breakfast before taking a long ride. In addition, take along something to eat, or at the very least, keep some money on you for a midpoint snack. Be sure to fill your water bottles with an electrolyte solution instead of plain water—most of these drinks contain enough sugar for a quick pickup.

As far as exactly what kind of food to eat to avoid bonking, it's impossible to say. Everyone's body reacts differently. Six-time Hawaii Ironman Triathlon champ Dave Scott used to eat figs during long races. Joanne Ernst, who won the Hawaii Ironman in 1985, somehow came up with the odd combination of red licorice and fortune cookies.

Something sweet, or at least "bready," usually helps; cookies, granola bars, energy bars and so forth are endurance favorites, but you really need to experiment. According to nutritionist Ann Grandjean, Ph.D., "Despite all the scientific progress that's been made in the field of nutrition, the only way to know what foods are best for any particular athlete is through trial and stomachache."

The good news for cyclists is that you have things a little easier than runners do. You can coast. You can stop along the way, grab a couple of candy bars, then roll along until the sugar kicks in. For the runner in the grips of glycogen depletion, there's no such thing as a comfortable pace. Plus, it's pretty hard to eat with your insides bouncing around.

Whether you run or cycle, however, keep in mind this warning from Ken Sparks, Ph.D., an exercise physiologist at Cleveland State University in Ohio. "Be aware that if you take in high sugar content during competitions, you run the risk of a sugar high followed by a blood sugar drop, which could cause hypoglycemia."

From an endurance perspective, your muscles are most effective while burning a combination of carbohydrate and fat. It's when your carbohydrate stores are exhausted that things get sticky, because fat alone can't supply energy quickly enough to bring you up to a competitive pace.

In the long term, then, training is the best bonk-preventer in the world. Best of all is long, slow training—those 50-, 60- or 100-mile weekend rides that condition your body to use fat more efficiently, thus preserving your precious stores of glycogen.

See Also: *Electrolytes, Glucose and Glycogen, The Wall*

Carbon Monoxide
What you can't see can hurt you

*A*n unflappable bunch, Southern California residents routinely scan their local newspaper's weather page for the PSI—a pollution standard index that measures the level of various noxious elements in the air. Others with less faith in the printed page simply poke their heads out the window. In areas like Los Angeles, with the nation's worst air pollution, seeing for yourself is often enough to keep you indoors. At times the entire skyline looks as if it's been belched from a diesel bus.

The problem with carbon monoxide, or CO, is that it's colorless, odorless and dangerous. And, of course, it's not confined to the city of Los Angeles. Wherever cars exist, carbon monoxide exists. It's produced by the incomplete combustion of gasoline in automobiles.

Carbon monoxide is of concern to us all, and triply so to anyone who plans to spend a lot of time exercising in the stuff.

This noxious gas has several harmful side effects. When inhaled, it diffuses rapidly into the bloodstream, where it combines with the hemoglobin in red blood cells. It then inhibits the transport of oxygen to working muscles, which inhibits your overall aerobic capacity.

Respecting CO's punchout power

An overload of carbon monoxide can have far more serious effects than a lousy day of training. An extensive study at the University of North Carolina found that people exercising in high levels of carbon monoxide could be risking heart attacks. Carbon monoxide seemed to increase the likelihood of abnormal heartbeats and other cardiac irregularities. The study was conducted with men and women who had histories of heart disease, but researchers concluded that carbon monoxide emissions were a potential risk to anyone who exercised outdoors.

The effects of an exercise jaunt in carbon monoxide are disturbingly long-lasting. Studies indicate that it can take almost eight hours to clear all the carbon monoxide from the blood after heavy exposure. Meanwhile, victims will feel such symptoms of physical distress as headaches or nausea.

Individual reactions to carbon monoxide poisoning will vary, but researchers agree on a commonsense exercise prescription. If you live in an urban area, try to exercise before or after rush hour to avoid the worst levels. If you insist on exercising despite high carbon monoxide levels, go easy and skip the intervals that day. Better yet, go inside. Run on the treadmill or ride the stationary bike at your local gym.

Los Angeles' South Coast Air Quality Management District issues a series of recommendations for various stages of air pollution. During Stage 2 alerts they recommend replacing vigorous exercise with walking and crafts activities. It sounds ridiculous, but serious conditions warrant extreme measures.

See Also: *Air Pollution, Obsession*

Cramps
Anti-cramp tips from the pros

C ramps have probably put a stop to more athletic endeavors than jobs, family and rainy weekends. It's unfortunate, because for the most part they're avoidable. Over a career spanning three decades and thousands of training and racing miles, coauthor Scott Tinley has rarely had problems with cramps. He attributes this in part to conditioning, since well-trained muscles are less likely to cramp. But he has primarily avoided cramps with a simple prescription.

"When I'm racing or training over long distances, I pay close attention to replacing lost fluids, electrolytes and glucose," explains Tinley.

Poorly trained muscles can contribute to cramps. So can trauma to a muscle, such as a sudden blow during exercise. But for endurance athletes, cramps occur mostly because of dehydration and a resulting electrolyte imbalance.

Usually, your body has a precise balance of electrolytes—ions of sodium, potassium and chloride—within its cells. This balance helps maintain the movement of fluid in and out of the cells. It also ensures proper muscle contraction.

If, during exercise, you lose enough electrolytes, you'll impair both fluid movement and proper muscle contraction. The result can be a sustained, continuous contraction of the muscle—otherwise known as a cramp.

Counterattack those cramps

To understand why water and electrolyte loss brings on cramps, you need to understand what happens when you lose both of these crucial elements through sweat. Sweat is nearly 99 percent water. The rest is a mixture of electrolytes.

Of all the electrolytes, salt will be your primary cause for concern. Salt, you'll recall, holds water. When you lose sodium, out goes the water as well, increasing the possibility of dehydration. You're also at higher risk of experiencing a cramp. In fact, some researchers believe most muscle cramping in endurance events results from salt loss.

Once you know how cramping develops, you can take steps to prevent it. Proper conditioning and hydration are certainly an important part of your arsenal against cramps. But scientists are seeking more answers about the phenomenon.

They have their work cut out for them, too. It's difficult to study cramps in the lab—they just can't be triggered at will. Clearly, however, fatigue and dehydration are linked with the experience of cramps.

"People who are untrained cramp more when they are doing something physical than people who are trained," says Bill Fink, a researcher at Ball State University's Human Performance Laboratory in Muncie, Indiana. "Other than that, the best advice we can give is to drink fluids. The problem is, there are so many theories as to what causes cramps that it's hard to prescribe a guaranteed cure."

If you do get a cramp, your best bet is to stop and stretch. Massage the area gently toward the heart for optimal circulation. When the cramp starts to subside, continue at a slower pace. Build slowly back to your original speed and hydrate aggressively from that point on.

While exercising, drink four to eight ounces of cold water every 10 to 15 minutes. How much you drink ultimately depends on your capacity. But if you want to avoid cramping and other symptoms of dehydration, keep that water jug close by during your workout.

See Also: *Dehydration, Electrolytes*

Cyclist's Palsy
Move it or lose it

*T*he pack is hunched low and hammering. You're tucked in the paceline watching the sweat funnel between your eyes and splash off your front wheel. Earlier, your fingers tingled. Suddenly you notice your hands have turned to stumps, endowed with all the sensation of a cement block.

What's going on? You've compressed the ulnar nerve at the base of your wrist. The condition you're experiencing is called "ulnar neuropathy," otherwise known as cyclist's palsy.

On the plus side, this can easily be avoided. First, make sure your cycling gloves and handlebar are well padded. When riding, change your hand position frequently (this will take the strain off other parts of your body, too).

And now, some don'ts. Don't clutch at the handlebar like a drowning man. Don't lean on the handlebar with all your weight. And if your fingers start to tingle, don't ignore it. Permanent nerve damage can result if you pinch off the ulnar nerve for extended periods of time.

A final word for mountain bikers. Because washboard terrain and ugly drops merit a firm handlebar grip in off-road riding, mountain bikers may experience a more serious condition known as de Quervain's disease. Pain and tenderness in the hands and wrists are preliminary symptoms—in advanced cases you may find it hard to grip anything.

What's the best treatment? Stop riding for a few weeks and concentrate on strengthening your wrists. Take time to do wrist curls, squeeze a rubber ball or stretch a rubber band between your thumb and index finger. They're all helpful.

Dehydration
A loss your body can't afford

Those who saw the first Olympic Marathon for women, held in 1984 in Los Angeles, will never forget it. Yes, Joan Benoit ran away from the field for an impressive win. But what many remember most about that oppressively hot day was the finish of Swiss marathoner Gabriele Andersen-Scheiss. Exiting the stadium tunnel, Andersen-Scheiss lurched onto the track. It took the stadium throng only seconds to realize something was seriously wrong. Andersen-Scheiss, however, was beyond caring. She shuffled around the track, her upper body leaning violently to one side as if it wished to veer off into the infield and lie down in the soft grass. Her legs, though, made resolutely for the finish.

Confused officials, unsure whether Andersen-Scheiss needed help, approached her cautiously, only to be motioned off with a weak but definite wave. Numbed by the drama, the crowd sat quiet. Andersen-Scheiss finally staggered to the finish, a victim of severe dehydration.

Of all the risks endurance athletes face, none is more common or potentially dangerous than dehydration. The rate at which people sweat varies widely, but it's possible to lose up to six pints of water per hour during vigorous exercise. If you don't replace that lost fluid, you're in for a case of dehydration. And once this occurs, your risks of heat injury and electrolyte imbalances rise.

Because your body is sensitive to even small changes in temperature, it responds quickly when exercise starts cranking up your internal heat. Heat receptors on the skin and within your body instruct the sweat glands to release perspiration through the pores. As the liquid evaporates on the surface, it cools the blood beneath the skin, and this cooled blood then courses back through the interior tissues and organs.

It's an effective system, but like the radiator in your car, it needs plenty of water to function properly. In fact, endurance athletes would do well to keep this radiator image in mind.

"Most people think of dehydration as water being lost from the body," says exercise physiologist Mary O'Toole, Ph.D., director of the University of Tennessee's Human Performance Laboratory in Memphis. "But from an endurance point of view, what's really important is the amount of water available for the blood vessels to circulate."

Lots of factors affect how much you'll perspire—heat, humidity, your body mass, the intensity of your effort, even the speed and direction of the wind. Also, there are genetic differences. Some people simply have more sweat pores than others—and men have more of them than women.

Training can also affect your rate of perspiration. Studies have shown that better-trained, heat-acclimatized athletes sweat more. They're better at cooling their bodies, yet, ironically, are more prone to dehydration.

Stay alert for warning signs

First and foremost, remember that thirst is *not* a reliable warning sign of impending dehydration. Thirst is your body's way of telling you that you need water.

It may be a terrific reminder to have a drink if you're mowing the lawn on a hot day. You'll stop, take a break and quaff down some juice or water. But if you're deep into a ten-mile run, it's another story. You'll have lost so much fluid already, your first harbingers of thirst may well come too late.

You don't have to lose much fluid before you start feeling the effects. When fluid loss during training or racing equals 2 to 3 percent of your body weight, your aerobic capacity and muscular endurance begin to dip. This isn't much weight loss—four pounds for a 150-pound man; three pounds for a 110-pound woman.

Dehydration's effects last longer than you might expect. One study of wrestlers showed a 30 percent drop in muscular endurance when 4 percent of body weight was lost after dehydration. A full four hours after rehydration, performance levels had risen to only half of normal.

Physical problems seem to accelerate with continued fluid loss. When it reaches 5 percent of your body weight, you may feel light-headed and weary. Cramps may begin, due to the onset of hyponatremia, or low salt levels.

At a fluid loss of 10 percent of body weight, your performance will be seriously impaired and health risks are acute. Nausea, dizziness, vomiting, loss of equilibrium, severe cramps and convulsions can result. Andersen-Scheiss had reached this point, and only prompt attention by medical personnel kept her from serious repercussions.

If percentages are confusing, here's a general guideline. If you experience chills, light-headedness and disorientation, says Dr. O'Toole, dehydration has progressed too far. If you're training and these symptoms appear, she suggests you stop, drink something, get out of the sun, wait until you feel better and then take a shortcut home. If you're racing, hitch a ride to the finish. At this point, discretion is definitely the better part of valor.

An ounce of prevention

You'll want to take an aggressive, day-to-day approach to be sure you're getting enough fluids. Prevention is the only cure for dehydration. Be alert to whispers of distress from your body; don't wait for it to scream. Simple carelessness makes chronic dehydration a problem even among experienced endurance athletes.

There's a simple rule of thumb to remember in your war against dehydration. (File it next to your radiator simile.) One pint of water weighs one pound. If you've lost two pounds after a workout, two pints of water should be consumed in short order.

Because weight loss is a fairly accurate measure of fluid loss, it's easy to gauge your fluid loss. Step on the scale before and after each workout—it takes but a few seconds, and it's worth every tick. See how much weight you've lost, then drink enough water to make up the difference. Eventually, you'll know roughly how much water you lose during exercise.

Generally speaking, endurance athletes should drink at least one quart (two pints) of water per hour during exercise (including swimming), then aggressively rehydrate after the workout is done. If you train regularly, you'll find that proper hydration before, during and after workouts will help you train better and recover more quickly. Weight loss, fatigue and lack of motivation may be signs of overtraining, but they should first be regarded as indicators of dehydration.

Drink up before competitions

What about preventing dehydration during long, hot races? How do you combat fluid loss then? Again, prevention, prevention and more prevention.

In the early years of the Hawaii Ironman Triathlon, contestants were stopped at designated spots along the course and weighed. By monitoring their weight loss, medical personnel could see if it was safe for the triathletes to go on. Unfortunately, some of the athletes—overzealous and blind to the dangers of dehydration—stuffed their shorts with pennies to make weight.

The wise triathlete can be seen carting gallon jugs of water around the week before the Hawaii Ironman. This might seem excessive at first glance, but it's good advice to drink "until your urine is clear and copious." It's far better to stay close to a bathroom now than to suffer with a full bladder during the race.

As for race day, start by drinking 13 to 20 ounces of water 10 to 20 minutes before the race starts, says Ellen Coleman, R.D., a Riverside, California, sports nutritionist.

"Drinking immediately before you race helps lower your body's core temperature and reduces the added stress heat places on your cardiovascular system," explains Coleman, who knows something of heat stress, having twice completed the Hawaii Ironman.

Once you're under way, remember our earlier admonition to drink at least one quart of water per hour. Coleman suggests drinking small amounts frequently—six to eight ounces of fluid every 10 to 15 minutes should do the trick. Cold fluids, says Coleman, are best because they empty more rapidly from the stomach. And contrary to popular belief, cold fluids will not give you stomach cramps.

If you decide to use a carbohydrate/electrolyte replacement drink, be sure it's one you know will agree with you. Race day is not the time to experiment with new drinks. There is a plethora of carbohydrate/electrolyte replacement drinks on the market, all claiming that they alone offer the staying power you desire. Because the manufacturers are after your dollars, they tend to inundate you with confusing information.

Coleman, an objective observer, clears up the picture. Any sports drink that provides 6 to 8 percent carbohydrate, some sodium and low fructose (high levels can upset your stomach, causing cramps, nausea and diarrhea), will do the job. And in many cases, water alone is enough.

"If you're exercising hard for over an hour, sports drinks can give you a performance edge that water can't," Coleman says. "But if you're exercising for less than an hour, water remains the most effective and least expensive fluid replacement beverage."

Understand, too, that in events like the Ironman that last longer than four hours and take place in hot, humid environments, it's probably impossible to prevent dehydration altogether. Fluid loss simply exceeds the rate at which your tissues can absorb water from your stomach. All you can do is stay alert—making sure you drink your six to eight ounces every 10 to 15 minutes and watching carefully for dehydration's warning flags.

Exercise and its effects on the body can be baffling. When it comes to dehydration, Coleman offers a final, wonderfully simple thought.

"Water," she says, "is our most commonly overlooked endurance aid."

See Also: *Cramps, Electrolytes, Humidity*

Frostbite
Staving off the Big Chill

During the 1982 Iditarod sled dog race—1,157 miles from Anchorage, Alaska, to Nome—a blizzard powered by 69-mile-per-hour winds pinned down race leaders in the tiny coastal settlement of Shaktoolik. The area is one of the coldest in Alaska, directly exposed to hellish winds that scream across the Bering Strait out of Siberia.

An impatient Eskimo native named Herbie Nayokpuk decided to push on. Twenty-two miles later, Nayokpuk and his sled dogs were halted by a blinding blizzard. Nayokpuk spent the night out on an exposed ice pack, hunkered down in his sled, buried in thick clothing. When rescuers discovered him the next day, Nayokpuk was numb but otherwise well.

Few of us would find ourselves in such a dramatic predicament, but it does illustrate that extremes of cold can be tolerated and survived.

At the other end of the spectrum is the story of a 53-year-old physician. Running for 30 minutes in below-freezing weather with inadequate protection from the waist down, this gentleman's case of frostbite gained notoriety for its location and the fact that the case was described in the *New England Journal of Medicine.*

Fortunately, the physician was knowledgeable enough to recognize the symptoms of frostbite, take appropriate measures and prevent serious injury.

When frostbite strikes, it most commonly affects the skin of the extremities (fingers, toes, ears, nose and face). One reason is that these areas are often exposed. A second reason is the body's attempt to protect itself in harsh conditions. To conserve heat in cold weather, your body shunts blood, and its accompanying heat, to your core tissues. Here it's protected from the surrounding cold. Deprived of this circulating blood, surface tissues are then more vulnerable to the cold.

Frostbite comes in one of two varieties—superficial or deep. Skiers often experience the symptoms of superficial frostbite—painful numbness on exposed cheeks and the tips of the nose and ears. Deep frostbite is far more serious, inflicting irreversible damage on underlying tissues. When circulation stops, the extremities actually freeze, and the skin turns white and hard to the touch, like a bar of soap.

Deep frostbite usually requires swift medical attention to avoid amputation of the affected body part. Secondary bacterial infections due to tissue death (gangrene) can be a serious complication of deep frostbite.

Preventing frostbite

As the tale of the frozen physician demonstrates, frostbite should be a concern to any athlete who plans to spend even a short time in the cold.

However, there's no need to be obsessive about it—consider the Iditarod, where participants successfully endure frigid temperatures that would have polar bears scurrying for cover.

Their strategy is simple: Cover up. In most cases frostbite prevention is a simple matter of dressing warmly. *Don't* rely on the body heat you generate while exercising to keep you warm. Noses, toes, fingers, cheeks—even male genitals—are at risk on a cold day, even when you're working hard. Protect your head and ears with a wool cap. If it's particularly cold or windy, make sure your entire face is protected. Some runners wear ski masks; others daub their faces with a light covering of petroleum jelly.

Wear gloves. If it's really cold, wear two pairs—and do the same with socks. And don't neglect your torso. The first priority of your body's warming system is your head and torso. If they aren't warm enough, your body shunts blood away from other areas to keep them warm—and presto, your extremities are courting frostbite.

Don't underestimate the power of a windbreaker—it can work wonders. The skin can't freeze if it isn't exposed.

Because you'll be perspiring despite the cold, you'd also be smart to wear polypropylene undergarments. This amazing synthetic fabric whisks perspiration away from the skin to prevent the cooling from evaporation from stripping moisture from the body.

Cotton or woolen underwear, on the other hand, will absorb sweat like a sponge. There it'll lie, damp and cold, against your skin.

All these layers may seem like a nuisance, but you can always remove some as you warm up. And they'll be there when you need them, as soon as the sun begins to drop or the wind begins to howl.

Actually, the greatest danger of frostbite for athletes isn't *during* exercise. "Athletes are generally producing so much body heat that they're not really at much risk while they're active," says Andrew Young, Ph.D., a research physiologist at the U.S. Army Research Institute of Environmental Medicine in Natick, Massachusetts. "The risk comes before and after exercise. That's when you have to be particularly careful."

First aid in the field

It's relatively easy to recognize the signs of frostbite—your skin will look white and opaque, and it'll feel cold to the touch. Don't massage it—you'll only increase the tissue damage. Nor should you rub the area with snow or ice—that, too, will only make things worse.

If you think you've been frostbitten, consider these suggestions from Dr. Young.

1. Get out of the cold if possible.
2. Remove wet or restrictive clothing.
3. Warm the frostbitten area by gently breathing on it or, even better, placing it next to warm skin.

4. Stick your fingers under your armpits or against your stomach. If
your feet are frostbitten, lay them across someone else's stomach.

Dr. Young cautions against placing the affected area in hot water or near
any artificial heat source.

"When the area is frostbitten, it won't have any sensation. You can actually cause it to burn and you won't even notice it," he explains. "The key is
to rewarm the affected part gradually. The safest, most effective way to do
that in the field is to put your frozen skin against nonfrozen skin."

Once you've done what you can, says Dr. Young, see a doctor as soon as
possible. Unless you have a lot of experience with frostbite, you can't tell
how serious the injury is just by looking at it.

See Also: *Hypothermia, Windchill*

Hamstring Pulls
The thigh that binds

*I*njury often seeks out the weakest link, which is precisely why playing
fields are littered with athletes suffering from sore hamstrings. When it
comes to conditioning, this muscle running down the back of your
upper leg is often neglected, and if you'll excuse the pun, the results can be
thigh-popping.

Most hamstring pulls occur because the hamstrings are overpowered by
the much stronger quadriceps muscles at the front of your leg. Muscle
groups work together when you're exercising. If one muscle is strong and
one isn't, the weaker muscle can be pushed past its limit. Endurance athletes are also especially vulnerable to hamstring pulls early in the season,
when the hamstrings are tight and weak and the mind is overzealous.

Hamstring problems are compounded by the fact that these muscles are
notoriously tight. Runners, for example, often have bow-tight hamstrings,
since the muscles go through a small range of motion during running. You
can increase the range of motion slightly by doing different kinds of running—fast and slow, uphill and downhill—but most experienced runners
address the hamstring dilemma through stretching and strengthening.

Strengthen those strings

The simplest hamstring stretch is probably familiar to you: Lie on your
back, keep your legs together and slowly bring them up and over your
head. Touch the floor behind you, if possible (never strain during any
stretch, particularly when it involves hamstrings).

For a variation, stand next to a waist-high table and, keeping both legs straight, put one leg on the table and bend your head toward your knee until you feel the strain. Hold for 15 to 30 seconds and repeat five or six times. When it comes to your hamstrings, a little stretching goes a long way.

Finding exercises that single out the hamstrings isn't easy, which explains why these muscles are often weak. Hamstring curls on a weight machine are probably the best specific strengthening exercise for this area.

What to do if you pull a hamstring? First, get off the leg. This is usually easy enough, since you'll feel as if someone's taken a blowtorch to the back of your thigh. Don't massage the leg right away, as rubbing will aggravate the injury. Immobilize the leg, ice it and wrap it as soon as possible.

Don't be a hero. Stay off the leg until the worst of the pain passes. Then—carefully!—try some light massage and stretching. Don't push too hard too soon. Remember, that's probably what got you into trouble in the first place.

Humidity
Managing the soggy swelter

I f you've ever exercised in hot, humid conditions, you might have an inkling of how Scott Molina felt during the run at the 1981 Hawaii Ironman Triathlon. After a 2.4-mile swim and a 112-mile bike ride on a swelteringly muggy Hawaiian day, the 21-year-old trailed race leader John Howard out onto the run. Molina pushed hard and began making up ground. Reports filtered back that Howard was struggling. Supremely fit, Molina, a strong runner, pushed harder.

It wasn't until about 13 miles into the marathon that Molina began feeling the effects of the heat and humidity. Leaden-legged, head buzzing, enveloped in a clammy-hot cocoon, Molina, one of the top triathletes in the sport, quit 17 miles into the run. He was carried back to the finish on a stretcher.

Although Molina's meltdown was caused partly by the oppressive heat, Hawaii's stifling humidity also played a feature role. We've already discussed how to manage heat. But humidity merits special attention. As Molina discovered, it can do you in if you're not prepared for it.

To stay cool, your body transfers heat from your core to the air. Blood is moved to the surface of the skin, where the heat can be relieved through sweating. Evaporative heat loss from the skin is the body's most important protection against heat stress.

Unfortunately, high humidity can prevent this evaporation as effectively as smothering your skin with a wet towel. When heat can't be dissipated quickly enough through evaporation, your internal temperature skyrockets. You've got to slow down or stop, or risk heatstroke.

If you're stubborn but particularly lucky, your body may intervene. Molina's saved him by dropping him face-first onto the pavement.

Meeting humidity head-on

While you can't avoid humidity, you can prepare for it. Your first priority is to get used to humidity before you race or train in humid conditions. It sounds simple, but like many simple rules, it's often ignored.

"If you're going to race in the heat, you have to train in the heat," says Dave Scott, who won six Hawaii Ironmans by combining talent with consummate preparation, including long training sessions in hot, humid conditions.

Humidity's effects can also be warded off with the same ploys you use to combat heat. Drink plenty of fluids. Wear light-colored clothing that breathes easily and a visor or an airy hat to keep your head cool.

And take advantage of aid stations. Grab the water they offer and pour it over your skin. On long training runs or rides, spray yourself with the water bottle you should always carry. If you're short on water, watch for hoses and spigots; it's better to clamber across someone's front lawn than to collapse in their flower beds.

On the bright side, you may be better prepared than you think. Some people simply sweat more efficiently. We're all genetically endowed with a certain number of sweat glands; a healthy supply can help carry you through humid conditions.

The fitter you are, the better you'll be able to handle heat and humidity. You'll begin sweating earlier and sweat faster, both of which help dissipate body heat.

Still, in some conditions of soggy swelter, even genetics and preparation might not be enough to save you. If you're dizzy, confused or experiencing cramps, nausea or clammy skin, don't be a hero. Play your trump card: Common sense.

See Also: *Acclimatization, Cramps, Dehydration, Electrolytes, Hyperthermia*

Hyperthermia
Heading toward meltdown

P erhaps the most startling case of hyperthermia on record involved U.S. marathon great Alberto Salazar. Running in the 9.6-mile Falmouth Road Race on Cape Cod, Massachusetts, Salazar crossed the finish on a hot, muggy day and collapsed. He was rushed to the medical tent, then to the hospital, where he was eventually given the last rites of the Catholic Church. His rectal temperature was said to be in excess of 106°F.

Fortunately, Salazar survived. But his close call illustrates possibly the most serious risk faced by competitive endurance athletes.

Hyperthermia is the extreme elevation of your body's internal, or core, temperature. Damage from hyperthermia can range from heat exhaustion, which can seriously impair performance, to life-threatening heatstroke. Severe heat injury occurs when the body's core temperature rises over 104°F.

Even under normal circumstances, your body's internal fires burn hot. Strenuous exercise stokes these fires as effectively as putting a match over a gas jet. When vigorous exercise produces energy for muscle contraction, it also releases up to 20 times as much heat as you generate at rest. Theoretically, this is enough to raise your core temperature one degree centigrade for every five minutes of activity.

Obviously, this doesn't happen—if it did, exercise of any sort would be a risky business, and endurance exercise would be fatal. Your body damps these metabolic fires through an effective cooling system that makes use of four interrelated processes: conduction, radiation, convection and evaporation. Compromise any one of these cooling mechanisms and heat injury can result.

To avoid hyperthermia, you'll want to understand how each of these cooling mechanisms works. The science part might be dry, but understanding these processes could someday be your ticket to survival.

Cooling down the skin

Both conduction and radiation transfer heat directly from the surface of your skin to the cooler air or water surrounding you. Each process can be effectively demonstrated. If you stand waist-deep in a cold swimming pool for 30 minutes, you'll get a good idea of how conduction works. The contact and the movement of water against your skin will rapidly move away body heat. Even in warm water, after 15 to 20 minutes your body loses more heat than it's producing. After 30 minutes, you'll have raised quite a few goosebumps and be thoroughly chilled.

Indeed, water conducts heat away from the body 25 times more efficiently than air. But let's not underestimate the efficiency of body heat radiating into the surrounding air. Just stand close to runners after they've finished a hard 10-K run and feel the heat radiating from their bodies.

Convection is the process of heat dissipating on the move; water or air passing across your skin whisks away body heat. Use a fan on a hot summer day and you'll feel convection at work.

We've saved evaporation for last because it's by far the most active and important method of cooling. Again, the mechanism is simple. Sweat evaporating from your skin cools the blood moving through tiny vessels under the skin's surface. Like coolant moving through a car's radiator, the blood circulating through your body collects heat from the interior tissues and organs in the body's core, then takes it to the skin's surface to be cooled.

Keeping water in

Most of the water streaming from your pores as sweat is part of your blood plasma, the clear portion of the blood. In fact, endurance athletes can lose around two quarts of perspiration an hour during vigorous exercise, siphoning away precious blood plasma at an alarming rate. When plasma decreases in volume, circulation slows and leaves less water available for the perspiration's cooling effects.

In addition, overworked sweat glands can fizzle out and stop producing perspiration, setting the scene for dehydration and hyperthermia. Losing just 2 percent of your body weight in fluid can cause your performance to taper off dramatically. Only by drinking can you replace this water.

Unfortunately, endurance contests often take place in hot, sunny, humid, windless arenas. This amalgam of conditions can combine to undermine your body's cooling system as effectively as taking a chisel to your radiator. Because circulating air is hotter than your body temperature, heat is conducted inward. Without a breeze, you have no means of moving heat off your skin.

True, humidity ensures that you'll have less evaporation of sweat from your skin. But you'll still sweat profusely, losing valuable moisture.

The best way to cope? Forget about setting a personal record. Slow your pace. You'll have to judge precisely how much you'll slow—everyone reacts differently to the heat. If you start feeling the first serious signs of overheating—shivering, goosebumps, chills—you should stop.

Since you're sweating profusely, it's also crucial to drink as much as you can. It's better to weather a sloshing stomach than find yourself in the medical tent.

Recognizing hyperthermia

Anyone involved in hot-weather exercise must learn to recognize hyperthermia's telltale signs.

Heat exhaustion comes first. Distinct signs include shivering, goosebumps or chills, dry, clammy skin, headache, nausea and an inability to sweat.

The most intelligent way to deal with heat exhaustion is to stop, get something to drink and find some shade. If you feel light-headed and think you might faint, find help quickly.

Err on the safe side. Don't push on and hope the discomfort will go away—heat exhaustion can quickly escalate to heatstroke, and by the time it does, you probably won't be in any shape to comprehend the danger.

Heatstroke is characterized by severe disorientation, loss of consciousness and convulsions. The condition can be fatal, and the popular practice of encouraging a stumbling, glassy-eyed, rubber-legged marathoner to cross the finish line is recognized by the sportsmedicine community as utter folly *and* a prelude to potential disaster. Ask Alberto Salazar.

If you suspect someone is suffering from heatstroke, lay the person on his or her back, elevate the feet and bathe the head, face, neck and shoulders with water—as cold as possible. If ice is available, wrap it in a T-shirt or towel and place it under the victim's armpits. Get medical help immediately.

Preventing hyperthermia

High heat and humidity present special problems for the endurance athlete. When the thermometer starts to climb, keep these thoughts in mind.

- Drink often during training and racing. Don't wait until you're thirsty. By then, your body is fighting a losing battle.
- Prehydrate aggressively during the week before a hot-weather race. Your urine should be colorless and abundant.
- If you know you're going to race in the heat, try to get acclimated. Don't leave your home in Anchorage the day before the Hawaii Ironman Triathlon and expect your body to adjust.
- Don't substitute showers, sprinklers and cold sponges for drinking. They feel good, but studies show they have only a marginal effect on lowering your body's core temperature.
- Wear ventilated shade on your head. Use a visor or thin fabric hat that allows air to get through. Since 40 percent of your body's heat is lost through the head and neck, it's crucial that air circulate around your head.
- Wear white or light-colored, loose-fitting clothing that reflects sunlight and allows air to circulate. Black spandex has its place—on the bodies of those perky types conducting the prerace aerobics clinic.
- Adjust your pace according to the weather. Don't push for a personal record in the heat. Don't be a hero. Your body knows better than you do when you've gone too far. Listen to it.
- Take extra precautions if the humidity is over 50 percent.
- Run, walk or ride—and, if need be, rest—in the shade when possible. If

you have a choice, run on a blacktop road surface, which absorbs heat, rather than on a cement sidewalk, which reflects it.

See Also: *Dehydration, Electrolytes*

Hypoglycemia
Avoiding the sugar crash

*M*any a grand tale has been told of cycling's grueling 2,000-plus-mile Tour de France. Some of the lesser tales are interesting, too. The one, for instance, of the cyclist who found himself without food in the middle of a long stage. Desperate, the cyclist moved through the pack, trying to obtain food from his fellow riders. Finally he procured a peanut butter sandwich. A sage competitor, he recognized the sandwich for what it was—a condensed source of carbohydrate and a sorely needed dose of glucose for his body's hungry muscles. So he was willing to pay the price—$150 for the sandwich.

Glucose is what fuels our efforts, and when it goes, so do we—which is what makes hypoglycemia, or low levels of glucose in the body, a problem for the endurance athlete who neglects his or her energy stores.

Here's what happens. As you exercise, your muscles use glucose for energy. A certain amount of glucose is already stored in the muscles as glycogen. The rest is siphoned from the blood. The amount of glucose present in the blood is regulated by the liver. If there's a need for more glucose, the liver jettisons it into the bloodstream, where the glucose can be rushed to its destination.

The problem is, your liver's stores of glycogen are very limited—it holds only about 90 grams. Glycogen reserves are almost completely depleted after about 1½ hours of continuous exercise.

If you've ever been caught short on energy supplies like our unfortunate cyclist, you're probably familiar with the signs of glycogen depletion. You feel weak and dizzy. Your thinking turns fuzzy. Your coordination is slightly off.

Why? Because your central nervous system, most notably your brain, depends almost entirely on blood glucose for energy. Your brain is sending an urgent message to your body to slow—or stop—activity so you'll conserve your remaining precious energy reserves.

In other words, you're "bonking" or "hitting the Wall."

Smooth out your sugar levels

If you're running a 10-K, hypoglycemia isn't a threat. If you're competing in an event that lasts two hours or more, hypoglycemia should be of some concern, but there's no need to be obsessed.

In fact, hypoglycemia is more of a threat to the sugar-scarfing slug than it is to the athlete, says exercise physiologist Mary O'Toole, Ph.D., director of the University of Tennessee's Human Performance Laboratory in Memphis.

"Hypoglycemia in the general population usually is a result of a reaction of perhaps too much insulin to simple sugars," says Dr. O'Toole. "But when you're exercising, you're burning the sugar that you take in, so that's not really a problem."

Maintaining your blood sugar levels during competition is easy, points out Dr. O'Toole. Just make sure you eat and drink during the race. Experienced athletes know this. After the Hawaii Ironman Triathlon, Dr. O'Toole took blood samples from the athletes. Most of them finished with slightly high blood sugar levels. Experience had taught them to be conscientious about their carbohydrate intake, both before and during the race.

Hypoglycemia can be easily avoided with a bit of planning. Three to four hours before the event, eat a meal high in carbohydrates.

Do not, however, stuff down carbs just before the event's start. Wolfing large amounts of glucose might provoke an insulin reaction. Your body, reacting to the onrush of high glucose levels, will secrete insulin to quickly lower those levels. This is precisely what slows you down after finishing off a box of bon bons, and it's precisely what you don't want. Studies indicate there may be an advantage to eating a small, energy-rich snack or swigging a small carbohydrate drink five minutes or so before the start.

Once out on the field of play, the ground rules are little different from the ones around the Thanksgiving table—eat and drink as much as you can hold. If you're in a triathlon, eating solid food isn't that difficult—do it on the bike where there's less jarring. If you're running a marathon, you can get more than enough carbohydrate from a sports drink. Should you choose to run something longer, drinks alone won't be enough—you'll need to start eating, too.

If you start to feel wobbly, a glucose drink can have a remarkably quick effect, restoring your blood sugar concentration within minutes. Incidentally, when it comes to eating and drinking, find out what works best for you during training.

A final important point. You can also help stave off hypoglycemia by adopting a sane pace. Take off at the start like a sailor freed for shore leave and you'll eat up your glycogen reserves right quick. Push at a moderate pace and you'll burn mostly fat for energy and maintain those blood sugar levels.

See Also: ***Bonking, Carbohydrate, Glucose and Glycogen, The Wall***

Hypothermia
Don't chill out

M ark Allen, triathlete extraordinaire, offers a case study of hypothermia. The event: a triathlon in Malibu, California, before the advent of wet-suits. The problem: a water temperature of 59°F.

"When we started back toward shore, my arms started feeling numb," says Allen. "It was as if my brain was telling my arms to do something, but the muscles wouldn't respond. Then my mind started getting foggy, and I started getting water in my mouth—I just couldn't control it. I had to turn over on my back so that I could breathe. It was scary. I'd swim for a while and then call for help, but there was no one around, so I just kept swimming. I'd never experienced cold like that before. I didn't know where I was."

Allen stumbled from the water, mounted his bike like a confused drunk and wobbled off. Soon after, he called it a day.

When it comes to endurance sport, hypothermia—the lowering of the body's core temperature to below 95°F—is most often associated with swimming. The reason is simple. Unless you're swimming at the Y, water temperatures generally hover well below your normal body temperature of 98.6°F. Even in warm water, after the first 15 to 20 minutes of immersion your body loses more heat than it produces.

To compound the problem, the body loses heat even faster while moving through the water. The convective effects of swimming cause the body to cool 35 to 50 percent faster than if floating motionless in the water.

This is precisely why survival experts recommend that people hoping to survive in cold water move only enough to keep themselves afloat. Moving your arms and legs increases the circulation of blood to your extremities, where the surrounding water promptly sucks it away.

When it comes to hypothermia, these same survival experts like to quote a sobering ditty they call the "50-50-50 formula." In 50°F water, 50 percent of the people will be dead in 50 minutes. While this is an alarming statistic, it also indicates the tremendous possible variation in how people will react to water's heat-sapping effects.

Experiencing hypothermia

Your body's first line of defense against cold is a process called "vasoconstriction." The blood vessels leading to your fingers, hands, toes and feet narrow, reducing circulation to those areas and minimizing heat loss. In a sense, your body is performing a kind of self-triage; in order to preserve your brain, heart and other vital organs, it sacrifices expendable parts.

Shivering comes next—again, a natural defense. Sensing cold, receptors near the skin send signals to your brain. Your brain instructs your muscles to generate heat by contracting and relaxing in rapid succession. Presto, you're shivering.

As your core temperature dips below 95°F, shivering becomes intense and your extremities, deprived of blood, go numb. At about this time, you will also experience the first signs of mental impairment; the "fogginess" that turned Allen panicky in the waters off Malibu. This is particularly danger-ous, since your sense of direction may also disappear.

When your core temperature falls below 90°F, shivering stops and the muscles become rigid. Disorientation becomes acute. Core temperatures below 86°F can be fatal, since your ability to deal with the situation is either severely impaired or missing altogether. Core temperatures below 78°F are fatal.

Most of us will never face life-threatening hypothermic conditions, but it's important to realize that hypothermia can come on subtly and quickly.

And it's not just a threat to swimmers. Hypothermia can also occur among landlubbers. Watch for signs on a cold day at the Boston Marathon, as hundreds of shivering runners peer woefully out from beneath Mylar blankets at the finish line.

In general, simply exercising won't guarantee that you'll avoid the effects of cold water or frigid weather. When your pace drops so low that you're no longer generating enough heat to keep warm, the process of hypothermia has begun.

Preventing hypothermia: clothing

On dry land the solution is simple, but like most simple solutions, it's often ignored. Wear warm clothing and plenty of it. Layer your clothing and make sure it's loose-fitting so air can circulate. Peel it off and put it on as the need arises. Think ahead, especially when it comes to long workouts. It's an unhappy cyclist who strikes out on a bright, sunny morning for a 100-mile ride wearing a T-shirt, only to ride into a cold, wet afternoon.

In the water, where the risk of hypothermia is at its greatest, remember that up to 40 percent of your body's heat can be lost through your head and neck. Even if the water is warm, it's a good idea to wear a swim cap. When the water temperature drops below 70°F, you might want to replace the cap with a neoprene wetsuit hood.

Wetsuits have revolutionized open-water swimming. The premise behind them is simple. First, the water enters the suit. Then, trapped between the rubber and your skin, it's warmed by your body heat, enveloping you in a body-temperature cocoon. For that reason, you should pay close attention to fit. A wetsuit should fit snugly—you don't want water flushing through your suit unimpeded—but it should be loose enough to allow for mobility.

When in doubt, go for the wetsuit. As long as you keep moving, it'll keep you warm in all but the most frigid conditions.

It'll also help you swim faster. Because wetsuits are buoyant, they relieve you of your struggle to stay afloat, allowing you to channel those energies into swimming forward. This might offend your sense of fair play—until you arrive at the start of your next open-water swim sans wetsuit and see that everyone else is wearing one.

Preventing hypothermia: tactics

On land, keeping an even pace can go a long way toward preventing hypothermia. Hikers, climbers and other experienced cold-weather sorts know that it's important to work at a level that keeps you warm but doesn't have you sweating profusely. Wet clothing can turn damp; when you stop moving, it can freeze.

For virtually the same reason, pace is also important for cold-weather athletes. Starting fast and then slowing to a crawl is a sure way to bring on hypothermia.

In the water, the best way to combat the cold is by keeping your cool. Exercise physiologists and military cold-weather experts have found a direct correlation between anxiety and the ability to tolerate cold. Simply put, mind does matter. If you dwell on your discomfort or dread the cold in advance, you goad your body into a state of heightened tension. This forces your circulatory system to work overtime and you lose more heat—precisely what you don't want.

Therefore, try to relax. It might be reassuring to consider a consoling piece of open-water history. In 1875, Englishman Matthew Webb became the first person to swim the English Channel. Webb not only survived, he thrived—despite the fact that his swim took almost 22 hours in water averaging 60°F.

See Also: *Open-Water Swimming*

Iliotibial Band Friction Syndrome
More than a pain in the knee

*T*his condition may be a mouthful, but plenty of athletes can pronounce it flawlessly. Unfortunately, iliotibial band friction syndrome—better known as IT band syndrome—is fairly common among endurance athletes.

The iliotibial band is a thick, strong sheet of connective tissue on the outside of the knee. Along with two muscles—the collateral ligament and the biceps femoris—the IT band supports the outside of the knee.

What brings on this syndrome? In most cases, a mechanical problem in your stride shifts the band slightly and makes it rub over the bony outside of the knee. You might start a run feeling fine, but as the IT band rubs over the bone and the friction increases, the band stiffens. And so does your knee.

Leg length differences (surprisingly common) are one possible cause. Bowed legs and high-arched, rigid feet can also produce IT band friction. Shoes that absorb shock poorly might also contribute to the problem.

IT band problems are painfully apparent—as soon as you start to run, you'll feel a sharp, localized pain in the area of your kneecap. Yet the pain will disappear as soon as you stop. La Jolla, California, sports podiatrist Joe Ellis, D.P.M., explains that the pain ends when the IT band is no longer rubbing over the bony outside of your knee. It'll recur, he promises, with a vengeance, as soon as you start running again. And downhill running will aggravate the pain even more.

Treat the knee with ice several times a day. Anti-inflammatories—aspirin or ibuprofen—can also help, but don't rely on them too heavily. By masking the discomfort, they may have you pummeling your injury before it's had a chance to heal.

You can also stretch to loosen the IT band. Timothy Noakes, M.D., of the University of Cape Town Medical School in South Africa, recommends two stretches to improve your IT band's flexibility.

1. While standing, place all your weight on your injured leg. Bend your upper body toward the uninjured leg without twisting your trunk. Do this for ten minutes once daily.
2. While sitting, place both hands on your injured knee. Then pull the knee gently across your body toward the opposite armpit. Do this for ten minutes daily, as well.

The actual mechanics that bring on IT band friction syndrome aren't yet fully understood. What *is* known is what aggravates it. Spare yourself and avoid the following:

- Downhill running.
- Sloped surfaces.
- Sudden increases in mileage.
- Excessive hard running.
- Hard surfaces.

Of course, these are all short-term solutions. To rid yourself completely of IT band syndrome, you'll need to identify what's causing it.

The onset of IT band syndrome can involve a number of factors. It's a complex injury. If you suspect you have this problem, don't be a hero. See a sports podiatrist.

And don't expect miracles. Unlike runner's knee and shin splints, which respond quickly to treatment, IT band friction syndrome can drag on for some time. Tap into your reserves of that sterling quality, patience, and let time help you heal.

Iron Deficiency
Not an equal-opportunity threat

*I*ron deficiency may be the most common nutritional deficiency in the world. Fortunately, for athletes, it's usually easily remedied. Most cases of iron deficiency result from a simple problem: low intake and high losses of the nutrient.

Endurance athletes are notorious for poor diets, perhaps because they believe that athletic efforts make them impervious to harm. Yet all athletes need their iron. It helps their metabolism work more efficiently, keeps up energy levels, boosts resistance to infection and keeps body temperature steady during exposure to cold.

Some research also indicates that iron deficiency can affect performance. "We used to think marginal iron deficiency had no effect on performance," says Susan Kleiner, Ph.D., a Cleveland-area nutrition specialist. "More recently, we've seen a significant effect in endurance athletes."

This should come as no surprise, since iron's a key player in moving oxygen through the blood. An essential trace mineral, it helps to form both hemoglobin (the oxygen-carrying component in red blood cells) and myoglobin (which ensures that your muscles can use oxygen). Any athlete who wants to work at peak performance won't lose time in correcting iron deficiency, if it exists.

Iron deficiency and athletes

How much of a problem can iron deficiency pose for athletes? A serious one, says Dr. Kleiner. "Iron is a big issue with athletes, particularly endurance athletes and women trying to keep a low body weight." Certain sports, she points out, such as figure skating, long-distance running and swimming, invite low body weight. Athletes in these areas have been known to run into problems of iron deficiency.

Women, she continues, are at special risk for iron deficiency. During their menstrual cycles alone, women can lose between 0.4 and 0.7 milligram of iron. Couple this with an iron-deficient diet, and the losses can mount up.

Diet is certainly one culprit. But there may be others. Experts are now studying the possible link between iron deficiency and "percussive exercise." This could be a potential risk factor for long-distance runners and others whose feet hit the ground repeatedly. Some studies of male runners have found that red blood cells explode in the feet during these long runs, depleting the body of some iron stores.

A third possible link to iron deficiency may be—of all things—sweat. Think about it. Endurance athletes who train and compete in hot weather may be losing a considerable amount of iron through sweat.

In one study observing male and female athletes who had worked up a sweat, Emily Haymes, Ph.D., professor of nutrition, food and movement sciences at Florida State University in Gainesville, found that the men sweated more profusely. But the iron levels in the women's perspiration were higher. And so, presumably, were the women's iron losses.

Why this is so is not yet understood. Nor is it clear how much iron is lost through sweat over specific periods of time.

Boost your Iron-Q

Becoming savvy about iron deficiency is your best chance of preventing it. First, find out where you fall in the spectrum of iron deficiency (if you're there at all). There are three levels—iron depletion (the mildest), iron-deficiency erythropoiesis (cause for concern) and iron-deficiency anemia (serious).

How can you tell if you're iron deficient? It's not easy. The overt signs—fatigue, listlessness and pallor—don't usually appear until your iron stores are almost completely depleted.

A blood test can ferret out iron deficiency earlier, but many athletes don't think about getting a blood test until unusual fatigue sounds an alarm. For that reason, Dr. Haymes suggests that endurance athletes get an annual blood test to check their blood iron levels.

One caution about blood tests, however. The standard version doesn't usually reflect the amount of *stored* iron in the body. "These only measure the red blood cells per volume of blood," Dr. Kleiner explains. "You'll need to measure iron stores with a more sophisticated test called a 'serum transserin' test, which your physician can order for you."

Still, the best way to address iron deficiency is to prevent it in the first place. And, for the most part, diet can go a long way to correct an existing problem.

"Proper diet is the key preventive measure," affirms Dr. Haymes.

Do you often wolf down lots of empty calories, such as sugary sodas and snacks? If so, give your iron intake a bit more attention. Meat, such as lean beef or dark meat from poultry, is a good source of readily absorbable heme iron. In fact, iron from red meat, fish and poultry is readily taken into the body.

If you're a vegetarian, you'll have to learn which nonmeat sources are richest in iron. Iron from vegetables is absorbed relatively poorly. Better sources include fortified breakfast cereals, dried fruits, dried beans and legumes. Some recommend cooking acidic foods, such as tomatoes, in a cast-iron skillet. The theory—still being debated—is that iron from the skillet is drawn into the acidic substance.

You can also enhance your iron absorption by including vitamin C–rich foods with your meal. When these are combined with vegetable sources of iron, chemical changes occur in the iron to increase its absorption by the body. If you're not a vegetarian, adding a small amount of meat will increase iron absorption even more.

Supplement wisely

What about iron supplements? If you're concerned about low iron intake, take a multivitamin/mineral supplement, says Dr. Kleiner. However, she cautions, don't let the supplement exceed the Recommended Dietary Allowance for iron. For women under age 50, it's 25 milligrams; for men, it's 10 milligrams.

Too much iron, in fact, can be poisonous, as stores building up in the liver could lead to a toxic reaction.

And watch what you take with your iron. Dr. Kleiner points out that high-potency wheat or oat bran cereals can interfere with the absorption of iron. And certain supplements, such as zinc, torpedo the body's attempts to take in iron. Your iron intake can even be sabotaged by lots of tea-drinking. Tea contains tannins, which block iron absorption.

The solution: Take your iron at a different time of day.

Is your iron really low?

Endurance athletes will be especially interested in a point raised by Priscilla M. Clarkson, Ph.D., a professor in the Department of Exercise Science at the University of Massachusetts in Boston. She explains that, although tests may show otherwise, some "low" iron blood levels diagnosed in athletes may not be low at all.

Plasma volume can expand from endurance training. When this occurs, there's no actual decrease in iron—the red blood cells containing iron are simply scattered about in a larger volume of plasma.

Most physicians are aware of this phenomenon, Dr. Clarkson emphasizes, but if they aren't, an endurance athlete might be falsely diagnosed as anemic, or iron deficient.

"These athletes have the same number of red blood cells as anybody else, but because their plasma volume is expanded, it may look as if there are fewer blood cells," Dr. Clarkson explains. "They may not be iron deficient at all."

In fact, a slight iron deficiency could be preferable to having too much iron. A 1992 study from Finland has brought grim tidings about *high* levels of iron in men. It revealed that high iron levels in the blood predicted an even greater risk of heart disease than did high cholesterol. This study could overturn current theories of heart-disease predictors.

The bottom line, as always, is the adage we all heard while growing up. "Moderation in all things" can be particularly applied to our approach to iron intake.

Obsession
Too much of a good thing

O ver the course of his career, professional triathlete Mike Pigg's dedication to training became legendary. Once, early in his career, Pigg faced a dilemma. His day called for a morning fishing trip and an afternoon wedding. Pigg wanted to get in his bike ride, so he hauled his bicycle onto the fishing boat that morning, windtrainer in tow. By the time the boat was under way, Pigg was cycling away, firmly ensconced on the bow. To keep himself from leaving the deck, Pigg grabbed the anchor winch and rode and bucked.

Eventually, the engineer, realizing Pigg wasn't going to travel conventionally, came out and lashed Pigg's handlebar down. Pigg spun out for 45 minutes, dismounted long enough to catch two good-sized salmon, then spun back in again. He went to the afternoon wedding, cooled it on his beer consumption and went running that night.

On hearing that story, an older and wiser Dave Scott, six-time Hawaii Ironman Triathlon winner, simply shook his head.

"I used to do that sort of thing," says Scott, "but now I'd leave the windtrainer at home and go fishing."

Both Pigg and Scott are professionals in a sport that requires a bit of obsession. The truth is, few worthwhile things in life are accomplished with a nonchalant attitude and half-hearted effort.

Still there's a dark side to obsession, and sport often seems to have cornered the market. Take the Los Angeles Raiders fan who, in one three-month period, spent $24,000 on game tickets, airplane travel and team memorabilia—money he stole in 24 bank robberies. Apprehended, the thief expressed a skewed sense of remorse. "I've embarrassed the team," the shame-faced man told the press.

A cautionary tale

Obsession, of course, isn't limited to spectators. The fitness boom of the 1970s created a cadre of obsessed athletes who, attracted by the health benefits of exercise, suddenly found they couldn't survive without their daily workout.

Endurance sports like triathlon, running and cycling seemed to attract the majority of these folks, who left a trail of ruined careers and broken marriages in their wake. Here's one tale, reflective of obsession as it applies to sport.

Bill Hippe's immersion in triathlon began innocently enough. In the summer of 1983, both his parents died. Upset by their deaths and his subsequent 50-pound weight gain, Hippe began a self-improvement program.

First he revised his diet. Then he began to exercise. His goal was simply to upgrade his general fitness level.

In the summer of 1984, Hippe competed in his first triathlon. He enjoyed it and trained harder. The next year, he placed sixth in the 35-to-39 age group.

Fueled by his success, Hippe got serious. He took on a cycling coach and a running coach. He also began training with top triathletes. Within three years, he was hooked on fitness. He called fitness experts for advice from home, while on the road—even at the pool. He averaged ten miles of swimming, 250 to 350 miles of cycling, and 40 to 50 miles of running a week.

In the spring of 1989, Hippe lost his job. "I was let go because I wasn't doing my work," he admits. A friend took him in when he couldn't afford his rent.

The crises continued. While running in a 10-K, Hippe sprained his ankle, then tried to run on it without adequate rest. This led to injuries severe enough to end his running and biking activities.

Finally, Hippe took stock of his life. He'd lost his job. He was hobbled by surgery on both ankles. He was 39 and unable to afford his own apartment. "I didn't realize how far I'd let other parts of my life slide until near the end," he says.

Hippe's story has a happy ending. Today, he's employed and planning marriage, and he avoids racing like the plague.

For others who might be tempted to follow the same path, Hippe has simple advice. "Sit back and look at the whole picture. If sport's your only focus, something needs to be changed."

Granted, Hippe represents the extreme. But the line between dedication and obsession can be a thin one.

Is your addiction positive?

On the other hand, psychiatrist and author William Glasser, M.D., calls the single-minded devotion to sports "positive addiction." In his book of the same name, Dr. Glasser encourages his readers to become addicted to running. Running, he writes, produces a healthy, non-self-critical state that leads to personal fulfillment and more.

"Will positive addiction save the world?" Dr. Glasser asks. "I doubt it, but I'm sure more of it would help."

Perhaps. But Dr. Glasser's book also quotes several runners whose pursuit of personal fulfillment has turned them into myopic exercise fanatics. They become depressed, guilty and angry if they miss a single run. This is hardly the stuff of positive addiction.

Obsession does have its place. While hanging onto the face of Half Dome in Yosemite National Park, a climber needs myopic focus. Those of us engaged in less life-threatening pursuits, however, need to draw the line.

Recognize the warning signs

Are there warning signs you can watch for to prevent obsession from taking hold? Definitely, says Joel Kirsch, Ph.D., sports psychologist and head of the American Sports Institute in Mill Valley, California. If you train when you're injured, if your training schedule is jeopardizing your family life and personal relationships, if you get edgy when you have to miss training, you could be heading for trouble.

"Those are all signs that you're carrying things too far," says Dr. Kirsch, "that you're fixated on your sport. Anything that interferes with your health or personal relationships in a negative way is an obsession."

That's not to say, he amends, that you shouldn't push your limits. Without such dedication, there'd be no Hawaii Ironman Triathlon or Western States 100.

"Remember, we used to think that women couldn't run marathons," Dr. Kirsch points out. "A lot of psychologists will see somebody who runs 100 miles and brand that person 'obsessed.' Not so. The person's simply testing his or her limits. However, if that person runs despite injuries or breaks up a marriage in the process, it's gotten out of hand."

If you fear you might be obsessive about exercise, the cure is simple. Break the cycle.

"Habits are tough to form and tough to break," says Dr. Kirsch, "but you have to break them if they're hurting you."

Despite the extremes of dedication required by professional athletes, coauthor Scott Tinley maintains a healthy balance in his life and a witty view of obsession. Here's his tongue-in-cheek list of warning signs of obsessive tendencies. Although it's on the light side, keep in mind that the list has serious underpinnings.

Tinley says you're obsessed when:

- You look forward to the Super Bowl because you know no one will be at the pool that afternoon.
- In any given year, you spend more time on your bike than in your car.
- The number of running shoes on your front porch rivals the number in Imelda Marcos's closet.
- Your idea of a dream vacation is going to compete at the New York City Marathon.
- You come back from a long weekend ride and your son asks your spouse who the sweaty person in the kitchen is.

The best athletes learn to keep their passion in perspective. They don't run on sore tendons. They don't dwell on the 15th mile of their last marathon over Thanksgiving dinner. You can't be focused on your sport all the time. If you try, you'll end up burning out and stopping altogether. It's better to realize that balance is ultimately more satisfying than doing that extra mile.

See Also: *Goal Setting, Overtraining, Prioritizing*

Overtraining
Knowing when to fold

Many dedicated endurance athletes don't need to be told what to do—they need to be told what *not* to do. Training for a marathon, a century bike ride or an Ironman triathlon would seem to indicate excessive measures. In fact, overtraining is almost part and parcel of pushing the endurance envelope. It's a fine line that separates good, solid training from illness, fatigue and recurring injury.

How much should you train? How hard? How fast? How often? What should you eat? When should you rest? Unfortunately, there are no specific guidelines—the answers to these questions are as varied as the thousands of people who ask them. Plus, the whole equation is skewed by the age-old endurance question—how can you identify your limits if you're not willing to step over the line once in a while?

"In order to perform well, you need to push the envelope," says former British track star Francis Nettle, M.D., now director of sportsmedicine at the U.S. Marine Recruit Depot in San Diego. "You have to stress the body enough for it to respond—and sometimes you go too far. It's often a matter of trial and error."

Even the most experienced athletes fall into patterns that lead to overtraining. The trick is to recognize the symptoms as soon as they appear, then ease off and make the necessary adjustments before all your hard work goes down the drain.

When workouts lose their luster

If you stop caring about your workouts, if it's a chore to get up in the morning and head out the door to run, if you'd rather have a root canal than get on your bike, you're probably overtrained. Flagging motivation is one of the first signs that you've gone too far.

Which is not to say you should be ecstatically approaching each and every workout, seven days a week. But if you regularly have to talk yourself into exercising, or you've felt your energy level plummet into chronic fatigue—be warned.

In one study of overtrained cyclists, a number of symptoms popped up, including a decline in performance and a lower sense of well-being. Heart rate during sleep rose significantly, while heart rate during exercise tests dropped.

Coauthor Scott Tinley admits that he, too, has been excessive in his exercise habits at times. When his wife, Virginia, was in the hospital expecting their first child, Tinley awaited the onset of her labor outdoors—on a 20-mile run.

He's put together his own list of symptoms of overtraining. If you suspect you're pushing yourself too hard, check off any of the following that might apply. Then reconsider your schedule. It may be a tad too ambitious right now.

- Your pulse rate when you wake up in the morning is more than ten beats per minute faster than normal (get in the habit of taking your resting pulse each morning—it only takes a minute, and it's a good measure of your current fitness as well as a potential warning sign of overtraining).
- You've been suffering from recurring colds; minor cuts and scrapes haven't been healing as quickly; your body temperature is slightly elevated—all signs that your body's immune defenses are down and you need rest.
- Injuries keep popping up—minor muscle strains and pulls and stress fractures, for example.
- Your weight drops suddenly.
- Your appetite wavers. You have to force yourself to eat.
- Your muscles are sore for days at a time.
- You're irritable and out of sorts.
- You feel as if you're working harder than ever, but your racing and training times are slowing.
- Your arms and legs feel heavy and your coordination is slightly off. You just can't seem to bounce back from yesterday's workout.
- You have trouble sleeping, or your sleeping pattern changes abruptly.

When stress throws you a curve

What many athletes fail to realize, says Tinley, is that overtraining and its miseries can result from a barrage of wearing stresses—not just excessive exercise. In fact, you don't have to train much at all to experience overtraining.

"Overtraining's not simply the result of too much physical training," says Tinley. "It's a situation where the weight of everyday stresses—work, family, health—exceeds your body's ability to recover and cope. Your whole system gets out of balance. You may have a relatively light training load but a huge amount of stress at work. The result is overtraining."

Pinpointing the physiological roots of overtraining is almost impossible. You could be suffering from chronic glycogen depletion, or dehydration, or electrolyte imbalances, or any one of a number of nutritional deficiencies.

Overtraining is usually the result of weeks of stress, but it can also be triggered by your failure to recover from a single strenuous event. You compete in a marathon. You take a day or two off. You start training again for your next race and, pow, exhaustion hits you like a 16-wheel Peterbilt.

Treat yourself to time off

The best cure for overtraining is rest. Take a few days off. Watch television. Come home from work, grab a beer and gab with your neighbor. Write to a college roommate. Rest easy; you're losing virtually no conditioning.

"An easy rule of thumb is that you get about a 1 percent decrease in physiological function for every day that you lay off," says John Duncan, Ph.D., associate director of the Exercise Physiology Department at the Cooper Institute for Aerobics Research in Dallas. "A few days off is hardly something to be concerned about."

In fact, the best athletes take days off all the time.

"To stay motivated, it's essential you take time off," says five-time Ironman champion Paula Newby-Fraser. "Before you become injured or miserable or burned out, take a break. When you come back, you'll be fresh and eager to train. I take days off all the time, even during the peak of the season. Everyone needs that."

If you insist on training, says Newby-Fraser, at least make it fun. She likes doing 90 percent of her training with partners. "By making it social, it's so much easier and more pleasant," she says. "It's 100 percent easier to push out the door."

And if Newby-Fraser's group pushes out the door only to find out they're tired and don't feel like training, they don't.

"We'll cut it short," says Newby-Fraser, smiling, "and go for breakfast."

If your energy level doesn't bounce back after a few days off and you're still feeling run down and tired after a week, you might want to see a doctor. Exercise puts tremendous stress on your body. You could be harboring a virus. Or you could be low on iron—a fairly common deficiency in endurance athletes.

If you're seriously overtrained, it could be weeks, even months, before you fully recover. Be patient. Accept the consequences of a hard-earned lesson. And remember—the most effective training comes from hard effort, followed by adequate recovery. If you don't recover, you can't push on to new levels.

"The process of restoration is where the real advances in conditioning take place," concludes Tinley.

See Also: ***Dehydration, Glucose and Glycogen, Obsession***

Pain
Dealing with discomfort

Some have dubbed endurance training "the science of pain management." When you think about it, few things come easily in the endurance arena, and perhaps that's as it should be. What would be the challenge of Mount Everest if Uncle Fred could ride a centrally heated gondola car to the top? What joy would there be at the finish of an Ironman triathlon if people arrived there by bus?

That's not to say that endurance activity must be painful in order to be fulfilling. On the contrary, if you can achieve your goal without suffering, all the better.

No elite endurance athlete wants to suffer. With ten miles to go in a race and victory assured, only a fool would face unnecessary pain and risk injury by pushing all-out to the finish, The exception, of course, would be a motive more pressing than simply winning—the chance to break a record, or the high of winning by as big a margin as possible.

Most endurance athletes regard pain as a valuable tool in the arsenal of achievement. The very best athletes have learned not only to accept it but to use it.

Four-time Ironman winner Mark Allen is famed for being able to take advantage of his own pain, and that of others. His nickname, "The Grip," short for "The Grip of Death," offers you an inkling of what it's like to train with him.

"Training enables you to be comfortable with pain—with the feeling of your body saying 'stop' but your mind pushing you through it," says Allen. "The more you get accustomed to being in that situation during your training, the more familiar it will be in a race. You'll be able to push all the way to the finish line because you've done it before—and you've recovered."

Allen doesn't pretend that pain can't be daunting. "I think that's the biggest fear, that the pain is so intense that it's never going to go away. But it does go away 10 or 15 minutes after you stop. I think a big part of working out is letting your body get used to the experience of going hard."

Often, he continues, the main difference between the best and the rest is the former's ability to live with pain—to accept it, work through it and push on.

"For me, I push until I reach a certain pain level, and that's when I know I'm going the speed I should be going," Allen says. "If I'm below that, I know I'm not going hard enough. The pain almost becomes a friend instead of an enemy."

Facing it down

The lung-searing, gut-wrenching pain of the sprinter is not the pain of the endurance athlete. Long-distance pain ranges from burning muscles at the threshold level of performance to the agonizing, whole-body hurt of extreme fatigue.

If you've ever watched runners push through the final miles of a marathon, you've seen this latter form of pain at work. Curiously, everyone's hurting, but the faster, more experienced athletes are still running—most of them looking a lot better than they probably feel.

It's only as you move farther back in the pack that you begin to see angry, determined-looking runners walking. They seethe with frustration. You'll see them alternately walking and running, clearly struggling mentally to find a way around the pain. Some of them have hit the Wall and are suffering from glycogen depletion; others are simply tired, bored and disgusted with themselves for stopping, or maybe for putting themselves in such a ridiculous situation to begin with.

Let's make a distinction here. The pain we're discussing is *not* the sharp, localized pain of outright injury—soft tissue damage, fractures, cuts and lacerations. If facing down the pain of effort is what separates true heroes from the also-rans, recognizing, and listening to, the sharply defined pain of injury distinguishes the wise from the foolish. Stumbling down a mountain with a broken leg to save yourself from freezing to death is heroic. Running a marathon on a stress-fractured leg is dumb.

Selecting your strategy

As Mark Allen suggests, one of the best lessons in dealing with the pain of endurance sport is to survive it. Once you realize it's not going to kill you, the urge to slow down or stop becomes less urgent. Through experience and hard work, you can almost acclimatize yourself to pain in the same way you might adapt to hot weather. It's going to be uncomfortable no matter what you do, but familiarity makes it easier to bear.

You can also choose from a menu of mental strategies to combat pain. Will it be dissociation today, or association?

Dissociation, or distraction, can take your mind away from your pain completely, letting your body run on autopilot while your mind takes a trip to the French Riviera, focuses on a card game with an imaginary foe or occupies itself with more pleasant things. One woman, fighting her way to the finish of the Hawaii Ironman Triathlon, willed herself to the line by contemplating her two favorite things—sex and ice cream.

The opposite approach is to concentrate on your pain, using it as an accurate measure of your effort, and then move on. Termed "association" by sports psychologists, this is the tactic Allen and most other successful athletes use so well.

Whether you're ignoring or accepting the pain, the bottom line is, you're trying to relax. Relaxed suffering might sound like a contradiction, especially when your heart's dancing about in your skull, but relaxing is indeed the best way to manage pain. It soothes your mind and halts negative thoughts that can quickly grind you to a halt.

Physically relaxing also allows for increased circulation, which helps improve your performance as your blood rushes oxygen to your muscle cells and whisks waste products away. You learn to relax, mentally and physically, through practice.

When it comes to managing pain, preparation is all.

"The only way to learn to work your way through pain is by doing it in practice," says miler and three-time Olympian Steve Scott. "You've got to challenge yourself in practice. That's what training is all about. If you're always training within your comfort zone, you can't expect to handle pain when a race comes along."

Ultimately, however, you'll have to be vigilant to distinguish what kind of pain you're feeling. Is it the result of pushing hard, or the sign of an injury? If you suspect the latter, hie yourself over to your local physician before hitting the exercise trail again.

See Also: *Ankle Sprains, Endurance Training, Hamstring Pulls, Iliotibial Band Friction Syndrome, Marathon, Runner's Knee, Shin Splints, Stress Fractures*

Prerace Jitters
Managing the butterflies

You've prepared impeccably for the big race. You've trained hard, eaten right. You should have fewer insecurities than Marky Mark. Why then, with the start just minutes away, do you feel light-headed, heavy-legged and just plain lousy?

Sports psychologists call it "arousal." We know it better as "butterflies." Left unattended, these sensations and emotions can turn what should be a great race into a forgettable experience.

On the minus side, arousal is unavoidable. On the plus side, arousal won't necessarily do you in.

"One of the misunderstandings of prerace jitters is that somehow they're dangerous, unnatural or unhealthy," says sports psychologist Michael J. Mahoney, Ph.D., of the University of California at Santa Barbara. "Jitters can be uncomfortable, but they also alert our systems to get ready for an all-out effort."

Use jitters to your advantage

Experienced athletes recognize the value of prerace jitters and worry if they're *not* aroused. They realize, says Dr. Mahoney, that arousal provides a competitive edge. For most of us, though, the problem isn't retaining our competitive edge as much as being swallowed up by it.

Befriending the jitters takes some mental gymnastics. It means having enough arousal to keep you on your toes but not so much that you fall apart. To put in a great performance, your butterflies should be flying, but they should be flying in formation.

Everyone achieves that proper level of arousal differently. Keep the following in mind, however, to optimize your efforts to conquer the jitters.

First, your appropriate level of arousal hinges on the type of event you're involved in. As a general rule, sprinters want to be highly aroused, with energy high. On the other hand, endurance athletes—whether running a marathon or cycling 200 miles—need relaxed muscles, so their level of arousal needs to be considerably lower.

How best to quell nervous energy before the start? Dr. Mahoney recommends taking deep, easy breaths, similar to sighs. Focus on the upcoming race. Feel the nervous energy coursing through your body. Realize that this edginess is perfectly normal. To reinforce your confidence, think about all the miles of training that got you to the starting line.

Then consider these words from basketball coaching great and sometime philosopher John Wooden. "I think the athletes who are bothered by fear and self-doubt are the ones who know they haven't done all they could to prepare themselves." He adds, emphatically, "Failing to prepare is preparing to fail."

See Also: *Mind Games*

Runner's Knee
Cyclists get it, too

Runner's knee, or chondromalacia, is a bit of a misnomer. Yes, it strikes runners, but cyclists are also fair game. If your knee feels stiff and achy after you sit, and if it produces more snapping, cracking and popping than your breakfast cereal, you may have chondromalacia.

The term sounds complex, but what's actually happened is simple. The cartilage lining the back of the kneecap has gradually been worn down. It sounds painful, and it is.

The runner's knee version of chondromalacia is usually brought on by excessive pronation. Each time your foot strikes the ground, your leg rolls in, throwing your knee out of normal alignment. Your patella, or kneecap, moves with it. Push the patella outside its normal path often enough, and the cartilage begins to soften and disintegrate. This is runner's knee—a creaky joint and a sandpaper feel under your kneecap.

Runner's knee can sometimes be relieved by temporarily cutting back on mileage and strengthening the quadriceps muscles. Strong quads cut down on patella movement and cartilage friction. To relieve the pain, ice the knee several times a day for about 15 to 20 minutes. Avoid icing it within two hours of your next run. You can apply ice to the knee as soon as you've finished.

For many, the ultimate cure for runner's knee is a simple shoe insert, or orthotic, to eliminate pronation. A serious case of chondromalacia will mean time off and probably a trip to a sports podiatrist to tend to the condition.

The cyclist's version

Endurance athletes don't usually associate chondromalacia with cycling. Yet one study holds chondromalacia responsible for 45 percent of all cycling injuries. Take cycling down to basics, and this isn't surprising. Cyclists bend their knees about 4,000 times in an hour's ride, creating a fair amount of stress there. Push too big a gear, go too many miles, climb too many hills, and this strain is compounded. Poor pedal adjustment is another major cause of cyclist's knee, says La Jolla, California, sports podiatrist Joe Ellis, D.P.M., who treats hundreds of sports injuries each year. Cyclist's knee can also be brought on by poor bike fit—if your seat's too high or too low, any kind of strain on your knee is compounded.

If cycling brought on your woes in the first place, try spinning in a lower gear. Avoid mountain goat climbs and excessive mileage. Go to the bike shop and have a qualified professional check your bike fit. Strengthen your quads with weight training.

Although it shouldn't bear repeating, as with any injury, rest is crucial. You may resist taking time off, but the discomfort of not running or biking can't compare with the pain you'll experience if you try to bulldoze your way through it.

Shin Splints
Coddling the tenuous tibia

S hin splints" is a catch-all term used to describe a variety of injuries. All of them revolve around the leg's shin bone (tibia), hence the name. But the root of the problem, and the pain it brings, can stray far and wide, involving the bone itself, or the muscles, tendons and connective tissues surrounding the tibia. You may have shin splints if you have pain or soreness anywhere around the tibia, from your knee to your ankle.

According to La Jolla, California, sports podiatrist Joe Ellis, D.P.M., shin splints are usually caused by muscles that aren't up to the stresses you're inflicting on them. They can also be caused by bone inflammation, muscle tears, stress fracture and nerve irritation.

Beginning runners, often overzealous, are especially prone to shin splints. Dr. Ellis estimates that this condition comprises about 7 percent of all running injuries among men and a whopping 20 percent among women.

Novice runners typically develop shin splints when they indulge in the three "toos"—too much, too hard, too fast. But shin splints can also be a result of biomechanical abnormality: Excessive pronation can cause shin splints.

Novice women athletes experience more shin splint problems than any other injury. With wider hips, women tend to pronate more than men—their feet roll inward when they hit the ground. This misaligned strike can lead to shin splints as well as other injuries.

Another problem is high heels. Calf muscles tend to shorten in women who wear them regularly. Walking with high heels creates a shorter stride; the calf muscle isn't stretched or worked as much. Muscles that aren't used regularly tend to shorten, and problems quickly follow.

"When one set of muscles is too tight, it fights against the muscles opposite," explains Dr. Ellis. "That's why women who wear high heels often get anterior shin splints."

People with flat feet often develop them, too. Ditto for people with rigid, high-arched feet; because their feet don't pronate enough to dissipate some of the stress, the shin absorbs almost all the shock. This results in bone inflammation.

Constantly running on hard surfaces can also foster shin splints—they're notorious among aerobic dancers and basketball players.

Recognizing shin splints

How can you tell if you have shin splints? Here's a good rule of thumb—if the pain eases off as you run, you probably have a muscle or tendon problem. Tendon and muscle inflammations are often part of shin splints, and your muscles especially feel the strain when they're cold and tight before you run. As you get further into the run and your muscles and tendons begin to stretch and loosen, the pain lessens.

In fact, says Dr. Ellis, in some instances you can run through shin splints if the pain is dull and mild—in this instance the pain may just represent bone and muscle adjustment to new stresses. Also, there are different types of shin splints, some more severe than others.

The most common type is the tendinitis version. Here the tendon in the shin becomes strained. You can run with this type, says Dr. Ellis, although you should probably cut back your efforts 30 percent until the tendon heals.

All other types of shin splints rule out running. If you're stubborn, your body will let you know right away that it isn't keen on exercise.

Periostitis, for example, is a form of shin splints where the bone covering actually begins to pull away from the bone. Says Dr. Ellis, "It usually hurts like hell."

Similarly, if your problem isn't shin splints but a far more serious stress fracture, the pain will usually bring you to your knees. Touch a stress fracture and you'll go through the ceiling.

If you have any question about what kind of shin splints you have, Dr. Ellis advises seeking professional help before going back to running. Unattended, they can lead to more serious stress fractures.

Sidestepping shin splints

As with any injury, prevention is the best cure. First and foremost, don't overdo. Ease gradually into whatever sort of running you are doing. Celebrating spring by going out and playing five hours of pick-up basketball is likely to shock your shin bone and its support system.

Take care of pronation problems. If you overpronate, buy firm, motion-control shoes with stable support on the sides to prevent your foot from turning in. If you underpronate, avoid shoes with anti-pronation devices and inadequate shock absorption. Don't do all your running on asphalt; do some of it on grass or trails.

You'll go a long way toward avoiding shin splints by conditioning your support system of muscles and tendons before giving them a workout. Weak or strained front leg muscles can lead to overpronation. You can fortify yourself against both by strengthening these muscles. Adds Dr. Ellis, "You also want to make sure you have plenty of flexibility in your calves to counteract all that strength up front."

Dr. Ellis offers two simple strengthening exercises. You can work the appropriate muscles by sitting on the edge of a chair or bed and lifting an unopened paint bucket with your foot. Or, if you haven't been to Sherwin-Williams recently, try heel-walking. Walk with your toes off the ground—50 steps with your toes pointed forward, 50 steps with your toes pointed in, 50 steps with your toes pointed out. You may look like a penguin, but you'll feel the benefits almost immediately.

Surviving shin splints

It's happened—you're a sadder but wiser victim of shin splints. Here's what to do next.

If the pain isn't severe, treat it with ice right after each exercise session, icing it down for between 15 and 30 minutes. Ice minimizes the swelling and inflammation caused by muscle or tendon strains. Ice will also increase the circulation in the deeper blood vessels, bringing more blood, nutrients and healthy cells into the injured area.

Take aspirin every three or four hours, suggests Dr. Ellis. If the problem's a strained muscle or tendon, Bob Wischnia, an editor for *Runner's World* magazine, offers a recipe for an innovative salve. Crush a few aspirin tablets, mix them into aloe vera gel and place a glop of the stuff right over the most painful part, leaving it there for at least a few hours.

Shin splints, in the final analysis, may be unavoidable. If you're new to running, you're apt to experience a number of pains, shin splints included, before your body adapts to the stress of running. Use common sense. If the discomfort is merely annoying, you can probably keep running. But Dr. Ellis strongly advises against running if there's any pain or soreness. Pushing through serious pain will lead to real damage.

If the pain doesn't go away, see a sports podiatrist or sportsmedicine specialist.

Reminds Dr. Ellis, "If you're having problems, you can't go wrong by having them evaluated. Unfortunately, it's human nature to push on, and that's where you get into trouble."

See Also: *Stress Fractures*

Snowblindness
Safeguard your sight

Snowblindness, points out Buck Tilton, isn't true blindness—but you might as well be blind, because your eyes hurt so badly, you *can't* keep them open. How painful is snowblindness? Tilton is graphic.

"Well," he drawls, "it feels like somebody took a handful of sand and rubbed it into your eyeballs."

Tilton should know. As director of the Wilderness Medicine Institute in Pitkin, Colorado, he's seen his share of snowblindness. He's suffered from it, too. In essence, snowblindness is sunburned eyes, explaining the intense pain that accompanies the affliction. The good news is, snowblindness is easily preventable. The bad news is, too many people get it anyway.

A simple cause and cure

Snowblindness occurs when sunlight is reflected off ice and snow (or in some cases, water) and into the eyes. Snow and ice are particularly ruthless reflective surfaces, bouncing about 85 percent of the sun's rays up into your eyes. Given the worst circumstances—midday on a bright, sunny day at high altitude—damage can be done in as little as an hour. The problem is, you likely won't know it—symptoms usually appear 6 to 12 hours later.

"That's what makes snowblindness so deceptive," says Tilton. "The first indication that your eyes have been burned is pain, and at that point it's too late."

Though the gritty pain can be intense—your eyes may also water, swell and turn red—snowblindness rarely results in permanent damage. Even in more severe cases, the pain subsides and normal eyesight returns within 24 to 48 hours.

What can you do if you become snowblind? As Tilton points out, your eyes will start the healing process on their own, foiling your attempts to open them by sending shafts of pain to your brain. Tilton recommends you cover your eyes, preferably with dark cloth patches, for 12 hours to further protect them from light.

You can also flush them with cold, clean water, but nothing else should enter your eye. Take aspirin to reduce the pain. If your eyesight hasn't returned completely after 12 hours, leave the patches on for another 12 hours. Healing usually occurs in 24 hours.

If the pain is intense, or if normal eyesight doesn't return within 24 to 48 hours, see a physician.

Still, the best way to handle snowblindness it to avoid it altogether.

"Sunglasses that don't let ultraviolet light through will prevent snowblindness," says Tilton. " There's really no reason to be snowblind."

If you're caught out in the snow without glasses or goggles, says Tilton, innovate. Find paper or cardboard you can tear or put a slit in, using a knife, your fingers or a stick. A temporary eye covering will do a serviceable job of protecting your eyes.

See Also: *Frostbite, Windchill*

Stress Fractures
When overtraining leads to injury

*I*t's usually pretty easy for Joe Ellis, D.P.M., a La Jolla, California, sports podiatrist, to pinpoint the cause when an athlete hobbles into his office with a stress fracture. Dr. Ellis casually asks about his or her training program. Then he asks for an objective appraisal of the program. Inevitably, both doctor and patient reach the same conclusion.

"Suddenly," says Dr. Ellis, "these people realize they're doing far too much."

Nothing causes injury faster than overdoing, and stress fractures are a perfect example. These are actually the worst kind of shin splint injuries, involving a microscopic break or crack in the bone. Like shin splints, stress fractures usually occur among overzealous athletes who do too much, too fast, too soon.

"Most people overtrain. That's why they have these problems," says Dr. Ellis, who sees his share of obsessive triathletes and runners. "Some people will develop stress fractures because of mechanical problems, but with a sensible training program, your odds of getting a stress fracture go down astronomically."

Unlike shin splints, which can have myriad roots, stress fractures are caused by a single, simple adaptation. The stress of increased exercise—whether it's a new addition to your program or a longer routine—triggers bone remodeling. In order for a bone to become stronger, it must break itself down first, jettison its components into the bloodstream, then regroup again in stronger and sturdier concentrations.

During this remodeling stage, the bone is weak. "At this point, if you keep exercising or increase the exercise, the bone will crack. Usually there's some soreness that precedes the crack—a telltale clue. Unfortunately, many athletes ignore it."

You don't need to be a podiatrist to know that stress fractures among endurance athletes are as common as sniping among politicians. Women are particularly susceptible to stress fractures—hormonal changes weaken the density of their bones, which are already smaller in girth than men's. Stress fractures occur in almost epidemic proportions among women distance runners.

Recognizing stress fractures

Stress fractures are sometimes hard for physicians to diagnose—because the crack is so small, an x-ray won't usually pick up a stress fracture for several weeks, until a bone callus begins forming around the crack. However, you might recognize it right on the playing field. When you touch the affected area, the pain will send you out of your skin.

"I've never seen a fracture that didn't hurt when touched," says Dr. Ellis.

Another stress fracture indicator is that the pain gets worse as you run. With shin splints, pain generally eases as you move through the run and your muscles warm up. If the pain builds through your run, says Dr. Ellis, you may have a stress fracture or be on the verge of one.

A good rule of thumb for any injury—and particularly stress fractures—is: If the pain remains or worsens, stop training and see a doctor.

The cure for stress fractures is also simple: rest. It takes about six weeks for bone to heal, although this can vary. It's imperative, says Dr. Ellis, that you let the bone heal completely. Resuming your running too soon will very likely refracture the weakened area. When to comes to stress fractures, caution is the best policy.

"If you understand the bone remodeling process, you'll understand why you don't want to overdo it," says Dr. Ellis. "When you get that bone soreness, don't increase your training. Train properly and you'll probably be able to avoid stress fractures entirely."

See Also: *Overtraining, Shin Splints*

Sun Damage
Fry now, pay later

*I*f you think overexposure to the sun doesn't deserve such bad press, consider the following statistics.

According to the National Cancer Institute, one in three people in Sunbelt states will eventually get skin cancer.

By 1992, melanoma—the deadliest of all skin cancers—had become the number one cancer among women ages 25 to 29. Men aren't immune, either. Researchers at Boston University Medical School report that the death rate from melanoma in men over 50 is now increasing faster than that of any other cancer.

The bottom line is, skin cancer claimed nearly 9,000 Americans in 1992.

When it comes to warnings about sun damage, there are plenty of facts to support them. There's no longer any doubt about the potential dangers of overexposure. Tanning oil manufacturers used to say, "Nothing flatters you like a tan." Today, a more accurate slogan coined by the American Cancer Society is, "Fry now, pay later."

The high cost of a deep tan

What makes sun damage so tricky—and so easy to ignore—is that its effects often remain dormant for 10 to 20 years. Dermatologists believe that 80 percent of the damage done to the skin usually occurs before age 20. You may have forgotten all that bare-backed broasting you did years ago, but your skin hasn't.

"Skin is sort of like an elephant," says Kevin Welch, M.D., a dermatologist at the University of Arizona Health Sciences Center. "It never forgets a ray of sun that hits it."

Listen to Dr. Welch and you'll realize that you needn't panic, but you should take precautions. The great majority of skin cancers—basal cell and squamous cell carcinomas—are generally easily cured by slicing away the growths. Rarely do these cancers metastasize, or spread. Even with melanoma, the deadliest form of skin cancer, there's a good chance of being cured if the melanoma is caught early and removed before it spreads through the body.

The bad news, in our society of sun worshipers, is that all three cancers are increasing at an alarming pace.

"The nonmelanoma-type skin cancers are increasing rapidly—they've doubled in the past ten years," says Dr. Welch. "The number of cases of melanoma have also more or less doubled in the last 15 years. The lifetime risk of melanoma is approximately 1 in 100 now for the average American, and it keeps going up."

Make the protection connection

How to best protect yourself from sun damage? Dr. Welch offers several recommendations for athletes, most of them grounded in common sense.

First, wear protective clothing. Hats are particularly important because they help protect tender, exposed areas like the tops of your ears, your nose and your lips.

Second, learn to rely on sunscreen, particularly "sport" sunscreens, designed to stick better and rub off less. Alcohol-based sunscreens also tend to stick better because the alcohol dries fairly quickly after it's been applied. Use SPF-15 sunblocks—they filter out 94 percent of the ultraviolet rays that spur on cancer. There's no need to scour the shelves for the super-protective stuff—SPF-50 is only 4 percent more effective than SPF-15.

The best sunscreen, says Dr. Welch, is perhaps the most traditional. "Zinc oxide paste, the old lifeguard stuff, is essentially the best sunscreen there is because it's an absolute block," he explains.

Don't skimp. Apply it everywhere you can, but especially to those exposed ears, nose and lips.

"The lip is an area that's often overlooked," points out Dr. Welch. "Lip cancer is one of the more serious forms of skin cancer, but it's easy to avoid with lip balm or sunscreen."

There are a number of other sun protection products athletes might want to consider. Sportswear manufacturers now sell "sunbreakers," tightly woven, lightweight fabric jackets that keep you cool but offer substantial protection.

Legionnaires' hats, with a patch of cloth hanging down from the back of the hat to cover the neck, are popular with sun-conscious runners. Some sunglass manufacturers offer special glasses that block ultraviolet light. These extend over your nose and cheeks.

But the best way to skirt sun damage is to avoid the prime sun hours as much as possible.

"The sun is strongest between 10 A.M. and 4 P.M.," warns Dr. Welch. "If it works into your practice schedule, it's better to be outdoors outside of that time period."

All of this might sound like grandmotherly harping, but the threat of sun damage shouldn't be ignored. Skin cancers are a very real problem. And the best solution is prevention.

The Wall
As real as a wall can be

Much ado has been made of the Wall, and anyone who has ever crashed into it knows why. It's that unforgettable moment when solid effort is replaced with arms and legs of rubber and a mind of mud.

The Wall is the point where your body's glycogen energy stores become severely depleted. Your muscles, deprived of their most efficient energy source, can no longer function rapidly. At best, you'll fall off to a stagger. At worst, you'll fall on your face. The term "hitting the Wall" was first coined by marathoners who, upon reaching a point around the 20-mile mark, did precisely that.

As a general rule, this glycogen crash occurs sometime after 90 to 120 minutes of exercise at solid effort. This equates to 75 percent of your maximum oxygen uptake, or VO_2 max.

This is only a rough window, but it's still fairly accurate, and it explains why many runners in the last six miles of a marathon look as if they've just closed down Bourbon Street.

Avoiding the Wall
If the Wall is the result of a glycogen crash, then the best way to sidestep this downer is to keep up your stores of glycogen. Though a daunting image, the Wall is by no means inevitable; it can be scaled on two fronts: first by boosting your glycogen supplies and second by conserving them as best you can.

Glycogen boosting is familiar to most athletes as carbohydrate loading. By gobbling down lots of carbohydrates before a long race or training session, you can effectively increase your muscles' glycogen supplies. The higher those levels are prior to exercise, the greater your endurance potential.

But even under the best of circumstances, you can store only a limited amount of glycogen. When it comes to avoiding the Wall, glycogen sparing, not glycogen stuffing, is your most important weapon.

Simply put, by exercising just below your anaerobic threshold—at an aerobic fat-burning pace—you'll tap into your body's ample supply of fat and burn it for energy, while conserving precious glycogen.

It's no coincidence that athletes who know how to race right at the edge of anaerobic effort generally finish strong. Nor is it surprising that inexperienced athletes who push into anaerobic, glycogen-gobbling efforts too early may not finish at all.

Finally, there's some speculation that the Wall might not even exist. William Morga, Ph.D. asked elite runners at the Cooper Institute for Aerobics Research in Dallas if they'd experienced it. To his surprise, they gave it little thought. Said one runner, "The key is to read your body, adjust your pace and avoid getting into trouble. The Wall is a myth."

See Also: ***Bonking, Carbohydrate Loading, Fat, Marathon, Pacing***

Windchill
Properly managing an ill wind

Warren Utes is 73 years old, a resident of Park Forest, Illinois, an avid runner and a perfect example of how athletes can manage windchill. Utes runs right through the worst of Midwestern winters, often leaning into windchills well below zero. Though others praise his doggedness, Utes sidesteps the acclaim. "It's not windchill unless it touches your skin," he says.

Precisely. When it comes to windchill, Utes illustrates two important points. First, athletes can weather substantial windchill. Second, they can only do it if they're well prepared.

What is windchill, anyway? Essentially, it's the effect of a cold wind on the surrounding temperature, and more to the point, on your rate of heat loss. A sunny, still day at 10°F can be almost pleasant. Add a 20-mile-an-hour wind to the equation, and suddenly the temperature is –25°F. Now add to that the windchill's impact on a skier hurtling down a hill at 25 miles an hour.

Still, athletes are at a substantial advantage when it comes to managing windchill. Exercise generates considerable body heat. The secret is to keep body heat in and the cold out.

The solution is simple—dress in layers. Layers of clothing provide an insulating barrier of air and can be removed as you heat up. No matter how cold it is, you'll still be sweating, so the clothes against your skin must absorb sweat quickly—polypropylene underwear is particularly good because it wicks away sweat that otherwise might keep you clammy. Use a windbreaker to top off your cocoon.

If it's really cold, try to make sure you're exposing as little skin as possible. Warren Utes may look like a mummy when he runs, but short of a few frozen tears ("It's like looking through a prism"), he's never had any problems with windchill. In fact, windchill can bring greater potential danger—frostbite and hypothermia—to the sedentary folk who stand around gawking at him.

See Also: *Frostbite, Hypothermia*

Part 5

Great Endurance Challenges

*I*t's no coincidence that this section appears last. Why sculpt your body into a ruthless engine of endurance if you can't put it to good use? Granted, events like the Western States 100, the Race Across America and the Hawaii Ironman Triathlon are as excessive as they sound. But most of the participants in these seemingly off-the-wall events once pooh-poohed them as insane before giving them a try.

Be forewarned. Endurance sport is an insidious thing. The once-ridiculous can become, in short order, intriguing. Suddenly, there you are standing in the dark in skimpy shorts with several hundred other excited souls wondering what brought you here.

Fortunately for you, the sports and events included in this section represent only the tip of the endurance iceberg. Twenty years ago, the marathon was considered the consummate endurance test. Today, marathons are run by octogenarians and quirky souls wearing suits made of pennies. And tomorrow?

In all honesty, we'll admit to an underlying motive. We're hoping that some of the events we've selected might entice you to join the march toward the endurance horizon. Somebody has to break down the barriers. Why not you?

Biathlon
Ski, shoot, win

B iathlon originated with the military traditions of Scandinavia, where soldiers in the field had to maneuver and fight in the snow. An Olympic sport since 1960, the biathlon combines cross-country skiing and rifle target shooting. Competitors carry their own weapons slung across their backs as they ski from target to target. It's not to be confused with duathlon, a run/bike/run offshoot of triathlon that became popular in the late 1980s.

Biathlon is extremely demanding from an endurance perspective. The aerobic intensity of cross-country skiing is challenging enough. Add to that stopping in midstride, calming your breathing and aiming and firing a small-bore rifle at an eight-inch target from 50 yards, and you've got a real challenge on your hands. Yet a special breed of men and women eagerly takes up the gauntlet every year.

In Olympic and world championship biathlon competitions, there are two standard distances for men: 10 kilometers, with two stops for shooting, and 20 kilometers, with four shooting stops. World-class biathletes complete the shorter distance in just under 30 minutes, while the 20-kilometer event takes a little over an hour.

There's also a 4 × 7.5-kilometer men's relay, in which members of a four-man team pass the rifle to a teammate at specified points along the course. Each competitor shoots both prone and standing. If a biathlete misses the target, a penalty is applied or an extra loop of the course must be skied, depending on the distance of the race.

Women's biathlon courses are set at 7.5 kilometers and 15 kilometers, with a 3 × 7.5-kilometer relay. The 1992 Winter Games in Albertville, France, marked the debut of women's biathlon in Olympic competition.

In a recent effort to draw more popular attention to their sport, especially in the United States, biathlon officials introduced a summer-season version of biathlon that involves running instead of skiing. The distance for both men and women in summer biathlon is three miles, with three stops for shooting.

Like its winter compatriot, summer's biathlon requires much stamina and rock-steady nerves. Don Kardong, a former Olympic marathoner with marginal shooting experience (one failed hunting trip 20 years earlier), tried the summertime version on a whim and developed a profound respect for biathlon's demands. Kardong sums up his thoughts on the event.

"The summer biathlon has three parts: fast running, straight shooting and fast shooting," says Kardong. "The three push against each other like three men in a tub. If one gets too rambunctious, the tub sinks."

Balance is the key.

Decathlon
Ten times the challenge

Quick now—which events will you find in a decathlon? Don't be embarrassed. Years ago, one of the world's greatest decathletes had no idea either.

When Bob Mathias, the first decathlete to win two Olympic golds (1948 and 1952), was a high school senior, his track coach approached him one day and said he'd read about an upcoming decathlon meet. Both Mathias and his coach thought this sounded great, though neither one of them could name all of the decathlon's ten events. Still, they reckoned Mathias—a versatile athlete who competed in almost every event for his tiny high school track team—had probably done five or six of them. Less than five months later, the 17-year-old Mathias won the 1948 Olympic decathlon in London.

The ten labors of Hercules

To clear up anyone else's misconceptions, the Olympic decathlon consists of ten events contested over two days. The first day includes the 100-meter dash, the long jump, the shot put, the high jump and the 400-meter run. The second day comprises the 110-meter high hurdles, the discus, the pole vault, the javelin and the 1500 meters.

The events were selected to ensure that the winner was indeed the finest all-around athlete, and the format was laid out—with breaks between the running events—to ensure that no one died in the process. Still, this amounts to an exhausting two days.

Dave Steen, a Canadian who captured the decathlon bronze at the 1988 Olympics in Seoul, Korea, claims he sometimes can't see for 15 minutes after he runs the 1500 to close out his two days. It's only fitting that the events that comprise the decathlon have been called "the Ten Labors of Hercules."

The roots of the decathlon can be traced back to the ancient Olympics in Greece, but the event didn't take its current form, or name, until two years before the 1912 Olympics. That first Olympic decathlon lasted three days because of an unexpectedly large number of entries. From then on, though, the decathlon was contested over two days.

There is no decathlon for women. The women's equivalent—currently ruled by 1992 Olympic champion Jackie Joyner-Kersee—is the seven-event heptathlon. Contested over two days, the hepathlon encompasses the 100-meter hurdles, the high jump, the shot put, the long jump, the 200-meter dash, the javelin and the 800-meter run.

Perhaps the most famous decathlete, and certainly the first to put the event on the map, was Jim Thorpe. An American Indian who, some argue, was the greatest athlete ever, Thorpe won the first Olympic decathlon at the 1912 Summer Games in Stockholm. While presenting Thorpe with a jeweled chalice and a royal bust, Sweden's King Gustav V made the decree that would become decathlon's label and the decathlete's consummate goal. "Sir," the King solemnly declared, "you are the world's greatest athlete."

Scoring for the decathlon is a convoluted affair. Athletes are awarded a specific number of points based on the speed, height or distance they attain. In 1962, decathlon powers-that-be adopted scoring tables that reward athletes for consistency rather than brilliance in just a few events. This ensures that the winner is indeed the most versatile athlete.

But this wasn't always the case. As late as 1960, American Rafer Johnson won the Olympic gold largely because he nearly tossed the shot put out of the stadium. Taiwan's C. K. Yang, who actually beat Johnson in seven of the ten events, had to settle for a silver.

When scoring changed to reward versatility, athletes were forced to expand their focus to all ten events. Where once they could do well by blasting their two or three specialties—and turning in mediocre performances in the other events—now they had to excel across the board.

And they have. In setting a new decathlon world record in September 1992, in Talence, France, Dan O'Brien, a solidly muscled 26-year-old from Idaho, launched the javelin 205 feet. He followed this by tossing the discus 159 feet, pole vaulting 16 feet, 4 inches and running the 1500 in 4:42. These performances earned O'Brien 8,891 points, besting the previous record—set by Great Britain's Daley Thompson at the 1984 Olympics—by 44 points.

Heroes, sung and unsung

Dan O'Brien is the most recent in a long line of illustrious decathlon stars—Harold Osborn, Bob Mathias, James Bausch, Daley Thompson, Bill Toomey, Bruce Jenner, Rafer Johnson, Christian Schenk, Juergen Hingsen, Dave Johnson. While you've heard of some, some you probably haven't.

Although Dan O'Brien and Dave Johnson attained high visibility before the 1992 Olympics as a result of Reebok's clever "Dan and Dave" marketing campaign, the decathlon has never been a sport to rivet the national consciousness, even during the Olympics. As Dave Steen once said, "If the decathlon were held separately from the rest of the Olympic track meet, I don't think too many people would show up."

Although 1976 Olympic gold medalist Bruce Jenner went on to a brief stint of cereal box appearances, decathletes have no delusions of fame and fortune. Thorpe died penniless, and most decathletes have followed in his footsteps.

Few athletes are willing to dedicate themselves to such a grueling event, but those who do often form remarkably close bonds. After the finale of the decathlon at the 1986 Commonwealth Games in Edinburgh, the crowds stood and clapped, waiting for winner Daley Thompson to take a victory lap. They waited and waited and waited. Only when all his competitors joined him did Thompson trot around the track.

Although the material rewards of the decathlon are few, apparently the personal challenge is second to none. "You never walk away from a decathlon totally satisfied," Bruce Jenner once said. "You may feel good about your performance, but you always see areas for improvement."

As of this writing, the world's greatest athlete is current world record holder Dan O'Brien. After breaking the record, O'Brien declared, "The world's greatest athlete has come back to America."

For now.

See Also: *Modern Pentathlon*

Duathlon
What? No swim?

Prior to the first duathlon, Ken Souza had been an aspiring triathlete with a legendary (albeit dubious) reputation in the water.

"He was a stone with arms," says a close acquaintance, who's kinder than most. Souza, duathlon's ruling figure since the mid-1980s, is frank about why he prefers run/bike events.

"Basically," he says, recalling one ill-fated swim, "I thought I was going to drown out there."

It's no secret that much of the appeal of duathlon is that you don't have to swim. When Dan Honig, founder of the Big Apple Biathlon Club in New York, put on his first event in 1984, 500 people showed up.

A biathlon club? Yep. Until 1990, the duathlon was known as the biathlon. But the term conflicted with the Winter Olympic cross-country skiing and shooting event, so biathlon's, er, duathlon's, powers-that-be adopted the new name, a moniker that didn't suit everyone's tastes.

"When you say 'du' to me, I either think of what's on the grass in the morning or what the dog leaves in the yard," huffed one top competitor.

Even though the sport's governing body, the International Triathlon Union (ITU), adopted the name, a number of run/bike events in the United States and abroad continue to use the name biathlon.

The first official ITU World Championship was held in Palm Springs, California, in 1990. The event featured a grueling 10-K run/62-K bike/10-K run course. The World Championships are now held annually, at preselected locations around the world.

Although no official distances have been established for this event, the most popular in terms of mass participation is 5-K/30-K/5-K. The sequence is usually the same—run/bike/run. Early race directors discovered that having 500 cyclists whipping across the finish line at one time was far too traumatic an experience.

Listen to the experts

How does one prepare for a duathlon? Here are a few gems of advice from two who know—Souza and long-time duathlon queen Liz Downing.

Souza believes you must first learn how to balance the two sports and get the most from each.

"Keep a running base you can sustain and still be fresh for cycling," advises Souza. "You've got to train like a runner and train like a cyclist, but you don't want to do too much of either."

Most duathletes are runners who find in cycling a respite from the pounding of running. For new converts to cycling, Souza recommends alternating days at first—a day of cycling followed by a day of running allows the legs to discover an entirely new set of muscles. Keep the bike in an easy gear and spin, spin, spin. Wait at least two weeks before running and biking on the same day.

"In the beginning, you're shocking your body," says Souza. "Cycling is something most runners just aren't used to. Take it easy. Cycling's a sport that lasts a lifetime. The first two weeks don't really mean that much."

Liz Downing, for years duathlon's superstar, set cycling's national 40-K record at 54 minutes in 1989. The next day, she hopped a plane to Seattle and won a major duathlon. Downing, like Souza, is a strong believer in using cycling intervals in training.

"Intervals allow you to put in quality training. If you put in enough quality, you don't have to do that much quantity," she says.

Downing incorporates a variety of intervals in her cycling training—going 2 to 3 miles all-out, then ½ mile easy; then hard for a minute and then easy for a minute; then hard for a final mile, then spinning ¼ mile easy.

Souza, on the other hand, has a thing for hills. He uses them to build cycling strength and improve his pedaling technique. Going at a slow cadence uphill, says Souza, you really feel the whole pedal stroke, pushing down *and* pulling up.

How much mileage you do is a matter of time and preference. As a general rule, Souza recommends a cycling-to-running mix of three to one. When you plan to run and cycle on the same day, Souza recommends starting with the run. Because running traumatizes your muscles far more than cycling, running first helps avoid injury. Topping the run off with a bout of cycling can also help loosen up your muscles.

See Also: *Interval Training, Triathlon*

English Channel
Swim to France in a day

The 22 miles from Dover, England, to Calais, France, are cold, treacherous and, as 22 miles suggests, long. There are more difficult marathon swims, but no other stretch of water has witnessed more displays of fortitude and foolhardiness than the English Channel.

As you might imagine, people subject themselves to the Channel for their own reasons, not all of them altruistic. In the late 1920s, Myrtle Huddleston attempted a Channel crossing in order to put her son, Everett, through college. When it became apparent Mom wouldn't make it, Everett purportedly brooded sadly in the escort boat. "I guess I will have to sell magazines," he lamented.

The first successful recorded crossing came in 1875, when a 27-year-old Englishman named, appropriately enough, Matthew Webb, struck out from Dover one August day. No sylph-waisted jock, he stood five feet, eight inches and weighed a chunky 204 pounds. His well-insulated frame came in handy, considering he spent a whopping 21 hours and 45 minutes breaststroking through water that averaged 60°F. His crossing galvanized the world, and Webb became an international celebrity. He basked in the limelight until eight years later when, attempting a prize-money swim across the Niagara River, he was swept over the falls to his death.

Thirty-six years passed before someone else made it across the Channel. This was not for lack of trying. Seventy-one swimmers—22 of them women—attempted the crossing before Thomas Burgess made it across in 1911, taking almost 23 hours. In keeping with the doggedness the Channel demands, that swim was his 11th attempt.

America's Ederle makes history

The first American to conquer the English Channel did so in 1926, making the grueling swim from France to England. That crossing stunned the world, and not only because it resulted in a new world record (14 hours, 39 minutes). The swimmer was a woman, a 19-year-old New Yorker named Gertrude Ederle. Women, of course, had tried to cross the Channel before, but the idea of a woman actually making it was unthinkable, even to some of the women who had tried.

Annette Kellerman, an Australian who made three failed Channel tries, had concluded that women might have the endurance to take on a crossing but would be short on the "brute strength" required. "I think no woman has this combination," she decreed. "That's why I say that none of my gender will ever accomplish that particular stunt."

Ederle proved otherwise, and like other successful Channelers, she did so doggedly. At one point, with heavy rains and strong currents lashing the Channel, Ederle's trainer, accompanying her in an escort boat, ordered her out of the water. Ederle refused. It's speculated that her father, also a passenger in the boat, may have stiffened her resolve by reminding her of the roadster that would be hers if she made the crossing. When she arrived at the finish on England's Shakespeare Beach, a wild crowd was there to greet her. Hundreds of drivers honked their horns; flares lit the sky.

Ederle wasn't the only woman to strike a blow for women's rights in the Channel. From 1957 through 1959, American Greta Anderson won organized races across the Channel. More than prestige was at stake, too. In Egypt, where swimming was a national pastime, King Farouk promised a lifetime income to any Egyptian who won. And more recently, on July 29, 1978, Californian Penny Dean set the Channel crossing record, for men and women, of seven hours, 40 minutes, which she still holds.

Unfortunately, the Channel has also seen its share of tragedy. In 1954, a steelworker named Ted May struck off across the Channel alone, towing an inner tube loaded with rum, chicken, sugar and biscuits. Foul weather forced May back to shore, but a few days later he swam off alone again. His body washed ashore a month later in Holland, a compass still strapped to his wrist.

Sadder still, in 1988, Renata Agondi, a 20-year-old Brazilian woman, died eight miles off the French coast when her coach refused to let her leave the water.

The makings of a winner

These days, the lure of the Channel still brings dozens of would-be conquerors to Dover each summer. The logistics alone are daunting. You can't simply wade into the Channel and strike off. The English Channel Swimming Association allows only a certain number of swims each summer, and in a necessarily rigid scheduling scheme, each swimmer has a scheduled day.

If that day comes and conditions are too rough, too bad. Though Steve Frantz of San Diego isn't likely to be mentioned in the same breath with

Webb, Ederle or Dean, he typifies the spirit of those who try to conquer the Channel. Frantz first tried to swim the Channel in 1987. He gave up after four hours, chilled by 57°F water and weakened by pneumonia. In 1988, foul weather canceled his swim.

But Frantz persisted. In August of 1990, he struck out for France again. The early hours of the swim passed without event, featuring scheduled feedings and unscheduled barfings. After 12 hours, about the time he had hoped to wade ashore, the 49-year-old was still three miles off the French coast. Currents would keep him there for the next five hours.

Frantz, however, refused to quit. Sixteen hours and 57 minutes after he left England, his hand scraped the bottom. He stood and ran the last 50 yards to shore.

Even now Frantz struggles to describe the euphoria that accompanied his finish. "It's hard to explain," he says of the feelings that overcame him as he stood on a dark beach near Calais. "It's like being tortured for a long period of time and suddenly it's over. I'd never felt so wonderful."

See Also: *Open-Water Swimming*

Hawaii Ironman Triathlon
Hot, hilly and hellish

*F*or triathletes, the Hawaii Ironman Triathlon is the grandpappy of them all. It's hard to pinpoint what makes the Ironman so popular, but many believe it's the location. While the ordinary tourist may skirt the bleak lava fields of Kona on the island of Hawaii, they're the perfect arena for endurance athletes who are ready to confront and hopefully vanquish their limits.

First, there's the heat, pounding down from a relentless sun, then radiating up from the coal-black lava fields, a simmering envelope that smothers you like a steamy blanket.

Then you've got the headwinds, drumming relentlessly in your ears, often slowing forward progress to little more than a crawl. There's also the monotony of a course resembling a bleak moonscape, with its black rock and wilting grasses.

And finally, there's the distance—a 2.4-mile swim, followed by a 112-mile bike ride and a 26.2-mile run.

The Hawaii Ironman seems to generate three universal feelings among the athletes who take it on—fear before the race, hatred during it and an absolute reverence afterward.

Some believe the arena is almost mystical. Before his 1985 win, coauthor

Scott Tinley drove out onto the course, walked into the lava fields along the road and quietly asked the Hawaiian gods for safe passage. Tinley says he isn't superstitious but admits that Hawaii's history and culture can produce a spooky feeling sometimes.

The early Ironfolk—unique as the race itself

Looking back at the early years of the Ironman is like peering through a kaleidoscope—the parts are all there, but each way you turn, they're a bit askance. The same could be said for many of the early Ironfolk.

"In those years, there weren't a whole lot of people who were really qualified to do the event," recalls Bob Babbitt, a competitor and journalist who has documented the Ironman since the beginning. "Basically, there were a whole lot of wackos."

Babbitt should know. He competed in the third Ironman in 1980, riding a $60 bike with rubber tires. Thinking the bike leg consisted of two 60-mile rides separated by a night's rest, Babbitt arrived in Hawaii with a sleeping bag. And he was better prepared than most.

Another competitor, John Huckaby, trumpeted himself as the only man to run the historic 25 miles from Athens, Greece, to Marathon three consecutive times. Unfortunately, his emphasis on running left little time for swimming. In fact, Huckaby didn't know how. The 2.4-mile swim ran parallel to the shoreline. Huckaby waded through the entire thing in knee-deep water, arms stroking furiously through the air.

During the 112-mile bike leg, Born-Again Smitty—an eccentric recluse who reportedly lived in a cave on Maui—was driven to the pavement when a passing truck's side mirror caught him flush in the back of the head. Bolstered by a firm belief in the Lord, Smitty popped back up, made a feeble attempt to stop the flow of blood and continued on his way, wrapping up the day with a 3:34 marathon. Determination has always been a keynote at the Ironman.

Nor were these eccentrics the only ones without a clue. Few athletes had ever tackled an event of this scope; fewer still had any idea how to do it. And so they displayed a stunning breadth of panache. Ironfolk stuffed their shorts with coins to make weight (in the early years, contestants' weights were closely monitored to avoid dehydration—if they lost too much weight, they were yanked from the race).

They also crammed guava jelly sandwiches and a horrendous concoction of defizzed cola, NoDoz and aspirin—aptly named "the Bomb"—into their mouths. The Bomb, incidentally, numbed part of the pain and sent the mind skipping with jolts of assorted stimulants. Not, obviously, to be recommended to saner folks.

Even at the front of the pack, the picture was askew. Dave Scott swam, biked and ran away with the 1980 race, weathered basketball jersey flapping in the wind, tube socks hiked almost to his knees. The following year, contender Scott Molina rode the bike leg wearing his father's T-shirt and black dress socks. The socks may have been his undoing. A mobile solar panel, Molina self-destructed early in the run.

"It was such a novel event," says Scott, who went on to win the Ironman five more times. "You went into it with your own conceptions or misconceptions of how to do it."

Ironman's origins (or: lunacy revisited)

How did this madness come about? The idea was first proposed in 1977 by John Collins, a Navy commander stationed in Hawaii. Collins attended the Oahu Perimeter Relay Run, a running relay around the island of Oahu. After the race, a group of athletes, Collins included, got into a heated discussion. Which group—swimmers, cyclists or runners—was the fittest?

Collins decided to lay the debate to rest in innovative fashion. Why not take two of Hawaii's most famous events—the 2.4-mile Waikiki Rough Water Swim and the 26.2-mile Honolulu Marathon, add a shortened version of the two-day, 116-mile Around-the-Island Bike Ride, and see? Eighteen men signed up for the inaugural 1978 race; 15 started, 12 finished. The winner, Gordon Haller, stumbled across the finish in 11 hours, 46 minutes.

Once a quiet, studious type with a degree in physics, Haller had shed his bookworm image in pursuit of competition and consummate fitness. An Oregonian, Haller trained for the 1978 race by swimming and running through fog, cold, rain, ice and snow. He also logged mega-miles pedaling his bicycle indoors on a windtrainer. Haller's winning time placed him among the Ironman's top ten finishers for the next two years.

Women first competed in the Ironman in 1979. They weren't wholly welcome. At the 1980 prerace meeting, one gentleman stood and demanded an explanation for this effrontery. Wasn't this called the Ironman? Then why were women competing?

This may have been less of a gripe and more of a thinly veiled plea. The year before, Lyn Lemaire became the first woman to complete the race. A national-caliber cyclist, Lemaire not only had the audacity to show up, she placed fifth overall. Had cramps not forced her off the bike to do some frantic massaging, Lemaire might have dealt machismo an even more crushing blow. At one point during the bike leg, she trailed leader and eventual winner Tom Warren by only five minutes.

Ironman in the '90s

Since those first days, competition has heated up appreciably. Lemaire finished the 1979 race in 12 hours, 55 minutes. Eleven years later, Paula Newby-Fraser won the women's race in 9 hours, 56 seconds; men's winner Mark Allen finished in 8 hours, 9 minutes. The progression has been dizzying. How dizzying? In 1979, Tom Warren won the race in 11 hours, 15 minutes. Ten years later, he finished in 9 hours, 42 minutes, good enough for third. And Warren was then in the 45-to-49 age group.

Perhaps even more amazing is the Ironman's burgeoning popularity. In 1990, 1,350 athletes from 49 countries competed at the Ironman, and organizers *turned away* several thousand more. Incredibly, so many people want in that Ironman organizers must reject entrants.

This has brought its own challenges. When the Ironman first instituted a limit in 1982, wannabe Ironfolk exhibited a fair bit of ingenuity. Race director Valerie Silk was offered everything from ski vacations to Super Bowl tickets; once she received a package of letters from a first-grade class, launching a plea for the father of a classmate.

Today, gaining entrance is an objective affair. You qualify at a designated "Ironman qualifier" race by placing within the top few in your age group. Or you can try your luck in a lottery. Now, getting to the Ironman is almost as difficult as finishing.

Because of its scope and size, the Ironman has been puffed full of hyperbole. The grand moments—Paula Newby-Fraser's stunning records, the epic battles of Dave Scott and Mark Allen—have certainly been grand, but they've often overshadowed events that more accurately mirror what the Ironman really is: flesh-and-blood folks trying to survive an arduous day.

Why would thousands of otherwise rational souls want to spend the better part of the day flaying themselves? Scott Tinley offers an answer.

"The race strikes a chord deep in the hearts and minds of endurance athletes," says Tinley. "It's almost as if they're called to the event, the lava fields crying out, 'Come on and give me a try and see if I can't beat you.' Finish the event and you gain a sense of personal knowledge and self-worth few people have."

Iditarod
The Last Great Race on Earth

How strongly do mushers feel about the 1,157-mile Iditarod Trail Sled Dog Race? Consider the case of John Suter. In 1988, Alaska's economy went sour, and Suter, a 38-year-old father of three, lost his job as a painter. He took his severance pay, tossed in his life savings, and spent the entire bundle—$30,000 in all—preparing for the Iditarod.

Suter also personified the individualism and free spirit typical of the mushers who take on the Iditarod. The best sled dogs are Alaskan huskies, a cross between the Siberian husky and Alaskan crossbreeds known as "village dogs." Eleven of the 20 dogs on Suter's team were poodles. In deference to the occasional – 90° windchills that tear across the Iditarod trail between Anchorage and Nome, Suter styled his poodles so their thick manes flared out like those of lions. Unfortunately, that year the weather turned unseasonably warm, and Suter's overly "dressed" poodles finished out of the running.

The Iditarod is named for the trail used by mushers in the early 1900s to hustle gold out of—and supplies into—the rough-hewn gold-mining towns hacked out of the Alaskan wilderness. In the local language, *Iditarod* means "far place"—precisely what Iditarod mushers must be thinking when they line up in Anchorage each year on the first weekend in March. Their destination: Nome, over 1,000 miles away.

The race was started in 1972 by a former Oklahoman named Joe Redington, perhaps because no native Alaskan was crazy enough. The trail passes by its namesake about halfway through the race. The gold-mining town of Iditarod flourished during the Gold Rush, swelling to 10,000 inhabitants, most of them men who reveled in sport of a different sort. A brothel is one of the few abandoned buildings still standing.

Because of its impressive and often unpredictable obstacles, the Iditarod is billed as "The Last Great Race on Earth." This is something of a misnomer. The howling winds and blinding snowstorms that spit on the 50-some mushers are anything but great, and things on the trail can get so weird that it hardly seems like Earth at all. Deprived of sleep—top teams run from 12 to 20 hours a day for 11 days and more—mushers often hallucinate.

A race for only the fittest

Real life can be even stranger. During the 1985 Iditarod, musher Susan Butcher and her dogs were assaulted by a pregnant moose (Butcher held off the starving animal with an ax handle, but not before the moose killed 2 of her dogs and injured 13 others). On another occasion, pinned down by a violent storm, Butcher chopped firewood in 80-mile-an-hour winds. This is not a race for the weak and giddy.

More than anyone, Butcher put the Iditarod on the map. Tougher and less yielding than bamboo, Butcher won the race in 1986, 1987, 1988 and 1990, which is not surprising since she's virtually dedicated her life to the event.

Butcher lives 300 miles north of Anchorage, in Eureka: population, six; running water, none; electricity, none. She lives in the 80-year-old cabin that once belonged to a Gold Rush blacksmith. Only in isolation, she says, can she maintain an uninterrupted focus on breeding and training sled dogs. She raises most of them from puppies, spending 12 to 15 hours a day feeding, exercising and massaging them after their runs. Not surprisingly, her rapport with her dogs is legendary. One musher accused her of using witchcraft and mind control on them.

There've been other gripes, as well. One male musher swore he'd walk back from Nome to Anchorage if a woman ever won the race. The chauvinist's loss was the T-shirt entrepreneurs' gain. A booming business followed for T-shirts that identified Alaska as the place "Where men are men and women win the Iditarod" and as "The land of beautiful dogs and fast women."

Though the dogs have their work cut out for them, their masters don't exactly recline on their sleds yelling "Mush!" They're too busy maneuvering 200-pound sleds full of gear and dog food. They also break trail through massive snowdrifts, cross miles of barren, rollercoaster tundra, plow through silent, frigid forests and climb steep ridges. Sometimes they push into winds so strong, their dogs strain as if trying to crawl under a door. Mushers can go for 20 hours a day without sleep, and when they take a break, they have to tend to their dogs' needs before they can rest.

Butcher herself runs up every hill along the course to ease the strain on her dogs; other mushers aren't always that fit or conscientious.

Sometimes mushers have to run farther than they expect. During the 1988 race, an unfortunate Swiss musher was knocked from his sled when he was clobbered by a low-hanging tree branch. He chased his team on foot for three hours before a stump snagged the sled and brought the dogs to a halt. Mushers can lose 25 to 30 pounds during the race. Still, all give the dogs their due. "The dogs are the real stars," states four-time winner Rick Swenson.

As a rule, mushers are not expansive sorts. The definitive definition of the Iditarod—apt and simple—is provided by poodle musher Suter.

"Man," says Suter, "when you're mushing down that trail it seems like it just goes on forever and ever and ever."

Marathon
Conquering the long haul

*L*egend has it that the first marathoner was a Greek messenger named Pheidippides. In 490 B.C. he was dispatched to Athens from the village of Marathon bearing news of a Greek victory over the Persians. Pheidippides ran the entire 24 miles across the plains of Marathon, announced the good word in Athens, then fell over dead.

To commemorate that effort, a marathon run of almost 25 miles was staged as part of the first modern Olympic Games in Greece in 1896. The Boston Marathon in the United States was held the following year.

However, it wasn't until the 1908 Olympic Games in London that the now-standard 26-mile, 385-yard distance was introduced. To please the royal family, the British Olympic Committee lengthened the route from Windsor Castle to White City Stadium in London by 385 yards. This would enable King Edward VII's offspring to watch the start of the race from their play area inside the castle walls.

For the record, John Hayes of the United States won the race with a time of two hours, 55 minutes, 18 seconds, following the disqualification of Diondro Pietro of Italy. Pietro, the first runner to actually cross the finish line, had collapsed before reaching the tape. He was helped to his feet and practically carried across the line by well-meaning but misguided race officials.

As for women, they remained off the Olympic marathon stage until the Los Angeles Games of 1984. By then, the women's world record for the distance (held by Norway's Ingrid Kristiansen) was two hours, 24 minutes, 26 seconds, a time that would have won every men's Olympic marathon race up until 1952. American Joan Benoit Samuelson won the inaugural women's Olympic marathon in two hours, 24 minutes, 52 seconds.

Long seen as one of the most grueling yet inspiring events on the world sporting scene, the marathon became the centerpiece of the running boom in the United States. It began when Frank Shorter raced to Olympic victory in Munich, Germany, in 1972. Within five years, tens of thousands of people from every walk of life had finished their first marathon. Some made the once-insurmountable distance look like a cakewalk: Before he died in 1988, Sy Mah, a soft-spoken Canadian, had run 524 marathons.

Training for the marathon

Let's not kid ourselves—although it's been conquered by nuns, octogenarians and your next-door neighbor, the marathon is still a daunting distance. Approach it with respect and caution.

Over the years, through trial and error, marathoners and running coaches have settled on a few training basics.

First and foremost, there's no need to abandon job, family and all other outside interests to adequately prepare for a marathon. The most important foundation of a successful marathon assault is the long, easy run. In fact, adding a long, easy run to your current running program is often all you need. Runners have finished a marathon by running as little as three miles a day and tossing in a long, easy training run once every two weeks.

How does this work? In his best-selling book, *Galloway's Book on Running*, author and runner Jeff Galloway (who has run a 2:16 marathon), lays this program out neatly. To run a marathon, says Galloway, you need to be able to run 26.2 miles. The only way to prepare for this is to actually run that far in training.

Lengthening your run

Extending your running mileage calls for commitment and consistency on your part. It'll help to log your normal weekly running mileage, paltry as it may seem, adding a long run every two weeks. Begin with a distance slightly farther than your longest training run.

Then, every two weeks, add one to two miles to that long run. Note the gradual increase in the distance of the long run while maintaining the distance of your regular training runs. Build up that long run until you're running 26 miles or a bit more.

Galloway points out that most first-time marathoners hit the Wall at precisely 20 miles because they're never gone that far before. Once the body and mind have experienced the stress of a marathon distance in training, they'll be prepared when it comes time to race.

Build up gradually to a long run of 26 miles. Do these long runs every two weeks, taking a week off in between to recover. Take a final long run three to four weeks before your race.

"You've got to run the long run slowly," says Galloway. "If there's one mistake people make, it's running their long runs too fast."

Galloway advises that the pace for your long run be at least two minutes per mile slower than your best pace for that distance. He also recommends taking walking breaks.

Novice marathoners particularly need these breaks early and often. If you're a beginning runner building toward your first marathon, Galloway suggests a minute's walking break every three minutes. In fact, he recommends these breaks for every level of runner.

"Even advanced runners who've run a lot of marathons should take a slow jogging break every ten minutes, slowing to a jog for a minute," says Galloway, who takes these breaks, too. "You'll be able to recover from the long run much more quickly. It doesn't detract one bit from the endurance you'll gain."

Accelerating your progress

Experienced marathoners who want to develop speed to improve their personal records can use the same long run foundation they used as a beginner. Just add speed and form work to it, suggests Galloway.

Marathon speed will come after you've run repeat miles, starting with three to five one-mile repeats. Your speed should be 20 to 30 seconds faster than your marathon race pace. It's a good idea to walk a few hundred yards after each interval.

You can build this interval session gradually, says Galloway, until you're up to 13 one-mile repeats. That session should be your last speed workout, two weeks before the race. Over the last two weeks before the race, you should begin to taper, decreasing your training mileage and cutting out hard-effort speedwork completely.

It's also important to include what Galloway calls "form accelerations." Good form, he points out, is crucial to maximizing your abilities and easing your running.

Entire books have been written on form, so we'll mention just three tips:

1. Run with your chest up.
2. Keep your hips forward.
3. Push off strongly with your foot.

This stance will align your body, eliminate improper form and reduce the chance of injury.

Do four to eight form accelerations of 80 to 150 yards twice a week, recommends Galloway. Try to concentrate on your form while running at a fast pace. Build into the acceleration, then ease out of it. Don't sprint, or you'll lose your focus on form.

Knowing when to taper off

Resting before the big race is crucial, yet it's often neglected by marathon runners who get paranoid about putting in miles. To run well, you'll need to be rested. Over the final two weeks, Galloway proposes cutting your weekly training mileage by 30 to 50 percent.

By the last week, you should be running below 30 percent of your peak mileage pace. Then, for the last 23 days, run only a few miles. Training hard over those last two weeks won't improve your fitness, says Galloway, and it's sure to tire you out.

As a final word, important to beginner and expert alike, Galloway offers, "Make it fun. If you do, you'll stick with it. And the benefits to your lifestyle can be significant and long term."

See Also: *Interval Training; Long, Slow Distance Training; Pacing; Peaking; Ultramarathon; The Wall*

Modern Pentathlon
Diversity times five

M odern pentathlon was the brainchild of Baron Pierre de Coubertin, the French educator who also established today's Olympic Games. De Coubertin used as his model for the modern pentathlon an unfortunate courier in Napoleon's army. The dedicated delivery man hopped on a strange horse, then had it shot out from underneath him, forcing him to dash through battlefields and swim rivers, all the while fending off the enemy with sword and pistol.

Needless to say, this was taxing stuff. The baron's athletic vision—minus life-and-death circumstance—is equally rigorous. Modern pentathlon is five disparate events contested over four days. Day one is toe-to-toe fencing. Day two features a 300-meter swim and shooting at stationary targets. Day three brings a 4,000-meter cross-country run. And on day four, there's equestrian show-jumping over a course pockmarked with obstacles.

Four days at the races

Modern pentathlon keeps its participants on their toes—literally. At the 1992 Olympics in Barcelona, Spain, U.S. national champ Mike Gostigian spent more than 12 hours fencing with over 65 competitors, all of them intent on running him through. Matches are won or lost on a single touch, so there was considerable mental anguish, too.

Gostigian woke the next morning, limbs still sore from a reservoir's worth of lactic acid, and swam an all-out 300-meters. That evening, he forced himself to stand rigidly while shooting at targets 25 meters away. Their silhouettes flicked to face him for a scant three seconds, during which time Gostigian had to raise his arm and fire off an accurate shot.

"I can't tell you how difficult it is to be so precise," says Gostigian, who tried anyway. "After fencing the day before and then swimming that morning, you've got lactic acid in your shoulders, you're stiff and you don't have the fine-tuned feeling in your fingers that's required for precision shooting. You go from pure adrenaline rush in the morning to having to be dead like a rock that evening."

The next day, Gostigian was forced to unleash the adrenaline again, tackling a billygoat cross-country course on legs feeling the wear of the past two days. On the final day, Gostigian had to mount up and negotiate a course pocked with 18 obstacle jumps four feet high—riding a horse he'd never seen before. How did he do it? Training, training, training.

"Pentathlon requires a lot of fine-tuned skills, plus supreme physical conditioning," says Gostigian. "You cover the whole spectrum of emotions and physical and psychological demands."

Nice work if you're a juggler

It's a daunting task to train for the pentathlon. World-class pentathletes must train from five to eight hours a day, six or seven days a week. A light day for Gostigian might be a 90-minute run, followed by an easy 45-minute swim and some shooting practice.

"Balance is the key to being a good pentathlete," he explains. "You have to find the proper training mix so you can maximize your potential. There are a lot of things to juggle."

And this, admits Gostigian, is much of the event's allure. "You can never get bored with a sport like pentathlon. It really keeps you coming back for more."

Pentathlon's Olympic history has been as unbalanced as its repertoire. During the ancient Greek Olympics, held over 2,000 years ago, the pentathlon included a running race the length of the stadium (about 200 yards), a long jump, a discus throw, a javelin throw and finally a wrestling match between the two athletes who had performed the best in the preceding four events.

Baron de Coubertin revised the Greek pentathlon for track and field by changing the 200-yard footrace into a 200-meter dash and substituting a 1500-meter run for the wrestling bout. His version of the pentathlete-as-courier debuted at the 1912 Olympic Games.

Changes will likely continue to bring pentathlon into the 20th century. Though women have been competing in international pentathlons since 1981, there's yet to be a women's pentathlon in the Olympics.

A move is now under way to generate more public interest by shortening the four-day format to a single day. It's popular in Europe, but elsewhere—including in the United States—modern pentathlon receives about the same attention as that accorded duckpin bowling and midget-tossing.

Yet, despite the event's lack of notoriety and support, U.S. contenders have done surprisingly well. In 1989, Lori Norwood became the first American to win the women's World Pentathlon Championship. In 1992, Gostigian became the first American man to win a pentathlon World Cup event, one in a series of international competitions held around the globe year round. Gostigian jokingly reckons an American winning an international pentathlon "is like some guy from Nebraska winning the world championship in surfing."

And if he had it to do all over again, Gostigian wouldn't hesitate.

"I think it's the most extraordinary sport out there. I've learned so much about myself—it's changed my life."

See Also: *Cross-Training, Decathlon*

Race Across America (RAAM)
Cycling's trial of tribulation

N early halfway through the 1983 Race Across America—3,170 miles from Santa Monica, California, to Atlantic City, New Jersey—Michael Shermer had built up a tremendous lead. Refusing to sleep, Shermer rode his bicycle all the way to Haigler, Nebraska—a whopping 1,500 miles—without stopping to rest.

His competitors were still strung out behind him, albeit a state or two behind, but Shermer had other concerns—namely his support crew. Shermer was convinced they were a group of aliens masquerading as his friends, conducting an elaborate plot to kill him. Riding along beside his support van, Shermer refused sustenance—how easy to poison a banana— and sporadically quizzed his enemies about intimate details of his past, things that only close Earth friends would know.

Nor has Shermer by any means been the only RAAM rider to act erratically. Short on sleep—RAAM riders typically sleep anywhere from 90 minutes to four hours a day—cyclists exhibit everything from outright paranoia to a profound appreciation for nature.

During the 1988 RAAM, cyclist Steve Born spent an hour lying in the middle of a Midwestern highway, spellbound by fireflies. Racing across a continent necessitates some obvious changes in habit. Offers former RAAM winner Michael Secrest, "The only time you should get off the bike is when you have to go to the bathroom or go to sleep."

A history of lunacy

Like most grand events, RAAM had an off-the-cuff beginning. In 1978, John Marino, a 28-year-old from Newport Beach, California, rode his bicycle from Santa Monica to New York, hoping to break the transcontinental crossing record of 13 days, five hours, 20 minutes. Shortly after Marino arrived at the finish (four hours under the old record), a reporter asked him the inevitable question: What next? Marino gave it some thought. Gee, he said, maybe we should make this a race.

The following year, four riders did exactly that—racing 2,968 miles from the Santa Monica Pier to the Empire State Building—and RAAM was born. More surprising, the event quickly blossomed from there. It was held each summer, and by 1988 there were 40 entrants. This was a sizable number considering RAAM's sole lure (the race offers little or no prize money)— the opportunity to stare down heat, cold, humidity, aridity, ennui, doubt, frustration, fatigue and aliens, simply to ride across the country on a bicycle as fast as possible.

Even Marino, who now serves as the race director, is somewhat puzzled by the event's popularity. Riders mortgage their homes, sacrifice jobs and relationships and train through all sorts of misery to qualify (RAAM has a series of 500-mile regional qualifying races), mostly to see what they are made of.

"It seems to appeal to an obscure side of human nature," muses Marino. "If you tell people that this is the toughest thing there is, they'll stand in line to do it. It's a phenomenon about the human species I haven't quite figured out."

There's no confusing the physics of the event. Depending on the year's route (the race has always started in California, but it has finished in New York, New Jersey, Georgia and Washington, D.C.), riders arc through more than a dozen states and a kaleidoscope's worth of weather and terrain. The ills they suffer are too long to list—the short list includes saddle sores, knee sprains, dizziness, vomiting and hallucinations that would make Timothy Leary sit up and take notice.

Occasionally, obstacles pile up all at once. During the 1991 race Paul Solon, a soft-spoken attorney, crashed 100 miles into the race. Solon was riding 40 miles an hour at the time—his bike flipped over several times with Solon still clipped into the pedals. Doctors later found a torn shoulder muscle, whiplash, a sprained left ankle, a loose bone chip in his left ankle, a sprained right knee and road rash from his butt to his shoulders.

Solon continued on for almost 1,000 miles before finally calling it quits in Cortez, Colorado. "After a while," he allowed, "it all got to be a little much." Race winner Bob Fourney rolled into Savannah, Georgia, in a time of eight days, 16 hours, 44 minutes.

Why they do it

Well, for one thing, the lowest lows can also be matched by the highest highs.

"RAAM is a period in your life when you can get more out of life than you've ever experienced," says Johnny Goldberg, whose thoughts are representative. "There's so much to experience—so much knowledge, so much performance, so much pleasure, so much pain. An entire spectrum of life, experienced in one race."

Cindy Staiger's RAAM experience is also representative. In 1987, Staiger's crew quit at the top of Utah's Strawberry Pass. Without support, she was forced to drop out. The following year, Staiger came back to win. When she reached Strawberry Pass, her crew threw a brief party, complete with champagne, flowers and toilet-paper banners.

But the most unforgettable moment occurred 100 miles from the finish. Assured of the win, Staiger stopped, got off her bicycle and began crying. One by one, crew members walked over and tried to persuade her to go on. Staiger waved them off. Finally, her father walked over and gently asked, "Don't you think you should go on?" Twelve days, three hours and 55 minutes after leaving San Francisco, Staiger wheeled up to the Washington Monument finish.

"I didn't want anybody to touch me or talk to me," says Staiger of her emotional pitstop. "It was just so long, it was so hard, there was so much work involved. Everything just came to a head and I had to stop. I just realized the impact of what was happening."

Tour de France
A recurring miracle

How fiercely do passions rage at the Tour de France? While leading the 1991 Tour, three-time winner Greg LeMond was charged by a Spanish spectator, upset that an American was winning Europe's most glorious sporting event. Still on his bike, LeMond clenched his left fist. The Spaniard charged into it, knocking himself out. LeMond was lucky. Five-time Tour winner Eddy Merckx was punched in the liver by a spectator during an arduous climb in 1975, a blow that effectively took him out of the race.

How popular is the Tour de France? Twenty million people line the course; two million alone crowd Paris for the finish down the Champs-Elysees. Those who disdain crowds repair to remote roadside meadows, watching the spectacle from tables laden with fresh strawberries, wine and cold chicken. Those who don't mind the elbow-to-elbow crush set up shop along popular sections of the race 24 hours in advance.

Everyone gets involved. During the 1986 Tour's epic battle between France's Bernard Hinault and LeMond, French President Francois Mitterand phoned Hinault and urged him to ride for the glory of France (LeMond won the race).

How tough is the Tour de France? One particular climb is legendary. L'Alpe d'Huez, an ascent in the Italian Alps, is 15 kilometers long, encompasses 21 switchbacks and climbs 6,000 feet. It's guaranteed, as the French say, to turn your legs *en compote*—"like applesauce." To make things even more challenging, the L'Alpe d'Huez assault comes at the end of a 100-mile ride that includes two other mountain climbs.

Riders do not lollygag. During the 1992 Tour—a 3,983-kilometer route encompassing France, Spain, Belgium, the Netherlands, Germany, Luxembourg and Italy—the 198 riders from 21 countries averaged 39.5 kilometers per hour. In nonmetric terms, we're talking about 24 miles an hour.

"I think this is the toughest sport in the world," LeMond told reporters after winning the 1990 Tour, a 3,414-kilometer grind. "No other sport combines endurance and intensity the way this one does. ... Here you have everything. You're tested on all your levels of athletic ability."

The price of greatness

All of this is fitting, for the Tour de France is cycling's epic—two weeks of racing and heated patriotism across more than 2,000 miles of Europe. The race takes place in daily stages and includes time trials (short rides, as little as 14 miles, where riders go all-out from start to finish) and longer road races, many over 100 miles.

At the end of each stage, the riders' time totals are added up. The rider with the fastest overall time rides the next day wearing the coveted *maillot jaune*—the yellow jersey worn by the race leader. This is unquestionably the cycling world's most prized item of clothing, and the heroes who have donned it are legendary. Five-time winners Eddy Merckx, Jacques Anquetil and Bernard Hinault. Three-time winner Greg LeMond. Twice-victorious Laurent Fignon. *Les geants de la route,* the French call them—"the giants of the route."

To win the Tour, however, means overcoming tremendous challenges. As part of the grind on mind and muscle, riders must spend up to ten hours a day on a bicycle. At race's end, you'll see men (no women compete in the Tour) who are no more than shells, sucked dry of all energy.

Take Greg LeMond. On his way to winning the 1990 Tour, LeMond raised huge blisters on his feet, dislocated a finger, cut his legs in a crash and ground away so much skin around his crotch that each night his masseur could hear him screaming in the shower.

It should be no surprise, then, that mind games are an integral, and daunting, part of the Tour. Riders talk of breaking each other's legs, and they come as close as they can to actually doing so without being arrested for battery. Tour champions are as legendary for their mental panache as they are for their resilient bodies—and sometimes more so.

Banty-size Bernard Hinault stood but five feet, eight inches tall, but his heart was bigger than all of France. Dubbed *Le Blaireau* (the badger), Hinault in the heat of battle was like a rabid animal on the scent. A single look from Hinault, whispered some, was enough to drain the courage right out of you.

On American soil, no rider is more synonymous with the Tour de France than Greg LeMond. LeMond first rode the Tour in 1984 and promptly shocked the European contingent by finishing third (not until 1981 did an American place in the top 50). He followed that with a second-place finish in 1985, then won the race outright in 1986 in a classic duel with Hinault, an outcome that left most of France in mourning.

Since the Tour's inception in 1903, French riders had won nearly half of all the Tours, and they fight to the death to retain this stranglehold. LeMond's father, Bob, put it best.

"This isn't just a bike race," said the senior LeMond during his son's 1986 win. "The fiber of everything French is at stake."

Pursuing "the permanent miracle"

LeMond would go on to win the race again in 1989 and 1990. His 1989 win probably qualifies as one of the most dramatic moments in sport. After more than 87 hours and 2,000 miles of riding, 50 seconds separated

LeMond from French Tour leader Laurent Fignon.

The Tour's final day featured a 24.5-kilometer time trial from Versailles to Paris. Riders would go off alone at two-minute intervals, with the last-place rider going first. Beating a world-class rider like Fignon by more than 50 seconds in so short a race was considered impossible.

LeMond started two minutes ahead of Fignon, who, as Tour leader, went last. The two ground toward Paris. LeMond chose not to be informed of Fignon's progress. Fignon, who heard shouted progress reports from his handlers, was at first shocked, then astounded as LeMond purposefully rode away from him, whittling precious seconds from Fignon's lead. Sensing drama in the making, the normally partisan Parisian crowd began shouting "De l'audace, LeMond, de l'audace"—boldly, boldly.

Head down, legs driving, LeMond rocketed across the finish, then turned to wait for Fignon. Minutes later, Fignon careened across the line and collapsed. His masseur, holding Fignon in his arms, was the first to tell the Frenchman. "Laurent," he said, "you lost the race." Second to LeMond by eight seconds after two weeks of racing, the normally stoic Fignon bowed his head and wept.

Like any great challenge, the stakes at the Tour are constantly being raised. In both 1991 and 1992, LeMond—and the rest of the field—was ground underfoot by Spanish rider Miguel Indurain. The average pace at the 1992 race—23.7 miles an hour—was the fastest ever.

The Tour is known among the French as "the permanent miracle," but as the race's history so aptly illustrates—suffering and glory excepted—there's little at the Tour that's permanent.

See Also: *Race Across America (RAAM)*

Trans America Footrace
The ultimate cross-country race

There are easier ways to see this vast country of ours, but none more thorough—on the run, coast to coast, for 3,000 miles.

Although the Trans America Footrace might sound like the ultimate fitness boom lunacy, its roots actually stretch back to the famed, and appropriately named, Bunion Derbies of 1928 and 1929.

These races were organized by enterprising promoter C. C. "Cash and Carry" Pyle, whose bad luck it was to launch his event at the beginning of the Depression. Perhaps because his fellow countrymen enjoyed hearing about those who were even less fortunate, Pyle's transcontinental races received extensive publicity. But the race received little of an event's lifeblood—money—and after two short years it was history.

The race was resurrected in 1992 and started, with little fanfare, on a gray June morning at California's Huntington Beach State Park. Runners were to pass through more than 400 cities and towns and cross 14 states, not to mention hoofing through such daunting topography as the Mojave Desert and the Continental Divide.

They'd run 28 to 64 miles a day, finishing, hopefully, 64 days after they started in New York City's Central Park. The promise of such novelty attracted 28 starters from seven countries.

The agony of da feet

Many of the entrants were actually prepared. Among the starters were Germany's Helmut Schieke, who had crossed the country on his own in 1971, and Scotland's Al Howie, who had run 4,533 miles across Canada, averaging over 62 miles a day. Schieke would finish seventh. Howie would be pulled out eight days into the race after medical personnel discovered that he'd rubbed the bottoms of his feet skinless.

Ultra runners have always taken stoicism to new heights. As Andy Lovy, M.D., a psychiatrist and member of the race's medical team, put it, "Seventy percent of this type of race is run in the mind. These guys don't put up mental barriers the way most people do. They smash them to pieces."

Indeed, such verve was much in evidence throughout the race, as runners plowed through ailments both minor and major. With three weeks to go, Maryland's Tom Rogozinski, the youngest competitor in the race at 24, was told that the intense pain in his foot was a stress fracture.

"Pain is pain, and that's all it is," retorted Rogozinski, who continued to finish third in 528 hours, 48 minutes. The toll on the racers' minds was equally daunting.

"After a while, the run became like a job on an assembly line," noted Milan Milanovic, a bearded Swiss who finished second in 527 hours, 16 minutes. "You spend 8 or 9 hours on the job and eventually you finish, exhausted, knowing you must do it again the next day."

Still, when Californian David Warady broke the Central Park finish banner to win the race after 521 hours and 35 minutes on the run, excitement was high.

Warady, a modest soul, did no chest-thumping at the finish.

"I'm not the fastest runner here," he told a reporter. "I just had less severe injuries than some of the others."

Triathlon
Three sports are better than one

Since triathlon's inception over 20 years ago, there have been many moments of grandeur. But few depict the sport's glory, humanity and grit better than the experience of Edson Sower.

Sower entered the 1987 Hawaii Ironman Triathlon undaunted by its distance—a 2.4-mile swim followed by a 112-mile bike ride and a 26.2-mile run—or by the fact that he was 70. Hawaii's heat and headwinds have never treated anyone kindly, and after nearly 18 hours on the move, Sower was struggling. A friend, waiting for him at the finish line, walked out into the night to accompany Sower for his last few miles. Both Brooklyn Dodger fans, they talked baseball, their conversation interrupted by Sower's periodic stops to vomit. Sower finished the race 7 minutes under its 18-hour, 30-minute cutoff.

This hardly sounds glamorous, but it's real life out on the triathletic field of play. Yet this is precisely triathlon's attraction. To persevere, and overcome, is a reward indescribably sweet. Sower remembers "floating" down the final 100 yards to the Ironman finish.

The birth of a multisport

Oddly enough, the sport of triathlon developed as a training alternative, initiated by bored runners in San Diego in the mid-1970s. It was inspired by the open-water swim/run/swim events that had long been a staple of Southern California lifeguard training and competition.

Triathlon exploded into mass popularity in the 1980s, driven largely by the popularity of Hawaii's 140-mile Ironman Triathlon. It then spread from California to around the globe— Europe, South America, Canada, Asia and Australia—spawning a cross-training ethic that replaced the running boom of the 1970s.

Today, triathlon is America's favorite multisport event. According to the Triathlon Federation/USA, over 2,000 triathlons are held in the United States every year.

Traditionally, triathlons consist of an open-water swim, a bike ride and a run. But multisport enthusiasts have never lacked imagination, and variations on the swim/bike/run theme are common.

Canoeing and kayaking, for instance, are frequently substituted for swimming. Contestants in the Mountain Man Winter Triathlon in Colorado race on cross-country skis, then on snowshoes, before speed-skating around a multiloop course.

Although there's no single, official triathlon distance, the most popular format for mass participation is the International, or Olympic, distance.

This includes a 1500-meter swim, a 40-kilometer bike ride and a 10-kilometer run. More than 4,000 triathletes compete each year in the international distance *Chicago SunTimes* Triathlon—the largest multisport event of its kind in the world.

Still, the Hawaii Ironman remains the premier event in the triathlon world. Founded by John Collins, a Navy commander stationed in Hawaii, the first Ironman was held in January 1978 in Honolulu on the island of Oahu. The event was a one-day combination of three major endurance events held in the Hawaiian Islands at that time: the 2.4-mile Waikiki Rough Water Swim, the two-day, 116-mile Around-the-Island Bike Ride and the 26.2-mile Honolulu Marathon. Four miles were lopped off the bike ride so that the run could follow the identical, start-to-finish route of the marathon.

In 1981, the Ironman moved to the town of Kailua on the Kona Coast of the Big Island of Hawaii, but the distances remained what they had been at Honolulu. The race annually attracts more than 1,200 competitors, tens of thousands of spectators, reams of media and numerous scientists and physiologists who, rightly enough, have come to see the race as a living laboratory for research into human performance under adverse conditions.

Yet the Ironman isn't the ultimate challenge. In recent years, athletes have taken on double and even triple Ironmans. While some might, with good reason, question the sanity of such undertakings, they underscore the basis of all multisport—to etch a path all your own.

Success starts in the mind

Successful triathlon training includes more than simply swimming, biking and running. It takes time to build a base and prepare the body for endurance training. Keep two words in mind when you first start training for triathlons: *Start slow.* Otherwise, your program can end before it starts—with an injury.

And do some serious thinking before you dash out the door. Know your goals. Figure out your strengths and weaknesses. Write down a training program, and make it convenient for you. If it's easy for you to get workouts in, you'll stick with it longer.

Log your progress by recording your workouts, otherwise known as planning your work and working your plan. This is especially important when you're just beginning. At first there'll be days when you suddenly want to challenge yourself with a long run. Don't.

There will also be days when you want to skip it all. Don't. Your well thought-out plan, right there on paper, will help keep you from getting injured, and from quitting.

With that in mind, though, leave some room for alternatives and creative workouts. Yes, you've got to be motivated and persistent, but you don't have to be myopic.

Coauthor Scott Tinley, who's been pushing himself out the door for over 20 years now, understands the training grind better than most. If Tinley isn't in the mood, he'll concoct any number of tricks. Instead of going for a long bike ride, he'll ride errands around town, sprinting from one to the next. Or he'll ride with friends and organize a Tour de Donut—riding 80 miles and stopping at five of the county's best bakeries along the way. Outright bribery is sometimes the only way to get that workout in.

"Nine times out of ten, when I finally get going, I'm glad to be out and doing it," says Tinley. And that tenth time? "I might get ten miles down the road and realize it just ain't gonna happen," he says. "I turn around and head for the barn so that I can live to fight again."

After you've been training for six months, Tinley recommends you step back and reassess your program. In fact, even if you've been training for eons, it's wise to make a periodic reassessment.

Have you improved? Are you ready for more difficult challenges? How much time do you have to train? Are you still as motivated as you were, or have your priorities changed? If they have, you may have to change with them.

Finally, don't get frustrated. Mastering one sport is hard enough. Taking on three requires—you guessed it—three times as much time.

"Be patient and persistent, and the results will come," says Tinley. "Learn to expect some bad days—this is hard work—and they won't throw you off as much when they happen."

Once you've decided why you're doing this in the first place, you'll face another important decision—how much time you want to devote to training. Of course, the answers to this question are as varied as the people who ask it. If you're an heir to the Wrigley fortune, time is not an issue. If you have a family of nine, time could be tight. Since you're probably somewhere in the middle, we'll answer the question you *really* want to ask: What's the bare-bones minimum I have to put in?

Tinley recommends a minimum of $1\frac{1}{2}$ to 2 hours a day, not much when you consider that you're honing not one but three sports. That sort of training, says Tinley, will get you in adequate shape to finish a race with a 1.5-kilometer swim, 40-kilometer bike and 10-kilometer run and still have fun with it. It won't, however, make you a contender.

Swimming: Get thee to a pool

The first stop—your local Masters swimming team. These recreational teams for swimmers of all ages (even 85-year-olds are still churning up the pool) have blossomed across the country. And for good reason.

Here you'll learn good technique. You'll also get the benefit of organized workouts—the best and most efficient way to get in your swim training. Swimming a mile every day at the Y is fine, but you'll never develop the necessary speed, stroke and conditioning without intervals and a coach

(continued on page 244)

How Far? Scott Tinley's Training Mileage Table

The following table offers some specific mileage guidelines for ten goal/ability levels. You'll recognize yourself in here somewhere. Find your level and check the training recommendations. They'll give you a good idea of where you want to be.

(D)—distance (H)—hard, steady (I)—intervals (R)—recovery

Level	Activity	Daily Distance							Total
		Mon.	**Tues.**	**Wed.**	**Thurs.**	**Fri.**	**Sat.**	**Sun.**	
1	Swim (yd)	1,200(H)	0	1,800(I)	0	1,500(I)	0	0	4,500
1	Bike (mi)	0	15(H)	0	15(I)	0	25(D)	15(R)	70
1	Run (mi)	4(R)	0	6(I)	6(I)	4(H)	0	8(D)	28
2	Swim (yd)	1,300(H)	0	2,000(I)	0	1,600(I)	0	0	4,900
2	Bike (mi)	0	20(H)	0	20(I)	0	35(D)	20(R)	95
2	Run (mi)	5(R)	0	7(I)	0	5(H)	0	9(D)	26
3	Swim (yd)	1,500(I)	0	2,000(I)	0	1,600(I)	750(R)	0	5,850
3	Bike (mi)	0	25(H)	0	25(I)	0	45(D)	25(R)	120
3	Run (mi)	5(R)	0	8(I)	6(H)	0	11(D)	0	30
4	Swim (yd)	1,750(I)	0	2,200(I)	0	1,750(I)	1,000(R)	0	6,700
4	Bike (mi)	0	30(D)	0	35(H)	0	50(D)	25(R)	140
4	Run (mi)	5(R)	0	8(I)	0(I)	7(H)	0	13(D)	33
5	Swim (yd)	2,000(I)	0	2,500(I)	0	2,000(I)	1,000(R)	0	7,500
5	Bike (mi)	0	35(D)	0	35(H)	0	55(D)	30(R)	155
5	Run (mi)	6(R)	0	9(I)	0	8(H)	0	15(D)	38
6	Swim (yd)	2,250(I)	1,500(R)	0	2,800(I)	2,250(I)	1,000(R)	0	9,800
6	Bike (mi)	20(R)	40(D)	0	40(H)	0	60(D)	30(R)	190
6	Run (mi)	6(R)	0	9(I)	0	8(H)	0	16(D)	39
7	Swim (yd)	2,500(I)	1,750	0	3,000(I)	2,500(I)	1,000(R)	0	10,750
7	Bike (mi)	25(R)	0	45(D)	50(H)	0	75(D)	30(R)	225
7	Run (mi)	7(R)	9(I)	0	7(R)	9(H)	0	16(D)	48

Level	Activity	Mon.	Tues.	Wed.	Thurs.	Fri.	Sat.	Sun.	Total
		Daily Distance							**Total**
8	Swim (yd)	3,000(I)	2,000(R)	0	3,500(I)	3,000(I)	0	1,500(R)	13,000
8	Bike (mi)	40(D)	20(R)	55(D)	60(H/I)	0	80	35(R)	290
8	Run (mi)	0	10(I)	4(R)	9(H)	6(R)	10(H)	18(D)	57
9	Swim (yd)	3,500(I)	3,000(I)	2,000(R)	4,000(I)	3,500(I)	0	1,500(R)	17,500
9	Bike (mi)	60(D)	35(R)	75(D)	40(R)	50(H/I)	90(D)	0	350
9	Run (mi)	0	12(I)	6(R)	10(H)	6(R)	10(H)	20(D)	64
10	Swim (yd)	4,500(I)	4,500(I)	2,000(R)	4,500(I)	4,500(I)	0	2,000(R)	22,000
10	Bike (mi)	70(D)	40(R)	85(D)	45(R)	60(H/I)	100(D)	0	400
10	Run (mi)	4(R)	13(I)	6(R)	11(H)	6(R)	10(H)	20(D)	70

Level 1. You're a beginner, with little or no experience. Or you're a survivor who simply wants to participate. Responsibilities other than triathlon have priority.

Level 2. You have an athletic background. You've completed a triathlon and you want to start getting serious.

Level 3. You have the time and will to train seriously. Family members are starting to give you triathlon equipment for Christmas and birthdays.

Level 4. You have several years of racing and training behind you. You feel comfortable saying "gear ratio." You go to bed at 9:30.

Level 5. You have serious thoughts about winning your age group. This is a good, solid level for the experienced triathlete with a firm commitment.

Level 6. Triathlon has become your number one priority. You show up for work, and leave work, in training gear.

Level 7. You have lots of experience. You may be training for an Ironman. You've finished near the top in your age group. You have two bikes and a garage full of finisher T-shirts and weathered bike shorts.

Level 8. You're almost a full-time athlete now. You're either independently wealthy or in immediate danger of being visited by creditors. You disconnect the phone at 8:30.

Level 9. Your spouse left you. You're scrambling for sponsors and prize money at races. Hopefully you're taking some of it home.

Level 10. You're a professional triathlete. Rent and bills are paid with prize-money checks and sponsor support. Or they aren't paid at all. You're committed. Or should be.

breathing down your neck. Plan to join an organized workout. Then expect to swim at least three days a week, at least 1,500 yards (a little less than a mile) per workout.

If you're an experienced swimmer or serious competitive triathlete, you'll need five days a week in the pool. Add to this a long swim in the ocean or lake on the weekends. Build to where you can handle 15,000 to 25,000 yards a week. You won't need any more. Improvements beyond that will hinge on speeding up your interval efforts, not upping your distance.

Biking: Work it into your routine

Expect to spend at least three days a week in the saddle. Remember, cycling is time-consuming, so you'll probably do most of your riding on the weekends. Your schedule might go something like this: a short, one-hour ride on Wednesday, a long ride on Saturday of three to four hours and finally, a medium-distance ride of about two hours on Sunday.

By definition, your long ride will take several hours, so go early in the morning. Riding from 6 A.M. to 10 A.M. leaves plenty of time for the remaining responsibilities in your day—kids, yardwork, shopping. The fact is, you'll find the pick-me-up of an early bike ride gives you extra pizzazz to keep you hopscotching through your day.

Tinley recommends keeping your total bike mileage at six times your running mileage. Are you running 30 miles a week? That means 180 miles of cycling a week. This ratio holds even for more serious triathletes, although it makes biking a seven-day-a-week proposition. But unless you're Greg LeMond, logging 500 miles of cycling can't be done in three days.

Running: Ease up on your mileage

Most triathletes come from a running background. The biggest problem here is holding yourself back. If you're a 50-mile-a-week runner, cut your mileage back to 30. Concentrate on balancing all three sports before you begin to bump up your running mileage again.

To the hardened runner, suggesting a cut in mileage is a bit like suggesting oral surgery. Relax. Your running won't suffer; in fact, it could improve. And if you're serious about triathlon, you'll need to devote time to those other two sports.

If you don't have a running background, start slowly. If you're overzealous, few sports will injure you more quickly. What minimum mileage should you aim for? Try four days of running a week for at least 20 miles total. The maximum? The best triathletes rarely run over 80 miles a week.

Tinley recommends scattering your four running days, allowing time to recover. For example, run on Tuesdays, Thursdays, Fridays and Sundays. On Tuesdays and Thursdays, focus on quality, either running intervals or taking hard, short runs. Use Friday for an easy run and Sunday for your long run.

That long Sunday run should be at least twice as long as the race you're preparing for, or twice as long as your average daily training run. Obviously, if you're training for an Ironman with its 26.2-mile run, you'd have to cover most of the county to get in twice the mileage. If your longest weekly run is 7 miles, run 14. Test your limits slowly.

Finally, when it comes to training of any kind, consistency is the key.

"It's the long-term training effect that will make you strong," says Tinley. "Not even the most talented athlete can come right out of the blocks and race well time after time without years of work. Getting the most from yourself means sticking with it."

See Also: *Cross-Training, Duathlon, Hawaii Ironman Triathlon, Overtraining, Pacing*

Ultramarathon
Pushing the limits

*I*t's not enough for some athletes to tackle the 26.2 miles that make up a marathon. So for those with a real yen to conquer the elements—and their own limitations—ultramarathons offer the ultimate challenge.

Arguably the best known of all is the Western States Endurance Run, 100 miles of hellish trail from Squaw Valley to Auburn, California. The route, mostly wilderness trails, covers some 17,000 vertical feet of uphills and 22,000 feet of descents. Temperatures on race day have ranged from 114°F to well below freezing, with snow at some of the higher elevations.

Even so, the event, held each June, actually turns people away. Other ultra races are also wildly popular—the Leadville 100 (Colorado) and the Old Dominion 100 (Virginia), to name just two. Although the better-known ultras are generally 100 miles, an ultramarathon, by loose definition, is usually any running race longer than a 26.2-mile marathon.

This open-ended definition leaves room for all manner of horrors. Take, for example, Australia's Westfield Run—1,010 kilometers across the outback from Sydney to Melbourne. This run also highlights the joie de vivre typical of ultramarathon events. For several years, the race was dominated by an affable Greek named Yiannis Kouros. At the May 1990 event, Kouros offered his 31 other competitors an 8-hour lead, then mowed them all down within 30 hours. Battling abysmal weather (high winds and scattered snowfalls) and napping every few days, Kouros emerged victorious in six days, 5 hours.

Ultra effort for ultra results

Although they don't get much attention, ultrarunners have produced some remarkable performances. In September 1989, soft-spoken northern Californian Ann Trason won the U.S. national 24-hour championship for men and women. She logged an amazing 143 miles over 24 hours.

Think all you have to do is plug on slowly? Trason puddle-hopped her first 50 miles in a rainstorm in 6 hours, 19 minutes—essentially two 3:18 marathons back-to-back. Her time at 100 miles was 13 hours, 55 minutes—equivalent to nearly four marathons averaging 3:39 apiece. All this was accomplished while cheerfully thanking lap counters at the end of each one-mile loop.

Perhaps the most remarkable ultra feat belongs to the monks of Mount Hiei in Japan. Reportedly, novice monks do a marathon a day for 100 consecutive days in a ritual designed to focus their minds. By the seventh year, the monks who remain are asked to run 100 consecutive 84-kilometer cross-country runs, followed by 100 daily marathons—all while dressed in traditional robes and sandals. According to John Stevens, who documented this ritual in his book *The Marathon Monks of Mount Hiei*, no more than 50 monks have gone through this ritual over the past 100 years.

What motivates ultramarathoners? There are more answers than there are miles. Here's one that's as good as any, from two-time Western States 100 champ Tom Johnson.

"America's a pretty easy society to live in," says Johnson. "Nobody really has to push their limits. It's amazing when you find out what you can do."

See Also: *Marathon, Pacing, Trans America Footrace, Western States 100*

Western States 100
The ultrarunner's ultra

W hen Herb Tanzer woke the morning of his first Western States, he was ready to run, all right. "I was so scared I couldn't believe it," Tanzer recalls. "I wanted to run away from the place screaming."

And these are the sentiments of a man who was talented enough to eventually win the race outright. Tanzer's anxiety, however, was understandable. Here are the ingredients for a Western States 100—officially dubbed the Western States Endurance Run.

Start with 100 miles of hellish horse trail across the Sierra Nevada Mountains from Squaw Valley to Auburn, California. Add temperature extremes that turn water from liquid to solid to gas. Sprinkle in climbs and descents that would discourage a mountain goat. Toss in darkness, depression and delirium.

Then try to handle all this while running in remote areas of the Sierra Nevada wilderness. For much of the Western States run, runners are in the wilds. Should something go wrong, horse and helicopter are the sole means of rescue. Contemplating the above brings a gleeful grin to Western types.

"The way I look at it, you either finish or they're going to have to drag you out on a horse or mule," chuckles Jim Pellon, the first runner to complete ten Western States races in a row. "You either finish and make it, or perish out there."

Sun and snow and squiggly things

Pellon, of course, is being somewhat dramatic—but not much. Few events are tougher than the Western States. The event traces its roots to the 100-mile Tevis Cup, a veritable endurance horseback ride over the Western States Trail from Squaw Valley to Auburn.

The Tevis Cup was perceived to be one of the most grueling endurance events in existence, until Tevis Cup rider Gordy Ainsleigh decided to leave his horse at home. Sans equine transportation, Ainsleigh covered the 100 miles in 23 hours and 42 minutes. Considering the fact that Tevis Cup participants, with horses, usually finished in the neighborhood of 22 hours, Ainsleigh's effort was quite respectable.

Three years later, in 1977, the first official Western States Endurance Run debuted with a field of 14. Only 3 runners finished, but the gauntlet had been tossed down. There are other ultraendurance runs—even other 100-mile runs—but the Western States is the grandpappy of them all.

A number of things make the Western States an attractive race to folks who enjoy next-to-impossible challenges. First, the arena, although hostile, is beautiful.

Second, runners get a gander at upcoming obstacles right from the start. Beginning in Squaw Valley, the course immediately climbs to 8,750 feet, often forcing runners to plow through snow even though the race is held in June.

Third, it's never boring. Over the next 96 miles, runners are treated to 40,000 feet of elevation change and commensurate shifts in temperature. During the middle of the day, the buzzing heat in some of the canyons is enough to set your shorts aflame. The trail is marked with yellow ribbons, but this doesn't stop even the most experienced runners from getting lost.

Sharp eyesight won't hurt, either. Negotiating the trail when you're fresh, during broad daylight, is one thing. Following it at night, after 14 hours of running have turned your mind to mush, can be a hair-raising affair.

It's not much better during the day. Prerace literature advises runners to keep an eye out for rattlesnakes, cougars and bears.

Ann Trason, a soft-spoken Californian who has won the women's race several times (women run the same course as the men), remembers following Jim Pellon down a steep hill only to see him suddenly leap straight up. "He screamed and jumped right over a rattler lying in the middle of the trail," recalls Trason, who came to a screeching stop, then gently shooed the snake off the trail with some well-placed pebbles. Shrugs Trason, "They have more right to be there than we do."

The fact is, ultrarunning attracts a peculiar kind of optimist, a sort of locker-room psychic who bends unpleasant thoughts the way magician David Copperfield bends spoons.

"You've got to think pleasant thoughts," reasons two-time champ Tom Johnson, who won the 1991 race in a remarkable record time of 15 hours, 54 minutes. "If you don't, you'll be destroyed."

The thrill of staying on your feet

If you think this is a race for only the crazed few, guess again. Since 1980, race officials have had to hold a lottery to decide who gets in. The only prize given is a highly cherished sterling silver belt buckle, awarded to every runner who finishes under 24 hours.

But as you may imagine, the potential rewards stretch far beyond the material. The Western States finishes in Auburn on a local high school track. Few finishes are more dramatic.

Most runners finish somewhere between 25 and 28 hours, spilling out of the wilderness to run a final few miles on dark town streets. Then they shoot out of the blackness and onto the brightly lit track in what will probably be remembered as a high point of their lives.

The diehards are now sporting taped toes and fanny packs stuffed with bananas, trail mix and tuna fish sandwiches. They've fought off heat, cold and an overwhelming desire to quit. To finish is their all-consuming purpose in life. The fact that it may take weeks, or even months, to recover bothers them not a whit.

Western States runners aren't generally folks who natter on. Tom Johnson recalls his first impressions of the Western States.

"I was amazed I could do it," he says. "I also realized 100 miles is a long way to go."

See Also: *Ultramarathon*

About the Authors

Scott Tinley

Scott Tinley is considered a true pioneer in the sport of triathlon. He began competing in 1976 when the sport was new, and since then has entered over 300 triathlons. He has won nearly 100 of them, and placed in the top three a record 30 times at Ironman races, Nice and the Budlight National Championship. His ability to win races at every distance—from the short course to the ultra—is one of his greatest assets.

In 1982, he won his first Budlight Ironman World Championship, setting a new world record. In 1985, he set his second record in this event. In 1985, he was voted "Triathlete of the Year" in a worldwide poll.

In 1990, Scott took the inaugural Ironman World Series with more consistent top finishes in four separate Ironman events. He finished a close second at the 1990 Hawaii Ironman and went on to win the Ironman World Series in 1991 and 1992.

These accomplishments helped him earn a top place in the world overall rankings for 1990, 1991 and 1992. To date, Scott has competed in triathlons held in 15 different countries and 20 of our 50 states.

When he's not competing, Scott keeps busy with the Tinley Performancewear clothing line. The company, of which he is vice president of advertising and promotions, is a leader in multifitness apparel. It is now part of Reebok International.

In 1988, Scott released a home video, *Triathlon Training with Scott Tinley,* and in addition to this book, he has written *Winning Triathlon* and *Triathlon: The First 15 Years.*

He expects to continue competing at the top for another five years.

His biggest fans are his wife, Virginia, his daughter, Torrie, and his son, Dane.

Ken McAlpine

Ken McAlpine is a freelance writer who has written for *Runner's World, Sports Illustrated, Outside, Triathlete* and the *Los Angeles Times.* He lives in Ventura, California, with his wife, Kathy, and their son, Cullen. He spends his free time boosting his own endurance by swimming, surfing and kayaking.

Index

Note: Underscored page references indicate boxed text. **Boldface** references indicate tables.

A

Acclimatization, 31–34
  altitude training and, 38
  open–water swimming and, 99–100
Acetaminophen, 49
ACSM. *See* American College of Sports Medicine
ADA, 141
Adenosine diphosphate (ADP), 7–8
  in anaerobic metabolism, 44
Adenosine triphosphate (ATP), 7–8, 135
  in aerobic metabolism, 8, 35, 44
  in anaerobic metabolism, 8, 44
  in muscle, 22
  restoring levels of, 52
Adipose tissue, 11, 32, 91, 133
Adner, Marvin, M.D., 49
ADP. *See* Adenosine diphosphate
Adrenaline, 7
Advil. *See* Ibuprofen
Aerobic exercise, 8, 14, 16, 44, 106. *See also specific exercises*
Aerobic fitness
  blood doping and, 51
  guidelines for, 29
  interval training and, 85
  measures of, 15, 45, 75–79
Aerobic metabolism, 8, 35, 44
Age, training and, 27–29, 28
Air pollution, 153–55, 154
Albuterol, 164
Altitude training, 36–38
Amenorrhea, 155–58
American Academy of Allergy and Immunology, 162
American Cancer Society, 209
American College of Sports Medicine (ACSM), 25, 62, 76
  anabolic steroid ban, 40

guidelines
  exercise, 29
  weight training, 117, 119–20
American Dietetic Association (ADA), 141
American Massage Therapy Association (AMTA), 95
Amino acids, 8, 149. *See also* Protein
  supplements, 125–27
Amphetamines, 39–40, 73
AMTA, 95
Anabolic steroids, 40–42, 73
Anacin-3. *See* Acetaminophen
Anaerobic exercise, 8, 14, 35, 43–45. *See also* Anaerobic threshold
Anaerobic glycolysis, 44
Anaerobic metabolism, 8, 35, 44
Anaerobic threshold, 45–47, 76–77, 211
Anderson, Bob, 109–12
Androgenic effects, of anabolic steroids, 40
Ankle sprain, 158–59
Anorexia nervosa, 159–61
Antioxidants, 127–29
Anxiety, exercise and, 10
AquaJogger, 116
Arginine, 72
Arrhythmia, cardiac, amphetamines and, 39
Aspirin, 47–49, 189, 206
Association, as mental strategy, 96–98, 200
Asthma, 154, 161–65
ATP. *See* Adenosine triphosphate

B

Baking soda, 72
Basal metabolism, 133
Benson, Herbert, M.D., 99
Benzedrine, 39
Beta-carotene, 128–29